1976

Creative
Children's Theatre
for Home, School, Church,
and Playground

Creative
Children's Theatre
for Home, School, Church,
and Playground

Maxine McSweeny

South Brunswick and New York: A.S. Barnes and Company
London: Thomas Yoseloff Ltd

A. S. Barnes and Co., Inc.
Cranbury, New Jersey 08512

Thomas Yoseloff Ltd
108 New Bond Street
London W1Y OQX, England

McSweeny, Maxine.
   Creative children's theatre for home, school, church, and playground.
   Includes bibliographical references.
   1. Children as actors. 2. Children's plays—
Presentation, etc. I. Title.
PN3157.M32   792'.0226   73-152
ISBN 0-498-01286-7

PRINTED IN THE UNITED STATES OF AMERICA

792.0216
M176

Contents

FOREWORD
ACKNOWLEDGMENTS
INTRODUCTION 13

PART ONE: *Children and Creative Theatre Activity*
1. Source of Delight and Spur to Development 19
2. Opportunities for Children to Participate 26

PART TWO: *Imitative Play*
3. Acting out Life 33
4. Playacting with Puppets 47

PART THREE: *Creative Drama*
5. Playmaking 57
6. How to Guide Improvisation 69
7. Stories and How to Act Them 88

PART FOUR: *Theatre*
8. Putting on Plays 123
9. Lead-up Activities 131
10. The Director Studies the Script 144
11. Call to Rehearsal 151
12. Staging the Play 166
13. The Excitement of Showtime 180

PART FIVE: *Plays for Children to Put On*

The Bird with the Broken Wing, adapted by Maxine McSweeny 191
The Wishing Shop, by Mildred Plew Merryman 195

Sleeping Beauty, by Maxine McSweeny   202

A Princess at Heart, by Maxine McSweeny   216

In the Kitchen Again   227

The Pudding Pan, by Katherine D. Morse   235

The Glorious Whitewasher, by Walter Hackett   240

Little Women, adapted by Maxine McSweeny   250

Gypsy Brew, by Maxine McSweeny   257

INDEX   265

Foreword

Creative children's theatre activity is a means of acquiring knowledge and of vicariously experiencing emotions aroused by the portrayal of events, both for the actor and the observer or audience. Drama, therefore, becomes a method of education, entertainment, or recreation. The use of drama in formal and informal education, as in a recreation program, is enhanced by the innate tendency to play at make believe—in short, to dramatize. All children possess this tendency to an extent that invites, even entices, parents, teachers, and recreators to utilize it for worthy accomplishment. Free expression in early years is so often conditioned by lack of appreciation and ridicule that when children become teenagers and adults drama too often is enjoyed only when they are in the audience.

Natural impulses become dwarfed from misuse or conditioned by experiences had in their early expression. Since the imitative and the dramatic impulse is one of the earliest to be manifested by the child, parents and others, who have supervision of children in their formative years, must take care not to unduly restrain the impulse and to guide its expression toward developmental goals. Thus guided it can become the means of enlarging the child's horizon of knowledge, appreciation, inspiration, and skill toward the enrichment of life to its end.

Drama is also one of the performing arts. That is the "showoff" part which often needs to be discouraged in the early stages. More importantly, theatre activity is a creative art naturally exercised for further development of one's power of expression, also for in-group adjustment.

Joseph Lee, founder of the playground movement in America, has said, "If you want to know what a child is, study his play; if you want to affect what he shall be, direct the form of his play."

This book has been written to inform parents, teachers in schools and churches, and play and recreation leaders how to direct the form of children's drama activity to encourage creative expression, and to aid social, mental, and emotional development.

The author brings great competence to the task derived from early professional education in the dramatic arts, followed by years of experience in story telling and recreational drama in the playgrounds and recreation centers of Los Angeles. In the latter capacity she was responsible for in-service education of a large corps of recreation directors.

George Hjelte
General Manager, Los Angeles
City Department of Recreation
and Parks (Retired)

Acknowledgments

The author expresses deep appreciation to

George Hjelte for guiding preparation of the manuscript, suggesting its title, and writing the foreword.

Minnette Spector for professional standards that pointed the way to goals and methods described in the book.

The many employees of Los Angeles City Department of Recreation and Parks who experimented with the book's materials and contributed to its ideas.

Howard Hill, Robert Meyers, Sterling and Mildred Winans for suggestions and critical analysis.

Frances Burgard for helping to develop certain projects and testing others in the classroom and the home.

Dena Rogin for editing the manuscript.

Tillie Olson for encouragement and technical assistance.

Elizabeth Ives for suggestions regarding music.

Acknowledgment is gratefully extended to

Greenwood Press for permission to quote from *Administration of Public Recreation* by George Hjelte, 1971

Child Life Magazine and Marion P. Ruckel for permission to include *The Wishing Shop* by Mildred Plew Merryman, copyright 1927 and 1955 by Rand McNally and Company.

Plays, The Drama Magazine for Young People for permission to reprint *The Glorious Whitewasher* by Walter Hackett, copyright 1949 by Plays, Inc.

Introduction

This book shows how to guide children in creative theatre activities. It is for parents, teachers in schools and churches, recreation directors, camp counselors, librarians, nursery school leaders, babysitters, and leaders of groups like Boy Scouts and Campfire Girls.

Here are step-by-step instructions for conducting different kinds of drama. One section tells how to increase the fun of such simple playacting as playing store. Another describes the playmaking of improvisation and acting stories. How to rehearse and present plays is described in detail.

HOW TO USE THIS BOOK

Persons in a hurry use it for reference. A mother needs ideas the playacting children can carry on by themselves. She looks at projects for imitative play. Social studies teachers plan for their pupils to dramatize scenes from history. They note the illustrations of a dozen ways to promote improvisation.

Playground directors and Sunday school teachers wanting plays for children to present refer to the collection of plays. Librarians read the outlines of stories and examples of how to make story play an exciting adventure.

Persons who have time read the entire book. They find answers to such questions as

How can children use their natural sincerity and ingenuity in creative theatre?

How do they progress from imitative play to playmaking, and finally, to putting on plays?

How does a director conduct rehearsals to promote players' joy and development, and to culminate in a good performance?

The book offers foundation for leadership that can make the most of creative theatre in children's education and recreation. This should aid students preparing for careers in these fields. The book's guidelines and cautions show administrators how to evaluate and upgrade their agency drama programs as needed.

The book is the result of practical experience. As drama specialist for Los Angeles City Department of Recreation and Parks I conducted courses and prepared bulletins for directors at one hundred recreation centers. I helped them adapt the activity to varied situations and facilities. These were testing ground for most materials and suggestions in the following pages.

Creative
Children's Theatre
for Home, School, Church,
and Playground

Part One

Children and Creative Theatre Activity

1

Source of Delight
and Spur to Development

Everybody acts, and he starts when he is a child.

There was Tim. He played astronaut. So did all the children in the neighborhood. In their houses and up and down the streets boys and girls acted outer space.

Tim's mother saw him climbing out the window. One end of her tape measure was around his waist. The other end was tied to the curtain cord.

"Get back in the house," called his mother. "What are you trying to do?"

"I'm spacewalking."

"You've got my tape measure on."

"I know. It's my umbilical."

Then there was Gwen. On her sixth birthday she received a toy medicine kit that included a hypodermic needle. She played doctor with Rachel and Sue. When Gwen was doctor the other two played they were obstreperous children on a visit to his office. In desperation Doctor Gwen said, "If you two don't behave, I'll give you thirteen shots all in the same place."

Sam's acting experience was different. He described it to fifth grade classmates in their first assigned speech. Its topic was "The Most

Thrilling Experience of My Vacation.'' Sam said his most thrilling experience was acting a story of Robin Hood.

For Beth acting meant anticipated pleasure. On the last day of her year in the first grade she said, ''Mommy, I hope I get Miss Wilson for second grade.''

''Why?'' asked Mother. ''I thought you liked all the teachers.''

''Oh, I do.''

''Then why do you want Miss Wilson?''

''Because in Miss Wilson's room they do plays.''

To eleven-year-old Frank acting meant playing Dragon in ''St. George and the Dragon.'' He was so enthralled with the role that he thought about it at home after rehearsals. Two weeks before performance he ran to the director.

''Look!'' he shouted and held out both hands. A popsickle stick protruded beyond each finger. Sticks were held in place by rubber bands.

The director asked, ''What are they for?''

''They're my claws—dragon claws. I thought of them at home.''

Happiness found in acting can be long remembered. This was demonstrated by Lucia. She left home early to be in the playground circus. Twenty years before, the circus had been a regular feature and was revived only this summer.

Children who wanted to be in it listened as the director described its acts. All except Lucia named the parts they wanted. The director turned to her, ''Lucia, which part do you want?''

''Not any of them?''

''Don't you want to be in the circus?''

''Yes.''

''Then what do you want to do?''

''I want to be the mother who rescues her baby from the fire.''

''But I haven't told you about that? How do you know it?''

''My mother told me about it. She played that part when she was a little girl.''

Tim, Gwen, Sam, Beth, Frank, and Lucia had various experiences. All are part of creative children's theatre.

Theatre Springs from Life and Action

Creative children's theatre is drama. And what is drama? Aristotle said it was the imitation of life and action. For example, boys engage in drama when they run down a hill to play Indian. Later they run down the same hill at the same speed just to get momentum from the slope. This is fun, but it is not drama. There is no attempt to imitate life and action.

A boy imitates the movement of tying a shoe lace to learn how to tie. This is not drama. But if he tries to act like Grandma tying a shoe lace he is dramatizing. He imitates life and action.

Delight of Being Someone Else

Children delight to play at being someone else. Below are some of children's desires and the ways creative theatre activity satisfies them.

Answer to the Cry for New Experience. From infancy children cry out for new experience. They want to feel a new shape or texture, look at changing forms and colors, and use muscles in untried ways. New sounds exert special appeal. The young like novel games and stories and discoveries they make for themselves.

Playacting offers new experience for mind, muscle, and feeling. Its possibilities include fresh contact with the past, present, and even the future. There can be new encounters that concern any place on earth and outer space besides.

Chance to Be Somebody Important. Life doesn't often let a child make decisions that control other people. He is usually the one under control. In drama he can be the person in authority as he plays teacher instead of pupil, doctor instead of patient, and king instead of subject.

Fun of Thinking. Trying to remember experience and translate it into drama challenges a child to think. The desire to act makes him want to remember, to solve problems, to imagine, and to make judgments. The joy of recall is apparent in the often-heard childish shout, ''I thought of it.''

Thrill of Accomplishment. Creative theatre lets players show what they know and what they can do. It requires them to take responsibility. They are pleased when they measure up.

Theatre Activity and Development

This activity is more than a way for children to play. It is a means of learning. Pleasure in drama promotes players' development —intellectual, emotional, social, physical, and spiritual. Persons who work with children cite examples.

One example was Maria, a twelve-year-old, newly arrived in the neighborhood of a playground. She visited it every day but was too shy to participate in any activities. She just watched. The drama class was rehearsing a dramatization of Tolstoi's *Where Love Is God Is*.

Maria was interested in the play about the gentle shoemaker. She watched every rehearsal, but she would not take part.

Then came an important rehearsal, and the boy who played the shoemaker was ill. Maria recognized the emergency. Quietly she said to the director, ''Do you want me to play shoemaker today? I know what he does.''

Maria played the part well enough to give others a good rehearsal. The regular player returned next time, and Maria offered to help backstage. Her one acting experience broke the spell of shyness. From that moment she participated in many activities.

Performance of a play gave another child the chance to think in an emergency. He was ten-year-old Martin playing the role of a kind farmer in a play based on Longfellow's poem, ''Birds of Killingworth.'' When other farmers resolved to kill the birds Martin was the only one who objected.

An offstage birdcall was to attract him from the meeting so the other farmers could proceed. No birdcall came. Players felt stranded. They could do nothing until Martin left. He knew he had to invent a reason and go. Every player looked helplessly at him.

He got an idea. He turned his head to listen and said, ''My wife's calling. I'd better go.'' He rushed off, and the play went on.

Creative theatre contributed to the intellectual development of the poet, Robert Browning. His poem ''Development'' describes it. The poem begins

My father was a scholar and knew Greek.
When I was five years old, I asked him once
''What do you read about?''

''The siege of Troy.''

''What is a siege, and what is Troy?''

To answer the boy's question the father told the story and helped Robert act it out. They piled chairs and tables to represent Troy's walls. Within the enclosure they placed the cat. She was captured Helen. Robert climbed on the table to play Priam. The poem tells how this acting eventually induced Robert to study Greek so he could read the story in Homer's language.

Such acting experience has benefitted children who did not become famous. There was twelve-year-old Catherine, a Girl Scout. Her troop was planning to present the same play Maria rehearsed, *Where Love is God Is*. Catherine wanted to play the tea seller, who gets so mad she breaks a bag of tea against the table. The director asked the girl why she chose that part. ''Because,'' said Catherine, ''it lets me act as mad as I feel. I can't do that any other time.''

Another incident concerns a boy of nine. He played Miser in Cornelia Meig's story, ''Twopenny Town.'' When the dramatization was over, other players praised him. ''You're such a good miser. You act just like a miser.''

At first the boy was pleased. Then he turned to the teacher and said, ''I'd hate to really be a miser.''

Incidents like these show how the challenges and opportunities of creative theatre promote children's development.

Drama Stimulates Intellectual Growth. The activity helps children use their minds because it challenges their attention. They can't participate unless they keep their "eyes on the ball."

Through participation children overcome shyness and fear of failure which handicap their mental activity. Stories and plays and the desire to act them take children's minds off themselves and their problems. Children who act must think about their characters and lines and react to what other players do.

Finally, drama gives children contact with great literature. From it they get stimulating ideas to think about. Literature becomes a part of the players' thoughts and feelings.

When a child contacts literature through dramatization he is not distracted by mechanics of reading. Leaders have reported the joy of a youngster who returns some time after dramatizing a classic. With enthusiasm he says, "You know that story we played? It's in my reader." He speaks the word *reader* with new admiration.

Learning to Harness Feelings. Creative theatre provides a protective framework within which a child can express strong feelings. He can see the effect of emotion on people—what it does to character, appearance, voice, and manner.

Building Strong Bodies. The self-initiated, informal dramatizing of children when they imitate grownup activities goes on for hours. It often includes vigorous and sustained muscular activity. This makes significant contribution to participants' organic and neuromuscular development.

Further, dramatic interpretation depends on a player's own body. He must learn control and relaxation, and develop good coordination to participate.

Children Work Together. Creative theatre requires cooperation from its players. Since there is no fun without cooperation the activity encourages it. Each participant knows what is expected of him. He knows also that his peers can see when he is too lazy or careless to do his part.

A requisite for working together is communication. Some of its tools are speaking, listening, good manners, and social graces. All are fostered by theatre activity.

Gaining a Sense of Values. This is the basis of spiritual development. Through drama a child contacts the good, the true, and the beautiful as living forces. They are personified in characters. A player feels the struggles of heroes. He becomes involved in their victory over the evil, false, or ugly.

Overview

These outcomes of delight and development are possible for the child who participates in creative theatre. But they are not automatic. Children may find in their drama disappointment instead of delight. The activity may cause withdrawal instead of self-confidence; discord, not cooperation; attempts to show off rather than honest effort; and boredom instead of enthusiasm.

Leaders, whether parents, teachers, or recreators, should be aware of the activity's potential for good or ill. They need to keep in mind the twofold function the activity can perform in a child's life. This function, is, first, to contribute to his delight by giving him a new experience; a chance to play a person with authority; the incentive to recall experience; the thrill of accomplishment;

Second, drama can aid a child's development by helping him to use his mind; understand and control his feelings; build a sound body; work with others; acquire a sense of values.

Such opportunities as these are necessary if creative theatre is to fulfill a vital function in a child's life.

2

Opportunities for Children to Participate

Leaders of children's drama should know its various forms.

Forms of Creative Theatre

Three main forms of creative theatre are imitative play, creative drama, and theatre.[1] They may be classified according to the planning that goes into them.

The first, imitative play, has no plan. It is so spontaneous that players decide what happens in their dramatization while they act.

The second form, creative drama, requires players to make a plan before they start to dramatize. They know in advance what happens in the dramatization. While they act, they invent their dialogue and pantomine.

The third form is called theatre. It consists of putting on plays. Its plan is so definite it provides dialogue, pantomime, and plot. Players memorize the plan and present it for an audience.

These forms fit another classification. This system is for recreation activities, and it groups them according to method of organization. Its first category is Informal Routine Activities. They "...require no special organization of players in advance and may be engaged in at the whim of the player."[2] Imitative play is in this category.

---

[1]Later chapters deal in detail with the three forms.
[2]George Hjelte, *Administration of Public Recreation* (Westport, Conn.: Greenwood Press, 1971), pp. 295, 297.

In the second category are Recurrent Scheduled Activities. They ". . .are engaged in upon appointment. They are usually group activities such as clubs, classes and contests in which so many members take part according to rules or conventions that a given time and place must be appointed for them." In this category are rehearsals and classes in acting, creative drama, and stagecraft.

Third category is Special Events. These are of a ". . .type requiring preparation for days and sometimes weeks in advance and terminating in a performance or demonstration." In this category are performances and demonstrations of creative drama and theatre skills.

Guidelines and Cautions

To provide maximum benefit for players leaders should observe the following guidelines and cautions:

1. All children need opportunity to participate—not merely the few with obvious talent or economic advantage.

2. Children should engage in all three forms of drama.

3. The enthusiasm and ingenuity children show in imitative play should carry over into creative drama and theatre.

4. There should be planned progress from the easy to the more challenging and difficult.

5. The broad base of activity should be creative drama. It precedes any attempt to prepare a play for an audience.

6. Participants should develop skills useful in daily living. These include ability to think creatively, speak clearly, and move with good coordination.

7. Stories and plays should have literary quality.

8. Facilities and supplies should be in good taste and suited to children.

9. No leader should be restrained because of limited facilities and supplies. Although adequate resources enhance the activity, ingenuity with materials pays big dividends.

10. The purpose of the program is always the delight and development of the participants. It is not to increase agency prestige, not to make money, and not to prepare for professional theatre careers. Some of these may result as by-products of a properly motivated program. But they

should not be the raison d'etre of the activity. When they are, the program moves into another orbit of utility.

Who Provides Opportunities?

Many agencies offer opportunities for children to participate.

There is the family. Parents encourage the activity when they do little more than show interest in it. They can help by choosing gifts that suggest imitative play. The next two chapters contain suggestions for promoting playacting at home. The same methods are useful in institutional homes.

Creative theatre activities have a regular place in the programs of public recreation agencies, camps, youth serving agencies, and settlement houses. Public elementary schools sometimes offer drama classes. More often they include creative theatre in other classes or promote it as an extracurricular activity. Drama workshops are occasionally offered by private elementary schools, college theatre arts departments, and cultural centers. Churches through their children's religious education programs sometimes offer both creative drama and theatre. Even hospitals have offered drama participation to child patients who were convalescent.

Creative Theatre as a Good Neighbor

Most agencies mentioned above sponsor programs that include many activities. Creative theatre has a place of its own. But it is also combined with other activities. Here are ways that drama can contribute to classes in other subjects.

Pupils in social studies dramatize incidents from the material they study. Putting on a play motivates projects in art and craft classes. These include decorating scenery and making costume accessories, hand properties, and posters. Drama adds to a singing class with dramatized ballads and pantomimed stunt songs. It stimulates improvisation in dance classes. Religious education classes use dramatization to portray the effect of religion on life, and events in religious history. In nature study drama offers the chance to dramatize nature myths and legends.

Creative theatre does even more for special events than it does for classes. Dramatizations provide frameworks for demonstrations of skills and knowledge of other activities. A play about singers lets children sing as part of its performance. Selected plays give dancers the opportunity to dance and gymnasts the chance to perform their acts.

A creative dramatization may be developed around the theme of a special event and rehearsed for presentation. An example is acting a story about dolls and preparing it for presentation at a doll show. Similarly, an episode about the flag is acted out and then formalized for a Flag Day observance. Appropriate plays can enrich the following special events: parties, doll shows, song fests, play days, amateur circuses, patriotic celebrations, religious holiday observances, dance or music recitals, campfire ceremonies, community or family nights, exhibits of crafts or hobbies, seasonal observances like May Day, Harvest Home, Winter Frolic, and Good Old Summertime.

While drama is enriching other activities it receives benefit from them. Combining with them offers additional opportunities to act and entices new participants into creative theatre. Dances and songs learned in other classes increase the appeal of a play presentation. Special events that include other activities with drama help to attract audiences for performances of the play.

And Now, the Leader

To conduct creative theatre challenges the ability and enthusiasm of a leader. Drama, more than any other program activity, provides occasion and need for a varied array of skills. It offers such a multitude of demands and opportunities that no leader attains the ultimate in virtuosity.

However, no leader of children is without attributes and experience that enable him to further children's creative expression through drama. A person who has the interest should not hold back for lack of previous preparation. Competence will improve for those bold enough to start and resourceful enough to find opportunities for guidance. This book and others are written to help him and can be a step in his preparation. Toward increasing competence the leader should equip himself with the knowlege and skills of drama.

Part Two

Imitative Play

3

Acting out Life

Imitative play is children's informal dramatizing of experience. Also known as dramatic and free play, its chief characteristic is freedom of players. They act what they want to act. They start or stop at any time. They exchange roles without spoiling their dramatizing. One player simply says, "Now, *I'll* be mother, and *you* be child." The play continues.

As for supplies, children do without any or use what is at hand. One player announces, "I have a bandage on my arm." The fact that he has no bandage bothers no one. When children do have an interesting object of supply it suggests a subject for play. They build their dramatizing around it.

One player finds a strip of white cloth. He asks, "You see this cloth? It's my bandage. You say to me, 'How did you get hurt?' " The other player does, and a dramatization is launched.

Children can create supplies. Girls play princess. One girl announces, "We need crowns. Let's make them of this paper." They tear strips of colored paper and pin them into head-size circles. These are crowns.

Problems of space are equally easy to overcome. The playing suddenly requires characters to journey to the next kingdom. The players are acting in a small living room. They circle the room once and arrive in the next kingdom.

The young actors give no thought to spectators. Children who come to watch are ignored unless they want to become players. The number of roles can be increased or diminished immediately to accomodate the number of aspiring participants.

What it Means to Children

Imitative play lets children play their way with few rules laid down by adults. This is a change for most children. Typically their situation is that of the six-year-old who wanted to eat dessert first. "No," said his mother, "eat your sandwich first. Then you can have your cake."

The boy whined, "Why do we always have to do it your way?"

In imitative play children create their own recreation. They play for hours without help from adults. This gives them experience with self-reliance, making their own decisions, and resourcefulness with materials. This form of drama is children's own effort toward creative expression.

Any Time and Any Place

Imitative play is usually available. There is a hardly a time or place that does not offer opportunity to engage in it. It can answer agencies' needs for recreation when no activity is scheduled. An example of such need is the elementary school that provided long lunch periods but offered no leadership or supplies for play. A seven-year-old pupil complained to her mother that time dragged during lunch hour. The mother asked, "What do you do after you eat your lunch?"

Drearily the girl answered, "Oh, first the boys chase us, then we chase the boys."

Two Kinds of Imitative Play

Imitative play comes in two forms. In one, children personally interpret the characters of their dramatizing. The other is a kind of puppet play. Children manipulate and speak for objects that represent characters. Imitative play with puppets is described in the next chapter. Most methods described here are also useful with puppets.

How to Give Encouragement

Adults can make children's imitative play more frequent, more fun, and more valuable. But they don't direct it. They offer suggestions in the same spirit one player does to another. For instance, a child says to a playmate, "Do you want to play circus?" The playmate plunges into dramatizing as he answers, "I'll be ringmaster."

The first responds, "I'll be lion-tamer," and playacting begins.

In the same way leaders use casual comments and questions to encourage imitative play. A mother speaks to a child with toy dishes, "Do you want to set the table with your dishes?" To a child playing with dolls mother says, "Is your baby crying?" or "Is it time to put your baby to bed?"

Mother can participate with young children without stopping her own work. She pretends to be startled when children sneak behind her. She keeps up running comment about her fears. Children appear and disappear and make strange noises. Mother jumps or squeals in simulated fright as she continues to peel apples or load the dishwasher. When children hide she calls them and talks about her fears when they don't answer. Children ride broomstick ponies around the kitchen. Mother commends them for skill and awards them medals for fine horsemanship.

Reminiscing with children about an experience often whets their desire to play it. Talk about a recent trip spurs children to play stopping at a motel. Then they unload the car and unpack their belongings for the night.

Suggestions by adults keep the play going after it has started. A playground director saw children playing circus. He noticed young observers who wanted to participate. He said, "Do you remember the circus had animals who jumped through rings of fire?" This suggested roles for newcomers. They joined the playing.

Leaders do not say much. They don't gather children into an organized group or give lectures. They just ask casual questions that begin, "Do you remember. . .?" or "What do you think. . .?" or "Did you like. . .?"

Vicarious experiences are a means of encouraging playacting. To provide them an adult reads or tells stories to children or relates adventures. He makes books available so children can read stories or look at pictures. He suggests television programs that have the capacity to start dramatizing.

Take Advantage of Current Interests. By giving notice of television programs a leader takes advantage of children's current interests. News broadcasts contain ideas for playing. News of a flood suggests climbing to escape rising waters or rowing to rescue marooned friends. Heat waves, blizzards, and tornadoes can be just as stimulating. So can news of Miss America Contests, space flights, and the Tournament of Roses.

Television serials and cartoons have provided material for countless sessions of play. When a good serial absorbs children's interest an adult can encourage it. He locates a cape like the hero's or other object that resembles one used in the program.

Supplies Bring a New Dimension. Supplies like the cape increase the thrill of playacting. After a television performance of Cinderella a settlement director put on a table supplies that suggested the story. They included lengths of bright fabric and old drapes that could be trains for royalty. There were rags and an apron for Cinderella, old costume jewelry for guests at the ball, gold paper for crowns, and a string tied to a nail so it could be struck at twelve o'clock.

When the first children arrived the director called, ''You can use the things on the table if you want to play Cinderella.''

Another director reported that she put out only a few supplies in the beginning. As playing progressed she brought new items to draw out new ideas and sustain excitement.

Excitement and new ideas are provided by supplies. For this reason the stock is changed frequently. Children always in search of something new should find it in supplies. The same old items in the same old place have little power to challenge play.

Something to Wear. Players revel in special costume effects. Their everyday clothes provide foundation. Over these, children put on assorted pieces of wearing apparel. Trying them on stimulates ideas for character and plot. Six-year-old girls found a billowy scarf among supplies. They used it to play spring breezes. Older girls later found the same scarf. It reminded them of the scarf Proserpina lost when Pluto carried her off to his underground kingdom. This scarf enabled Mother Ceres to find her daughter. So the girls played Ceres and Proserpina with the scarf.

A few mufflers, mittens, and hoods started other children to play about a book they had read. It was *Snow Treasure*[1] and told how Norwegian children saved a supply of their country's gold during the Nazi occupation. They put it on sleds and coasted to safety while enemy soldiers watched without suspicion.

Scarves, hoods, and mittens are only costume accessories. Yet they gave impetus to hours of play. The accessories seem almost as effective as complete costumes. When a child puts on a piece of costume he tends to identify with the character immediately. From the character he gets ideas for situations to be played.

Makeup Supplies. These supplies should include materials for false hair such as crepe hair, raffia, excelsior, clean floor mops, and cast-off wigs. Simpler than a wig is a fringe of false hair material fastened to protrude below a cap or hat. Some of the same materials are useful for mustaches, beards, and shaggy brows.

Most women have in their makeup shelves an unwanted supply of lipsticks, rouge, eye shadow and liner, and face powder. These are treasures for imitative play.

Face putty can be an unexpected bonus. It can change the shape of a nose or add a wart to a fantastic character. A selection of closeup pictures of faces gives ideas for using putty as well as other makeup.

Not to be forgotten are clean-up supplies. Among them should be cleansing tissue, old rags, cold cream, paper towels, soap, and water. Children should be warned not to use their clothes or costumes for removing makeup.

Masks. These are akin to makeup. They range from half-masks that cover little more than the eyes to animal heads that cover the face, head,

[1]M. McSwigan, *Snow Treasure* (New York: E. P. Dutton, 1942).

and neck. With masks should be kept crude nose and ear appendages seen at Halloween.

Children make many kinds of masks. Some are made of paper bags, flour sacks, and worn pillow cases. Features are applied with crayon or paint. Half-masks are easily cut from construction paper. They can be cut in whatever shape desired with holes cut out for eyes and extensions to fit over ears like eye glasses. Another way to attach the mask is to insert round paper clips on either side. Tie on each clip a piece of string and tie the pieces together at back of head.

Something to Carry. Objects that actors carry in a play are called hand properties. Such properties provide delight in imitative play. What a person carries often shows his character, occupation, or life style. A woodman holds an ax; a fairy, a wand; the hunter, a bow; the gardener, a hoe; the soldier, a gun. A child who finds one of these items is apt to begin at once to act the character it suggests.

Toys are often made to suggest objects grownups use. Children desire them for imitative play. Little girls want toy dishes to add to the fun of playing house. Medical kits start sessions of playing doctor or hospital.

Children receive some of these objects as gifts. They also adapt what they find. A child finding a discarded steering wheel on a trash heap can hardly be restrained from playing truck driver. A broomstick gives the same thrust to playing horse and rider.

Leaders can salvage items for imitative play and even improve them. One parent attached the cutout picture of a horse's head to his son's broomstick pony. He also tacked on a strip of cloth to serve as bridle.

A recreation director did more. She taught eight-year-old craft pupils to stuff an old sock for a horse's head. They attached paper ears to the heel of the sock. The stuffed toe was the nose. The ankle of the sock was tied around the broomstick to provide the neck.

Supplies are almost essential in playing store. For playing drug store there should be empty bottles children can fill with colored water, and pill boxes for little round candies. To stock a grocery store there should be cereal boxes, coffee cans, jars, bottles, and paper bags. Colored pictures of cakes and pies are for bakery play. Jewelry stores have discarded costume jewelry, rings made of clover, and necklaces made of pods and seeds.

Among simple, commonplace objects that stimulate imitative play are blank checks, receipt pads, rubber stamps and ink pads, trading stamps, play money, alarm clocks, bowls and spoons.

Taking Advantage of Environment. Almost any place holds suggestions for imitative play. An elevation is invaluable whether it be a step, platform, curb, dirt bank, or sandpile. These suggest a daring leap by a circus performer, a tower from which Rapunzel can let down her long hair, or a hilltop from which to send signals.

A mere fence corner is useful. It serves as a corral or hitching apparatus for ponies. A clump of bushes provides shelter from weather, enemies, or animals. The sturdy branch of a tree is a home for Swiss Family Robinson or a refuge from floods.

One mother drapes a sheet over a cord stretched three feet above the ground. Stones on the sheets's four corners hold the sides of the sheet apart. Inside is a tent for camping out, hiding, or playing Indian or frontiersman.

Indoors also are settings for play projects. The kneehole of a desk is a secret hiding place. The dining table with a cloth hanging well over its edge is a cozy place for playing house. So is a space between the sofa and big armchair.

Large objects temporarily on the premises suggest play projects. They serve in the same way as stage properties in the theatre. Wooden boxes sturdy enough to hold a child's weight become a platform. A refrigerator packing box becomes a boat, house, or spaceship. A sawhorse serves as a pony or bridge.

Permanent play equipment is another resource. The slide is the means to escape from a burning building. Swings are satellites that cirlce the earth. On climbing apparatus made of pipes or metal strips children play birds, mountain climbers, cliffdwellers, or monkeys.

Wheeled toys are part of the equipment in most homes with children. They have uses in imitative play. A wagon becomes an ambulance or delivery truck. Tricycles are messengers' bicycles or racing cars. Roller skates may represent skis or wings on Mercury's heels.

Noisemakers. Sound effects provide another stimulus. Nature gave children equipment for many sound effects they use to full advantage.

Most boys can whistle like steamboats, beep-beep like auto horns, ack-ack like machine guns, and boom like cannons. Children make startling percussive noises with tongue and palate that suggest situations for play. They create pertinent sound effects just by stamping feet or clapping hands.

In addition to the personal equipment they have, children are adept at finding it. They locate bells, clappers, whistles, and all the noisemakers that come with carnivals or Halloween.

Other supplies they create. Woodblocks are covered with sandpaper to be rubbed together for a locomotive sound. A thin piece of metal is rattled for thunder. Coconut shells make the clatter of horses' hooves. All of these sounds remind children of projects to act.

To Get Supplies. Supplies for imitative play come from three main sources. The first consists of toys children receive as gifts. When these are outgrown they should be given to younger children or to agencies like recreation centers. Alert leaders salvage such supplies when neighboring families move or do spring housecleaning.

The second source is in what children locate for themselves. When they bring their discoveries adults should show appreciation and listen to plans for using them.

The third source is what children make. A by-product of imitative play can be an incentive for crafts. An example is the pony head children made of a sock. Craft supplies in their turn suggest content for dramatizations. Among materials that should be offered at different times are crayons, paints, brushes, paste, scissors, and a variety of papers. The latter include salvaged gift wrappings, newspapers, cardboard, and construction paper.

Sample Projects for Imitative Play

Restaurant Play. To get it started try some of the following:

1. Let children cook hamburgers or pancakes; make sandwiches or mud pies; model food items of clay; decorate paper plates; cut out papers for order slips, credit cards, and dollar bills; make chef caps, waitress

headgear, and aprons of paper; print menu cards; make a grocery carton into a play stove.

To keep it going try some of these:

1. Provide blank checks, bill folds, or handbags for customers.

2. Help children locate tables, benches, stools or chairs, pencil and pad for waitress, cashbox for cashier.

3. Suggest locations of discarded dishes, knives and forks, plastic flatware and wire clothes hanger and clothespins for holding chef's order slips.

4. Permit use of spatula, egg beater, mixing bowl and spoon, and a bell to let chef signal "Order ready."

5. Seek out grownup clothes and accessories in which customers can "dress up."

Bakery Play. To get it started try some of the following:

1. Let children cut out colored pictures of bakery products; stack grocery cartons for display shelves; play with dough (real or play or clay); bake biscuits or cookies.

To keep it going try some of these:

1. For customers, offer same supplies as for restaurant play.

2. Suggest where to find string, wrapping paper, and sacks.

Bus Trip. To get it started try some of the following:

1. Take children on a bus trip.

2. Locate steering wheel and stick for shifting gears.

3. Let children make a fare box (out of a box that has cellophane on one side); cut out papers for tickets and transfers.

4. On placards let children paint signs reading, "Move Back in the Bus" and "Fare 25 cents."

5. Provide a cap or jacket from an old uniform for the driver.

6. Point out seats that can serve driver and passengers.

To keep it going try some of these:

1. Offer customers the same supplies as in restaurant play.

2. Help children locate shopping bags, sacks, boxes, birdcages, animal cartons, suitcases, umbrellas, and anything else passengers might carry. (Such items suggest incidents for playing).

3. If children think of items help locate them.

4. For the starter, who calls bus routes and signals the driver to start and stop, provide a whistle and cap.

5. Stimulate ideas for getting an auto horn, money changer, and ticket punch.

Delivery Truck Play. To get it started try some of following:

1. Suggest this play when children play with a wagon or have just received one as a gift.

2. Provide string, wrapping paper, gummed paper tape and labels, receipt forms, pencil and pad. Children may make the receipt forms and labels.

3. Suggest that they bring their toys for delivery items.

To keep it going try some of these:

1. Get an alarm clock to serve for a doorbell ringing.

2. Provide housewives with clothes for dressing up like restaurant customers.

Service Station Play. To get it started try the following:

1. Suggest it as an outgrowth of delivery truck play.

2. Point out a curb or other elevation for grease rack.

3. Let children make credit cards, receipt slips, and trading stamps.

4. Suggest drawing an outline of a gas pump on a refrigerator packing carton.

5. Suggest the location of castoff pieces of hose for dispensing gas, air, and water.

To keep it going try some of these:

1. Provide sound effects equipment like rotary egg beater and auto horns.

2. Let children use hammers, screwdrivers, and oil cans.

3. Let them have any old tires and tubes that are available.

Beauty Shop Play. To get it started try some of following:

1. Introduce after children have observed what goes on in a beauty shop.

2. Let children rummage for appropriate items among castoff beauty

supplies. Among these can be nail polish and remover; cotton; cleansing tissue; hair rollers, pins, and clips; makeup supplies; brushes; combs; mirrors; shampoos; and color rinses.

3. Make available tables, chairs, and pans of water.

4. Offer customers same costume resources as in restaurant play. They also need protecting cover cloths.

To keep it going try some of these:

1. Suggest appointment book, toy telephone, pencil, cashbox and play money for clerk.

Fashion show Play. To get it started try some of the following:

1. Suggest playing it after children have seen a fashion show, live or on television.

2. Provide cardboard and cord for making microphone for commentator and programs for guests.

2. Suggest some elevation for models to use as runway.

3. Provide for models all the costumes and accessories available.

To keep it going try the following:

1. Bring out more clothes for models.

2. Let children use record player for background music.

Olympic Games Play. To get it started try the following:

1. Suggest this play when television and periodicals are displaying pictures of the games and contestants.

2. Let children cut from metallic paper circles of gold, silver and bronze to provide medals for winners. If no metallic paper is on hand make them of cardboard and color with yellow, grey, or brown crayons.

3. While children work tell them of Olympic Games traditions.

Offer a thick candle or candle holder to serve as the torch that opens the games.

To keep it going try some of these:

1. Play recorded band selections on record player.

Offer garments appropriate for contestants in swimming, skiing, skating, and track.

3. For spectators offer grownup clothes for dressing up.

Experiences that Suggest Imitative Play

By providing experiences, adults indirectly do much to improve opportunities, incentives, and content for imitative play. Here are lists of experiences that often result in sessions of play.

Things that Happen at Home
Company dinner
House guests
New car
New baby
New furniture
Holiday celebrations
Antics of pets
Somebody sick
Somebody lost
Leak in roof
Water turned off
Electricity off
Moving day
Telephone calls
Listening to stories
Reading books
Looking at pictures
Watching television

Events away from Home
Party
Picnic
Wedding
Recital
Ball game
Fair
Overnight camp
Pet show
Circus
Church service

Theatre
Parade
Street carnival
Concert
Political rally

Visits to
Park
Playground
School
Store
Beach
Market
Neighbors
Relatives
Farm
Mountains
Lake
Railroad yard
Zoo
Motel
Service station
Beauty shop
Barber shop
Airport

Watching the Following People at Work
Astronaut
Brick mason
Plumber
Fireman
Frogman
Ambulance driver
Usher
Animal trainer
Doctor
Dentist

Life guard
Orchestra leader
Airline stewardess
Postman
Teacher

4

Playacting with Puppets

Children use almost any small object for a puppet. They propel a stick up a sandpile for a boy climbing a hill. They move an expensive doll for a young lady going to a party. Child puppeteers speak for her, lift her hands in gesture, and move her about.

Like personal imitative play puppet playacting grows out of experience. The same experiences provide material for both. Only puppets make the difference. They are the important item of supply. All other items relate to them. Many kinds of puppets are used.

Paper Doll Puppets

There are several ways to get paper doll puppets and their clothes.

1. Cut out paper dolls and clothes from magazines.

2. Save commercially manufactured paper dolls, which otherwise might be cast aside after a few sessions of play.

3. Make paper dolls by tracing outline of doll on stiff paper and cutting it out. Features are drawn or painted, or a face is cut out and pasted on.

4. Cut pictures of dolls or people from fashion magazines and mount on stiff paper.

5. Make paper costumes for them. They too can be cut from fashion magazines if extensions are cut to fold over doll at shoulders and hips.

6. Make other costumes of colored paper. Cut outline of doll from

shoulder to hemline. Include shoulder and hip extensions to attach costumes to doll. From paper of different color cut collar, cuffs, belt, braid, and other trimmings.

7. Make costumes of fabric scraps. Cut a piece of fabric a little wider than the doll and long enough to fold over its shoulders and reach hemline front and back. Cut out circle to go over head. Fasten a narrow strip around waist for belt. This may be trimmed with lace, buttons, embroidery, sequins, or glitter attached with glue.

8. Make costume accessories and objects to carry. Draw outlines of purses, hats, shoes, jewelry, and flowers on paper of desired color. Cut out complete with tab extensions so they can be attached to the doll as desired.

9. Cut from fashion magazines or catalogues complete pictures of men, women, and children. These constitute an entire family of dolls. Cut several pictures to represent each member of the family. Different pictures of him provide him with a variety of costumes. When several children play with this type of doll each child cuts out enough picutres to represent every member of a family in several outfits. The life of an entire community can be enacted. Families visit one another, meet at the beach, the zoo, the lake, and at parties. These dolls may be stored between pages of a magazine. Each family has its own magazine, and each member has special pages between which his clothes are stored.

10. Make furniture of small gift boxes.

11. Create forests or gardens with leafy twigs in little jars or cans of sand.

Stick Puppets

Almost any stick can become a puppet from a toothpick to a walking stick. Here are ways to enhance sticks for puppet purposes.

1. Glue to the stick a cutout face, or draw one with crayons.

2. Give the stick hair made of cotton, yarn, string, raffia, or shredded paper.

3. For arms wind a pipe cleaner once around the stick and extend both ends a suitable length.

4. Wrap paper around the stick for a costume. Capes and robes are easy. Add a belt for shape and for holding costume in place.

5. Attach headgear made of paper or fabric: a crown for a king; a chef cap for the cook; a pointed cap for an elf; a shawl for an old woman; and kerchief for a young girl.

6. Wind pipe cleaner arm around any object puppet carries.

7. Make simple hand properties by cutting them from construction paper.

8. Play with stick puppets in moist sand. It lets them sit or stand and leave footprints when they walk.

9. Model sand furniture, houses, tunnels, hills, and bridges.

10. Use old-fashioned two-pronged clothespins for stick puppets. It is easy to paste pants on them for men puppets.

11. Picnic spoons of wood, plastic, or paper can be treated like stick puppets. The bowl of the spoon offers an ideal place on which to paste or draw a face.

Finger Puppets

Always available for puppet play are a child's ten fingers. He has only to bend their joints to have puppet characters nodding and bowing. Here are techniques for enjoying finger puppet play.

1. Draw faces on soft pads of flesh near fingertips. Use lipstick, eyebrow pencil, or eye liner.

2. Make headgear similar to that for stick puppets, and perch it on fingertip.

3. Make finger puppets of Mother Goose characters, and act out the rhymes. Draw Wee Willie Winkie's face on the pad of middle finger. Perch on it the pointed end cut from a paper cup for a peaked night cap. For nightgown wrap a piece of cleansing tissue, toilet paper, or paper napkin around the finger. He can "run through the town" any place his puppeteer wants to take him. To play Jack Horner draw his face on right index finger. Let right thumb be Jack's thumb which he sticks into food that child holds in left hand. To play Miss Muffet draw her face on left index finger. Around right index finger wind a black wire or

blackened pipe cleaner for spider. His puppeteer can readily make him come along and "frighten Miss Muffet away."

Fist Puppets

With this kind of puppet a child's fist is the body of the puppet. Its head is a ball two or three inches in diameter. In the ball is hollowed out a place to hold the puppeteer's finger to a depth of two inches. Here are suggestions for fist puppets and how to play with them.

1. Make a ball of clay or commercial modeling material. Insert the finger to form the hole. Make this big enough to hold the finger with a cloth folded over it. On the ball place clay for nose, chin, and ears. Shape eyes and lips. When the clay is dry paste hair on top of ball. (Use any materials suggested before.) Paint a face.

2. Place center of a small handkerchief over right index finger and insert in hole. Extend thumb and long finger so tips show beyond handkerchief. These are the puppet's hands The handkerchief is its costume. It has no feet, but the puppeteer can make it bow, clap its hands, pick up objects, and travel wherever he wants to take it.

3. Make a fist puppet for each hand and play Punch and Judy, Alice in Wonderland and White Rabbit, or other story. When several children play each manipulates his own puppet to represent a character in their story.

4. Use for the puppet head an apple, a potato, carrot, or ball of wood, rubber, or styrofoam. Cut the hole with an apple corer or knife, and carve features.

5. Instead of a handkerchief use a piece of fabric that suits the character. Cut slits through which finger and thumb protrude. This holds costume in place. For a tall character use a square of cloth large enough to hang over child's forearm.

Commercially Manufactured Dolls

Children frequently use these dolls as puppets for imitative play. They come with built-in incentives for play. The baby doll walks or talks. The deep sea diver has a hose through which to blow air to him. Teenager dolls have contemporary wardrobes that permit exciting changes of costume. Such dolls should be saved and passed on to other families or recreation agencies. When they are worn from hard use the redecoration of them can provide an interesting craft.

Sample Projects of Imitative Play with Puppets

"Three Little Pigs" [1] *Play.* To get this started:

1. Tell or read to children the story, "Three Little Pigs."
2. Take them to the movie.
3. Let them look at pictures books that contain the story.
4. Sing with them songs from the movie.
5. Make fist puppets for Three Little Pigs and Wolf. Use potatoes for heads of pigs and upper part of a carrot for wolf.
6. Make stick puppets for men who sell straw, wood, and bricks.
9. Make pigs' houses by drawing and cutting them of construction paper. Cut extensions on both sides of each house. These are bent back so houses stand erect. Look at picture books for house styles.

Puppet Play with "Three Little Kittens." [2] To get it started:

1. Let children look at illustrations of poem in nursery books.
2. Read or tell the story to them.
3. Recite the poem.
4. Use styrofoam balls to make fist puppets of Cat and Kittens. For

[1]*Tall Book of Nursery Tales* (New York: Harper & Row, 1944), p. 110.
[2]*The Tall Book of Mother Goose* (New York: Harper & Row, 1942, p. 25.

eyes insert pins with colored heads. The nose can be a clove. Below it fasten pipe cleaners for whiskers.

5. Let four children manipulate the puppets and enact the poem. If only two children are present each can manipulate two puppets—one on each hand.

6. Use the puppets for all kinds of kitten play. Let the kittens meow and stretch, lap milk, and play with string.

7. Create a mouse puppet, and play cat and mouse.

Finger Puppet Play with "Snow White." [3] To get it started:

1. Tell or read the story to children.
2. Take them to the movie.
3. Sing with them songs from movie.
4. Provide a book with illustrations of the story.
5. Let children make finger puppets for characters. They can draw faces on their own fingers and on one another's. For greater puppet agility put face on index finger, and use thumb and long finger for puppets' hands.
5. If only two or three children play, put all the dwarfs on the fingers of one child. The seven dwarfs usually move as a unit.
6. Let the wicked queen hold a shawl over her head to disguise herself when she visits Snow White.

Pilgrim and Indian Puppet Play. To get it started:

1. Tell stories of the Pilgrims' landing and their first Thanksgiving. [4]
2. Show pictures of them.
3. Suggest that children create settings for these events in the sandbox or on the beach.
4. Pile sand to represent Plymouth Rock. Make a great hollow beside it to represent the Atlantic Ocean.
5. Make Pilgrim and Indian puppets of clothespins. Use the old-fashioned kind with a head, body, and two prongs. Paint or draw faces on clothespin heads.

[3]*Grimm's Fairy Tales* (New York: Grosset & Dunlap, 1945), p. 166.
[4]A. Dagliesh, *The First Thanksgiving Story* (New York: Chas. Scribner's Sons, 1954).

6. Costume Pilgrim men by coloring body and prongs black or dark color.

7. Costume Pilgrim women by wrapping a piece of dark cloth or crepe paper around body of clothespin. Twist a wire around fabric at neck to hold fabric in place. On the head paste a tiny fold of white paper for a cap.

8. Paint costumes of bright colors on Indians. Give each a headdress of feathers. Make it by folding paper several times and cutting feather shapes. Leave them attached near bottom. Procedure is the same as for cutting a string of paper dolls. Color the feathers in assorted hues.

9. Don't stop for arms. Let children get quickly to acting.

10. Load Pilgrims into a shoebox Mayflower so they can sail the Atlantic and disembark at Plymouth Rock.

11. Stick the Indians in moist sand on shore so they can watch.

12. Move Pilgrims inland where they build sand houses, tables, and benches, and invite Indians to the Thanksgiving Feast.

Follow-through

Each session of dramatic play, whether with or without puppets, ends with a cleanup. Children do not walk away leaving supplies scattered about. They are told in the beginning that all supplies are to be picked up and put away. Play should conclude so this can be done without rushing. When children are very young the leader guides their efforts. Cleanup should be a time of happy talk about the play and plans for future dramatizing.

Part Three

Creative Drama

5

Playmaking

Playmaking, or creative drama, means to make up and act plays. Its participants may be called playmakers. They should have the same spirit of adventure they have in imitative play. But playmakers must exercise greater self-discipline. There are other differences between these two forms of creative theatre.

How Creative Drama Differs from Imitative Play

Players Act According to a Plan. Unlike imitative play, creative drama requires players to plan before they begin to act. The plan can be short, but it is definite. It is neither written nor memorized. It is only discussed until participants agree on it.

Playmakers Work as a Team. They cooperate when they plan and when they act. Each child has opportunity to contribute his ideas, and he pays attention to the ideas of others. The plan results from teamwork.

In dramatizing, each player accepts a definite responsibility. To discharge it he must coordinate his efforts with those of others. How unlike imitative play! There each child acts to suit himself. If he doesn't like what other players do he ignores them and acts as he chooses.

Players Try to Excel. They want to do their best in both planning and acting. After performing a dramatization once, participants offer ideas for improving it. So does their leader. Then they repeat their performance to improve it.

The effort to improve is not to please an audience. It is like a game. When children play "hide and seek" they try to do their best. They run their fastest and use their greatest cunning to sneak back to base. Concern for spectators has no place in such a game. Neither has it a place in playmaking.

Forms of Creative Drama

There are two forms of creative drama. One is improvisation. In it leader and players together create their own plot for a dramatization.

The other form is story play. Here players take their plot from an existing story. It may be an old favorite or one they hear for the first time the day of the dramatization.

The two forms are so closely related as to be often combined into one project. For example, players develop an improvisation to the point that it is a complete story. Then, their final processes of planning and acting are identical with those of story play.

In its turn story play can be served by improvisation. Its players find they need a scene that they must invent to explain a situation or show what characters are like. To achieve it they use techniques of improvisation.

What Playmaking Means to Children

Playmaking offers children experiences deeper and more thought-provoking than those of imitative play. Success in the more difficult form brings a thrill unknown in imitative play.

The 1960 White House Conference on Children and Youth considered the activity important. It recommended: "Every child should be given the opportunity to participate in creative dramatics under qualified leadership."

UNESCO approved the activity as a technique to help solve psychological problems of European children after World War Two.

Where It Takes Place

Creative drama requires little in the way of space or supplies. It may be conducted indoors or out. It needs only a place that is quiet and that permits children to move about. Among places frequently used are classrooms, clubrooms, the corner of a park or playground, and a family living room.

The Leader Makes the Difference

Success of creative drama depends not on the place but on the leader. He gives direct leadership. His efforts determine whether creative drama succeeds or fails in its attempts to achieve drama's goals for participants. His task is not to create something and hand it to children. But he must bring the activity to life and set it on the right course. He has responsibility to:
1. Choose suitable program material.
2. Present it so as to challenge children's imagination.
3. Guide them in making a plan.
4. Organize them for dramatization.
5. Help them grow in ability to think and act.

How to Choose Program Material

The devices a leader uses to stimulate children's ideas for dramatization are called program material. It may be found in personal experiences and in all the arts. The leader usually considers a variety of material before he makes a choice. There are questions he should ask concerning possible material.

Do I Like This Material? If a leader can answer ''yes'' he knows the material stimulates his own interest and feeling. Unless it does he cannot hope to use it to stimulate others.

Does It Deal with Specific Images? There is greater challenge in a specific image than a generality. For instance, the statement that people are hungry does not stir the imagination as does the following: One family had so little food that they lived on berries their little son searched for every day in the woods. Here is a character as well as a situation to start a flow of ideas.

Hearing about this boy, children think about him, how it feels to be hungry or alone, and how brave and generous he is. They soon have ideas for dramatization.

A teacher once showed pupils a picture of a rockly landscape and said, "What do you think about all those rocks?" The children did not respond. With another group she asked a different question as she displayed the picture. "What do you think of this rock that looks as if it had been hurled into place?" Children began to think about who hurled the rock, and why. This brought ideas for a dramatization.

Does It Suggest Struggle or Conflict? Drama needs an element of conflict. Characters should encounter obstacles or complications as they try to solve their problems. The struggle need not be physical; it can be emotional or intellectual.

The Mother Goose rhyme, "The Queen of Hearts," involves conflict. The king and knave struggle for possession of the tarts. "Little Miss Muffet" is based on confrontation between the little girl and a spider. The spider wins. "Jack Horner" is a pleasant rhyme but lacks conflict on which to build a dramatization.

Drama should treat life in moments of crisis. The leader looks for material that involves a clash of opposing forces.

Does It Suit Age, Ability, and Interests of Participants? Material should be mature enough to challenge children's interest yet simple enough for them to understand. Above all, it should be within their emotional understanding. Pangs of a jealous mother-in-law do not stir feeling in a ten-year-old. Neither can children be expected to understand sorrows of unrequited love.

Material within children's emotional understanding can be adapted to different age levels. An example is "The Queen of Hearts." Chapter 7 shows how adults used this rhyme. Five and six-year-olds can use it to equal advantage. The two dramatizations will differ but all ages can understand the feelings of king, queen, and knave.

Children's ability to adapt material for dramatization is another consideration. Beginners and young children should have short planning sessions so they can move quickly to acting. Their material should require little adaptation. Older children need something that challenges them to concentrated effort even in planning.

Children's interests as well as age and ability influence choice of material. Chapter 3 describes use of current interests for imitative play. Creative drama leaders can use many of those suggestions.

One recreation director took advantage of a current interest when she learned children were studying Columbus at school. To her creative drama group she introduced the poem "Columbus" by Joaquin Miller. History study gave these participants a background of facts about the explorer. From the poem they learned of his feelings and struggles. Their dramatization reflected both their knowledge and understanding.

Another leader saved ideas for use in different kinds of weather. This put children in the mood for her selection. On the first hot day of spring she showed creative drama participants Brian Wildsmith's picture storybook, *The North Wind and the Sun.* They dramatized it with enthusiasm.

Does Material Suggest Interesting Characters for Children to Play? The greatest thrill of creative drama is acting. This means there must be parts to play. They should be roles that appeal to children. The hungry boy who gathered berries should offer such a role. Characters he might meet in the woods could be of equal interest.

If Material Is from the Arts, Is It of Recognized Merit? Material from the arts should be good art. This is true whether the selection is literature, music, visual arts, or other. Leaders report that children often reveal naturally good taste. When offered a choice between what is fine and what is mediocre they frequently choose the best. Program material from the arts should have recognized merit.

Does Material Offer Variety? In a course of several sessions there should be variety of program material. There are many ways to achieve it. A leader may relate personal experiences or ask players to tell theirs as a beginning for dramatization. To help them recall he asks questions like these: "Have you ever slept outdoors?" "Were you ever afraid?" "What games do you play?" "What happened when you played?"

For other sessions material is from the arts—a variety of arts. For the first session a leader may use a story, at another, recorded music, and later, a picture.

A sure way to attain variety in program material is to choose what relates to the time of year. Every day is the anniversary of some historic event or the birthday of a famous person. Dramatizations may be based on the event or an incident in the life or times of the person.

Holidays as they occur suggest varied program emphases. Religious holidays suggest stories of religious history. Civic holidays offer patriotic poems, stories, music, and pictures.

The four seasons offer equally varied material appropriate for summer, autumn, winter, and spring.

Presenting Material so as to Challenge Players

Program material is presented to start creative drama in the same spirit as ideas and supplies are offered to stimulate imitative play. Presentation methods differ, but spirit is the same.

When girls use a Dutch door as a counter for playing store in imitative play they do not think of themselves. They think of the half-door and ideas it suggests for play. In the same way boys get from their bicycles impetus to play Indianapolis 500. Just as the Dutch door and bicycle initiate imitative play so program material promotes creative drama.

How does a leader present program material to give this challenge to playmakers?

Be Prepared. This is the first requisite of the leader about to introduce program material. If the material is in a book the page is marked for quick reference. When recorded music is used the record is in place, and the electric cord is plugged in.

The leader who tells a story knows what happens next throughout the tale. He doesn't let Red Riding Hood get to Grandma's without telling that she met Wolf in the woods. Participants are distracted by hesitation or fumbling of any kind.

Enjoy It. A leader chooses material that he likes. He shows this and makes an effort to focus attention on features in the material that stir his pleasure in it.

One caution must be mentioned. The leader does not merely state that he enjoyed the material. He points up those features that gave him joy. Listeners have a right to be annoyed when someone says, "I heard the funniest thing. I just laughed and laughed." They want to hear what caused the laughter so they too can laugh. For this reason a leader makes vivid the details that stirred his sense of humor, wonder, or admiration. Then his listeners can be moved to deep feeling that is apt to stimulate imagination.

A leader has the same spirit in presenting material he would have in telling a joke to friends. He enjoys the joke and wants to share it so they can enjoy it with him.

With players the leader's purpose is to stimulate their creativity toward planning. To do this he presents material that stirs their feeling enough to draw attention away from themselves. The material then stimulates players' flow of ideas. A teacher once complained, "I couldn't get my class to create anything. I said, 'Now class, I want you to be creative. You can make a play about anything you want.' They didn't say a word."

This teacher might understand her class if she thought about an unhappy hostess who described her dull party. To a friend she said, "As we sat down to dinner I said, 'Does any one know a good joke?' Apparently no one did. Then I asked if some one had an interesting experience on his vacation. No one said a thing. Yet I've known these people to be lively and entertaining."

The teacher and hostess should understand that neither adults nor children get much impetus to create by merely being told to do so. They are motivated when experience gives them ideas they want to share. Leaders remember this when they present program material.

How to Guide Planning

Children about to plan a dramatization should feel the same elation as when they start imitative play. The leader sustains the enthusiasm by showing appreciation for their ideas and making full use of them. He is careful not to humilate children because their suggestions are not useful.

To stimulate ideas the leader asks the question about the program material and how to use it for dramatization. These are not like examination questions to discover what participants know. These are to make the children want to think. First questions call for little more than opinion. Since answers are easy they let children gain confidence. The first question is something like, "Do you like this material?"

The second may be, "Why do you like it?" This causes players to do analytical thinking. Then come questions about characters: What people are in this situation? Why are they here? Might there be other characters? What are they doing? How do they feel toward one another? Do these feelings change?

The next group of questions concerns characters' looks, attitudes, mannerisms, and habits. Each question is a topic for short discussion, a chance for children to express ideas and opinions. All children do not speak on each topic, but all have the opportunity to speak on some of them. Questions come fast enough to keep discussion lively. Occasional pauses give children time to think. This variation in tempo adds excitement.

When children speak the leader looks at them and listens. If no answers come, he asks a simpler question. It may require only an opinion or an obvious "yes" or "no." Some of these questions he directs to children who have not spoken. He looks encouragingly at them but not long enough to embarrass. He continues to include them along with others as he directs questions to the entire group. He discourages too many answers from the same children by looking more frequently at others.

The leader laughs with the children when there is humor in a question or answer. He is careful to let participants know that he laughs at their cleverness. He does not laugh at apparent mistakes; nor does he permit children to do so. If laughter becomes boisterous a leader attempts to control it by a slight raise of his hand in a gesture for silence. He follows this with a challenging question.

Consideration of each topic concludes with a group decision about the plan for dramatization. When opinion about plot and character is unanimous the leader moves to a new topic. If children disagree he states the question and takes a vote. Majority opinion prevails, and they are ready to move on.

Planning periods should be short. Only a bit, or scene, is planned before dramatization begins. For beginners and young children a scene may be planned that takes only two or three minutes to enact.

Planning phase is complete when participants know (1) what happens in the scene; (2) where and why it happens; (3) what characters are involved; (4) why they react as they do; and (5) when to begin and end the scene.

To Organize for Dramatization

The activity should pick up speed when organizing begins. It takes less time and thought than required to plan content. To organize for dramatization the leader helps children to

1. Arrange the stage.
2. Prepare offstage effects.
3. Review cues.
4. Assign individual responsibilities.

Arrange the Stage. It is necessary to decide which area will serve as a stage. Participants should be aware of lines, even if only imagined, that separate the stage from observers, and from backstage. In the latter space, which is both behind and at sides of the stage, players wait to make their entrances. Children who create offstage effects are also stationed backstage.

Stage entrances are designated with a box, chair, or mark on the floor. The same methods locate stage properties. These are big objects that are part of the setting. If they are tables or chairs or other convenient items they are put in place. Otherwise their location is marked, or other objects substituted. Chairs are used for thrones; boxes for tables; and floor lamps for trees. A small bench makes a bank; chairs provide seats in a bus.

The leader appoints specific children to put properties in place or mark their location. This is a good task for a child who does not seem confident enough at first to play a role. He is dignified with such title as property boy or girl or member of the stage crew.

Prepare Offstage Effects. Responsibility for sound effects is assigned. Children who discharge it can be called sound technicians or stage crew. Sound effects may require equipment. To obtain it children experiment with different ways of achieving the desired sound. Sound effects technicians try out suggestions and place needed equipment backstage.

Review Cues. Then comes the time to agree on cues. A cue is the signal for a specific word or action in the dramatization. Cues indicate the time for players to enter and leave the stage, for specific dialogue, pantomime, and sound effects. Players also agree on a cue to begin and conclude their scene.

Review of cues gives opportunity for quick review of the plan. The leader asks, ''What is the signal to begin our dramatization?'' Children may decide on a stamp of the foot. Often they suggest a sound that relates to their scene: the sound of a bell, an animal, a musical instrument, or a storm.

As cue review continues the leader asks, ''What characters are onstage when the play starts? Who comes next? What is his cue to enter? Do other characters come? When? What are cues for offstage effects? Does any one leave during the scene? When? What is the last thing you say and do?''

Assign Individual Responsibilities. Choosing the child to play each role is done quickly and quietly. Players should not attach undue importance to it. Each understands that he will play different roles in subsequent performances.

Children usually speak for roles they want to play. Unless there is reason to deny them the leader assigns the roles of their choice. The first performance should be a success so as to increase confidence of all. The leader keeps sufficient control of assignments to assure fairness of opportunity. Sometimes he asks a child to play a particular role for his good or the good of the dramatization. Children often suggest roles for one another. During an entire session each participant has his turn at a variety of tasks.

The creative drama leader adds to the responsibilities of observers. These are the children who watch a performance while they wait their turns to perform. To them the leader says, "Watch the players. See whether they tell the story we want our scene to tell. Do they make its story clear? Is it interesting? Is it exciting?"

Observers can also assist with sound effects. These should be sounds for atmosphere rather than for moving the story forward. The latter are performed by sound technicians backstage. Observers create sound like wind, rain, voices, or distant music. Children who observe should feel personal responsibility to perform their duties.

Just before dramatization begins one child is selected to signal time to open and conclude the scene. If there are few participants this can be the job of the sound effects technicians. He also calls "Places" a minute before the signal to begin.

With this call everyone goes to the place of his assignment. Players onstage at the opening are there. Those who enter later wait at proper entrances. Property boy checks properties and leaves the stage. Sound effects boy with his equipment at his side is ready backstage. Observers are in place in front of the stage.

The leader also has a place. He sits among the observers, or stands behind them. This position lets players know they are on their own. It lets the leader know immediately of any distraction caused by observers so he can correct it. By the leader's attention to the dramatization he encourages players and sets an example for observers. Getting into place takes but a minute. Then players enact their scene.

During the performance the leader notes what players do well and where they need to improve. He does not interrupt. If players reach an impasse he stops the performance to lead them in a short discussion.

Together they discover what went wrong and how to remedy it. The scene is played again from the beginning. At its conclusion the leader leads the applause. Observers join it.

Helping Them Grow in Ability to Think and Act

As applause dies down players and stage crew take seats among observers. The leader sits with them. They talk first about what was good in the dramatization. The discussion is short. Again the leader uses questions to stimulate thinking. Of the questions listed below only a few would be used in any one discussion.

First questions build confidence: What did players do well? In which part were they best at telling the story? When did you feel what the characters felt? How did players show how characters felt? What did the stage crew do to help? These early questions give no opportunity for adverse criticism.

Questions are then directed to players. How did the observers help the play? Did the stage crew help? How did players help one another? Players are then asked to tell what problems they encountered. They describe what they would do to improve as a helpful hint to the next players. The next questions help all participants devise ways to improve their plan.

Questions do more than stimulate children to think of ways to improve. Questions put them in the mood to learn. When one cannot discover an answer for himself he is apt to listen for answers offered by others.

Above questions are for beginning as well as for experienced participants. Of the experienced, a leader asks additional questions. Some of them are to promote serious study of characters: Did players speak and move in character? Did they act like their characters even when they were not speaking? Did players tell about their characters with eyes and body as well as with words?

For experienced players there are also questions of tempo and climax: What is the most exciting moment in the scene? How can it be made the most exciting? What can players do to increase suspense up to this point? Do players show an interest in what other players do? When do they talk and speak faster? When should they pause?

This little evaluation period after each bit of dramatizing should be short, happy, and thought-provoking. After participants offer suggestions for improvement the director adds his own. To players who have just completed a performance the evaluation period should give a sense of achievement and point direction. Observers learn from it how to build on accomplishments of others.

6

How to Guide Improvisation

In improvisation players and leader contrive the plot for their dramatization. Described below are illustrations of procedures leaders use to guide improvisations. Some examples occurred as related. Others have been combined or modified or devised to demonstrate methods.

Wind Storm

Mrs. Farrell, a fifth-grade teacher, started her class on improvisation with an experience for all pupils to share. She let them listen to recorded wind sounds. As she turned on the record player she said, "Listen! What sounds are these?" In a minute she turned off the sound. "What did the sounds remind you of?"

Answers came in a chorus: "Wind." "A windy day." "A storm."

The teacher stated, "You heard the wind. Try to feel it. How does it make your ears feel? Your eyes? What does it do to your hair? Does it make your ears hurt? What do you do to protect them? Did you get dust in your eyes?" They demonstrated answers.

She continued, "Now try to remember some time when you were in a strong wind. Where were you? Did you like the wind? Think about it for a minute." She paused. "When I play the sounds again, show how you felt about that wind." Remaining in their seats pupils acted their feelings about a wind they remembered.

Mrs. Farrell watched them and spoke above the wind noise. "Shirley, your back is good. You round it to protect you from cold. Tom wrinkles his nose to show he doesn't like the wind. John's hand is up to protect his ear. Susan, your eyes show you are happy. And Dan likes the wind. He lifts his face to feel its full force. Look out! Here comes a big gust! Now it's stopping." She turned off the sound and gave children a chance to talk.

"Tell us where you were when you felt the wind." She nodded to one child after another as a signal to speak. She wanted short answers. To children who did not speak she directed a question or comment. "Barbara, were you on a hill? Jeff, you seemed to be on a ship. Rachel, were you on the playground?" She got a response even if only a smile.

The teacher then gave them another problem. "When you hear the wind again, decide which way it's coming from. Is it blowing against your back? Your side? Your face?" During this short exercise she managed to praise children she had not mentioned before.

Then came a more difficult challenge. "Until now you've been sitting in the wind. Did you ever try to walk against it? Would you feel it more? or less? Which is easier—to walk with the wind or against it? When you hear the wind this time you are to walk against it. You in the first two rows, walk from the windows to this wall." She turned to children in the other two rows. "You are observers. See what you can learn about the wind by the way the players walk against it."

Mrs. Farrell encouraged players as they walked. "It's a strong wind. You hate to start, but you have to get to the wall. There, Victor has started. Carmen is out there. Observers, watch them."

As soon as players reached the wall she told them to return to their chairs. She said to the observers, "What did their faces and bodies tell you about this storm? Bessie's wind had a particular quality. What was it? Yes, she felt a cold wind. What did you learn from the way Ignacio turned up his collar, from the way Ralph gritted his teeth?"

Mrs. Farrell then gave the observers their turn. They walked with wind at their backs as they moved from wall to windows. The first players then had a chance to tell what they learned.

This session gave fifth-graders their first experience with creative drama. Not until the second session did they begin to develop plot and character. Then they played they were pioneers who had to get out of their covered wagons to lighten the load. They walked against the wind as they climbed the steep mountain trail. They played the different members of a family who rejoiced when the youngest son ran back to tell them the summit was near.

Leading Children from the Easy to the More Difficult. Mrs. Farrell used several methods to progress from what was easy to the more difficult. First there was progress in the way she asked children to respond. In the beginning they answered simple questions. Next, they were asked to respond in pantomime. This began by merely using eyes, then proceeded to use of faces, heads, and hands, and finally, entire bodies.

The next step involved position. Children remained inconspicuously in their seats for their first interpretations. Later they had to stand and move about the room.

Early exercises permitted all to work at the same time so no one felt he was the focus of attention. As participants gained confidence Mrs. Farrell asked half the class to work while others watched.

This gradual progress in the first session built the confidence necessary for individual work in the next session.

Sweaters and Jackets

Miss Diets, a playground director, used children's sweaters and jackets to stimulate their thinking for improvisation. The children were six- to eight-year-olds. The day was so cool that all wore wraps.

The director began by reciting the familiar rhyme:

> The north wind doth blow
> And we shall have snow.
> And what will the poor robin do?
> He'll tuck his head under his wing, poor thing!
> He'll tuck his head under his wing.

Then she asked: "What did the robin do to keep warm? What do you do to keep warm on a cold day?" Children answered that they wore sweaters or jackets. Miss Diets continued: "Do you ever get so warm when you play that you want to take off your jackets? What do you do to cool off?''

Answers varied from letting jackets hang down over arms to throwing jackets on a bench.

Miss Diets said, ''Don't tell me any more. I want you to show me what you do. First, show how you feel when you get too warm. You wish you didn't have your jacket. Decide what to do, and then, do it—whatever you want. Last, show how much better you feel.''

Miss Diets followed this with a series of improvisation problems that involved sweaters and jackets.

1. ''You're in the house. You remember you left your sweater outdoors. You don't want to go out again. It's cold now, and you have no other wrap. But you must get that sweater. Show how you hate to go, and how you make up your mind to start. Your yard is on this side of the bench. Don't go beyond the bushes. Where do you look for your sweater? Where do you find it? Ready?''

2. ''This time you remember your sweater after you're in the house. But there's a difference. It's now dark outside. You hate to go out now even more than you did before. When you get outside you find several sweaters on the bench. You don't know which is yours. You can't see its color. How do you recognize it? Do you feel its collar? Count the buttons? Feel whether it's fuzzy or slick? Put it on, and show how good the warmth of the sweater feels.''

4. ''Do the same story with this addition. Pick up the wrong sweater. When you get in the house you realize your mistake. Go outdoors again, and find the right one. What do you do then?'' She assigned this to one child to do alone.

Miss Diets again recited the poem about the north wind, and asked the children about snow. ''How do people get about in snow? Why do children go out in snow?''

Answers to the last were ''To ski.'' ''To coast.'' ''To run errands.''

Next questions concerned accidents and what happened to children who fell in the snow. These brought ideas for characters and story, which children acted. In it several children were skiing when one girl fell with a sprained ankle. Girls tried to care for her while boys skiied away for help. They returned with crutches on which the girl hobbled home.

After the session was over Miss Diets saw the children continue to play accidents in the snow. This imitative play had been stimulated by their improvisation.

A Crash

Mrs. Redburn, mother of eleven-year-old Julia, devised a crash to start improvisations at Julia's party. Mrs. Redburn arranged with two young sons to push a kettle of nails off a table when she gave the signal. She went into the next room with the girls and said, "Listen!" Then came the crash.

When the girls recovered from their surprise, Mrs. Redburn asked, "Did that frighten you? What did it make you do?" Half-hysterically the girls described their sensations.

"Have you heard a crash like that before? Where did it occur? Where could it occur?

Among the answers were in a mine, a tunnel, a ship, a tower, a kitchen, and a street.

Mrs. Redburn formed the girls into three groups of three or four each and instructed them. "Each group is to make a play about a crash. Let your play show answers to these questions: Where are you? Why are you there? Who are you? When you hear the crash do you want to run toward it or away from it? What happens after the crash?" She gave the girls ten minutes to plan their scenes.

Each group presented its scene for the others. One girl from each group had a chance to cause the crash for other's scenes.

Something Burning

Children's sense of smell was challenged to start improvisations at a children's cultural center. Miss Kolesky, the director, had conducted a creative drama course for two months. The pupils were nine to twelve years old. She put an old pan of eggshells on an electric plate in an adjoining room. She signaled a volunteer to turn on the heat under the pan.

To the class Miss Kolesky said, "Don't tell me with words what you are beginning to notice. Show me, and show whether you notice it with your eyes? Your ears? Your nose?''

The odor of burning eggshells was immediately apparent. The director continued, ''You show that you smell something. Stay in your chairs. Show me the answers as I ask questions. Do you like that odor? Will you show that you're trying to decide what causes it? Where does it come from? Do you want to move toward it, or away from it? Good.'' She signaled to turn off heat.

''Now, answer with words. Is this a pleasant odor? What could cause it? Do all agree that it smells like something burning? Can you remember any smell like it? What was the cause? What did you do? What did other people do? Did you ever rouse in the night, and smell something burning? Were you afraid? Tell us about it.''

Individual children told experiences with fire. Miss Kolesky went quickly from one child to the next so no one talked too long. Then she gave them an improvisation exercise to do without leaving their seats. ''You are asleep. You are roused by a strong odor. Waken gradually. Take your time, and try to decide what causes the smell. Close your eyes. Here comes the smell of burning.''

As pupils worked, the director made comments. ''Myra, you find it hard to waken. Bob is trying to remember where he is. I'm glad you thought of that. All of you, think about that odor. What can be the cause of it?''

These students were not beginners. They needed a more difficult challenge. ''Repeat your scenes, and add to them. Get up, and investigate. Feel smoke in your eyes. Try to find your way across the room. It is filled with smoke. You can barely see. Feel for furniture. Continue toward the front of the room until I shut the door. That's the signal to return to your chairs.''

After they did the exercise Miss Kolesky prodded children to recall walking in the dark. ''Do you walk fast? Do you bump into things? How do you protect yourself? Are you shocked to find you can't see? Think about this as you do the exercise again.''

Miss Kolesky then promoted a discussion for plot development. She asked, ''Where are you sleeping when you smell this burning?'' The only answer was a bedroom so she persisted, ''Where is this bedroom? At home? In a hotel? A mountain cabin?'' They agreed on home.

The next task was to develop characters. ''Who are you? Are you a member of the family? A guest? Are you mother, father, or child? Decide which you want to be, but don't tell. Decide also what kind of person you are. Do you panic easily? Are you so disorderly that you can't locate your belongings? What do you take with you? Each of you will have a chance to show the rest of us what character you choose. Tell us as much as you can about this character by the way you act in a house on fire.''

Myra was the first to volunteer to do this scene alone. When she finished, the other pupils described what her acting told them. They knew the character was a child because Myra called for her mother and picked up a doll. They could tell it was a doll by the way she cradled it in her arm. She was an orderly child because without hesitation she grabbed the doll from the foot of her bed. She showed she was a gentle child by the way she carried the doll.

Each pupil in turn acted the scene with a character he chose.

Excerpt from a Conversation

An excerpt from an overheard conversation provides a clue for an improvisation. So does a conversation quoted from a book or newspaper. The conversation can be that of only two people, or more. It may be chosen to fit the number who desire to participate.

The talk should stir curiosity and be general enough to permit a variety of interpretations. It may be invented by the leader, or it may be found in a story or play. When participants hear the conversation they should feel all the excitement of eavesdropping. Who has overheard a short conversation without thinking, ''I wonder what they were talking about?'' To wonder in this way is just what a creative drama leader wants participants to do.

He promotes and guides this wondering until children suggest circumstances and speakers. The leader asks questions like these: What people do you think are talking? Where are they? What is happening while they talk. What happens after their conversation?

Here are two conversations that should start improvisations:

1. ''There she goes.''
 ''Catch her.''
 ''Send her this way.''

2. "I'll never get used to being invisible."
 "Who on earth are you?"
 "I can hear speaking, but I can't see anybody."

A third conversation was chosen by the mother of three children. She used it while they waited for emergency car repairs. They sat in a park near the service station. Mother began, "I overheard three people talking. I couldn't see them, but this is what I heard:

"Have you lost it?"
"I can't find it any place."
"What did I tell you?"

Mother asked each child to tell what he thought was lost. Twelve-year-old Rose thought it was a will. Tom, a year younger, said it was probably a safe-cracking tool. The youngest, Babe, guessed a ring.

Mother said, "Let's make three short plays. In the first the lost article will be a will; in the second, a tool for opening a safe; and a third, about a lost ring." The children were ready to go to work. They asked Mother to repeat the conversation. Then they repeated it with each child speaking one line. This gave them a chance to think about what people might be talking.

That was the topic of Mother's first questions. "Who are these three people talking about a lost will? Did one of them have the will and lose it? Have they ever seen it? What will happen if they don't find it? Do they search for it? Where? What did they talk about before the conversation we know? Do they find the will? Who finds it? Does the finding end the play?"

Answers to the questions quickly provided characters and plot. Then the children acted the dramatization. The same questions with slight variations helped the children develop stories about the tool and the ring. The children also acted these two stories.

A Situation in a Sentence

A single sentence can provide the device to make children want to create an improvisation. The sentence should be the climax of a situation.

The following have proved successful:

An injured bird disappears.

Boys throwing sand prevent children from playing on swings.

Mother finds her son's torn coat.

A teacher suspects pupils of cheating in an examination.

Children hear cries for help from an abandoned well.

Mrs. Mack, director of day care center, used the sentence about a bird with five- to eight-year-olds. Two factors influenced her choice. The twenty-five children in the group recently found a baby bird fallen from its nest. They gave it food; the next day it was gone. The other reason was that an improvisation about birds could provide roles for all twenty-five children.

At the beginning of the session Mrs. Mack reminded children about their experience with baby bird. As they reminisced she asked questions that she hoped would result in improvisation. "Do you think other birds found the baby bird? How did they happen to discover it? Were they flying close to the ground? Do you think they played little games as they flew? Would they sometimes touch the ground and take a few hops? Let's play we are birds and do the things you suggest. Fly from the farthest tree to this clump of grass and sit in it."

Mrs. Mack joined them in their flight. Without her suggestion children made birdlike sounds as they flew. She heard "cheep cheep" from almost every child. Once they were seated on the grass Mrs. Mack started a discussion about the baby bird. "Did it cry for help? Is it afraid? Does one bird come so close he almost touches the baby? As other birds come does the baby tell its troubles? Where is its mother? Do birds feel sorry for the baby? How do they show this?

"Let's play it again and find the baby. Who'll be the bird to see the baby first? Cora will. Who wants to play the baby? All right, Peggy. Sit in this clump of grass until the birds find you."

They agreed that one bird would say "cheep cheep" as the signal to start the scene. Children played the scene to the point of feeling sorry for the baby.

Then they sat and talked about how birds could help the baby. They decided to bring straw to keep it warm and some berries to feed it.

To help children plan a conclusion Mrs. Mack asked, "What will happen to the baby in the end?" Children decided that the baby bird was found by its mother, who made a nest for it there in the grass. The children acted the entire scene.

Participants' Experiences

Telling their own experiences can result in children's improvisations. To help them recall events a leader mentions a challenging topic. Here are suggestions:

> When I was afraid.
> When I got my dog.
> When I lost my pet.
> When I started to school.
> When I moved into a new neighborhood.

The first topic was used by Sharon, a college girl, who was summoned to babysit with five children. They ranged in age from seven to twelve. Sharon put the children in the mood for the topic by reading to them James Whitcome Riley's "Seein' Things at Night."

As soon as she finished, the children began to tell of strange shapes and sounds that had come to them at night. The children laughed when they told Sharon how frightened they had been. She laughed with them, and asked, "What were the sounds like?"

The children hesitated as they answered, "Different kinds." Sharon suggested that each child find a piece of equipment to make the kind of sound he had heard.

She said, "You can use your voices, your hands, or any objects you find for sound effects." For five minutes the children separated to locate equipment and practice frightening sounds.

When they returned, each child was ready. One created the sound of tramping feet by beating a book on a grocery carton. Another wailed in a tremulous, high-pitched voice. A third child made a squeaking noise by dragging a piece of chalk across the chalkboard. Other sounds were achieved by pounding a fist on the door and by rubbing together two pieces of sandpaper.

Sharon then asked the children if they could put on garments and accessories to resemble the terrible shapes. They could, and they wanted to try. Again they separated. Their return showed the youngest boy with a knitted stocking cap stretched over his face. The oldest boy said he had been frightened by a creature with a big head. To imitate this he put a plastic motorcycle helmet over his face, and peeked through the two little air holes. The older girl tied a scarf over her face and let the long ends float behind her as she ran. The younger girl wore a dish towel over her head and arms. She extended her hands and opened and closed her fingers in convulsive, clutching movements. The middle boy blew up rubber gloves and tied one on each wrist for an apparition of a four handed monster.

Sharon called the children to her and asked, "Would you like to make a play with these strange people as the characters?" Since they would, she started the project with this question. "What could happen to make all these creatures come into the same room?" The children were unanimous in the idea that they would come to frighten a child at night.

After further planning Sharon played the role of a sleeping child. One by one the frightening shapes came in and made their frightening sounds. Sharon awoke and recoiled in fright. Then the children acted the climax they had planned. The weird creatures didn't want to frighten the child. They were only playing ghostly games and wanted her to play with them. The play ended as Sharon played "Looby Loo" with all the creatures.

Games

Traditional games of running, chasing, and hiding contain suggestions for improvisation. These games usually include struggles which can represent dramatic conflict. Here are some familiar games that can provide a basis for improvisation: prisoners' base, hide and seek, stealing sticks, pom pom pullaway, run sheep run, three deep.

Mr. Mukarsky was the activity director in a home for boys. Of all the activities he conducted the boys liked best the twilight game period.

One night a sudden rain forced them to take shelter in the playroom before the play period was over. They had been playing hide and seek. Mr. Mukarsky said, "Do you boys want to do something new with hide and seek? They stopped talking long enough to hear what he had in mind. He went on, "There's a mystery in this game. Why do the players run away from home base to hide, and then, sneak right back? If people did that in real life, what would you think they wanted?'' The boys did not answer. Mr. Mukarsky kept trying. ''Do they want to spy on the person who is 'It'? Does 'It' have something they want to get?''

A few answers came. The boys showed interest. Mr. Mukarsky asked more questions. He allowed time after each question for the boys to think about answers. ''Who is 'It'? Does he have some kind of treasure? Why does he try to catch the other players? Is he afraid they'll steal something, or discover a secret?''

The boys showed they were intrigued by this mystery in a commonplace game. Almost every boy had a theory to explain the situation. The theory that they all liked was that 'It' was a scientist who had developed medicine to cure all sickness. Boys thought the other players were doctors who wanted a supply of medicine and the formula. This explained why they ran, hid, and then sneaked back as soon as 'It' left.

Mr. Mukarsky asked, ''Why does the scientist count while the others hide?''

One boy answered, ''He has to stir the mixture fifty strokes.''

''Why do the others hide?''

''They've been spying and don't want him to see them. When he leaves they sneak back to steal the medicine.''

''What do the doctors do when they reach the medicine?''

''They smell it and touch it, and one tastes it. They try to lift the big kettle it's in.''

Then came questions about the scientist. ''Why does he leave his precious kettle?''

''He hears a noise outside.''

Mr. Mukarsky concluded, ''We'll play hide and seek like this. But we have to decide how it ends. Does the scientist capture the doctors?''

The boys wanted him to catch one and learn from him what the doctors wanted. They said, ''Then he gives them the medicine. He wants everybody to have it.''

Grab Bags

One hundred girls at a play day developed improvisations from grab bags. The twelve-year-old girls were separated into ten groups, each with a girl captain and an adult leader. Miss Withers, the play day chairman, let captains draw slips of paper from four paper bags.

In the first bag each paper bore the name of a place. Included were a motel office, toyshop, haunted house, laboratory, and tunnel. Papers in the second bag carried a stated time, such as Saturday afternoon, Christmas morning, your birthday, midnight, time to get up, first day of school, and Hallowe'en. Third bag papers contained names of people. Among them were Santa Claus, Columbus, policeman, bus driver, peddler, witch, housewife, and neighbors. Fourth bag papers described weather conditions: blizzard, fog, hurricane, rainstorm, tropical heat, and fair and warmer.

Miss Withers explained that each group would use the information on its four slips for a dramatization. Captains took the papers to their groups. All set about planning scenes to present for one another.

After they had planned for only a few minutes Miss Withers called the captains to rummage through large boxes. Some contained costumes and accessories. They included skirts, caps, crowns, ribbons, capes, collars, trousers, shoes, tights, sheets, drapes, masks, veils, costume jewelry, scarves, and aprons.

There were other boxes that contained hand properties. Among them were badges, hangers, tools, engine parts, gunny sacks, and pieces of crepe paper, butcher paper, and newspaper. There was also an assortment of noisemakers from auto horns to musical instruments.

Each captain could choose items she wanted from the boxes. From them the girls got more ideas for their scenes. The adult leader of each group helped with questions, comments, and final decisions. She made sure there was a part for every girl.

As soon as scheduled planning time elapsed all girls assembled at play day headquarters. They sat in a semicircle to watch as each group presented its scene.

Miss Withers found the grab bags so successful that on another occasion she used them at a Sunday school picnic. Pupils of varied ages attended with other members of their classes. Miss Withers used only one grab bag. The slips of paper in it contained proverbs. Among them were:

One in the hand is worth two in the bush.
A stitch in time saves nine.
Where there's a will, there's a way.
A rolling stone gathers no moss.
Early to bed, early to rise makes a man healthy, wealthy, and wise.

After participants had a chance to think about the proverbs they had drawn, Miss Withers presented the boxes of supplies. These were similar to those at the play day. Supplies and proverb together stimulated members of each class to plan and present an improvisation.

Poems

A poem has been used previously in combination with other devices. It can also stand alone as motivation for improvisation. Following are titles of suitable poems:

"Opportunity," by Edward Sill.
"Columbus," by Joaquin Miller.
"The Blind Man and the Elephant," by Edward Saxe.
"My Cat Timothy," by Rose Fyleman.
"Three Little Kittens," from Mother Goose.

Mr. Young tried another poem with his Sunday school class of twelve-year-old boys. It was "A Nation's Strength," by Ralph Waldo Emerson.

> Not gold, but only men can make
>   A people great and strong;
> Men who for truth and honor's sake
>   Stand fast and suffer long.
>
> Brave men who work while others sleep,
>   Who dare while others fly—
> They build a nation's pillars deep
>   And lift them to the sky.

Mr. Young wanted the boys in his Sunday school class to enjoy the music and message of the poem. He prepared carefully before he met with his class. He read the poem aloud, first, for sheer enjoyment, a second time, to comprehend more fully its meaning, and again to feel its rhythm and the music of its words.

Its pace was slow and heavy. It invited the reader to take time to think. The rhythm of a pile driver was suggested by the strong beat of the lines.

The teacher noted contrasts between the words *gold* and *men,* and again between *stand fast* and *sleep.* When he read the clause, *only men can make,* he held the sounds *m* and *n* to make it musical.

The poem made him think of various people who had made America great and strong. Some were famous. Others had led little-known lives. He formulated questions to help children think of heroic people they knew, or had heard about.

When the class met, Mr. Young read the poem with all the feeling his study of it had roused in him. After concluding he asked, "What does the poem say a nation needs to make it strong?" No one answered. The boys seemed under the spell of the poem. The teacher persisted, "Does a nation need gold to make it great?"

Several boys said softly, "No."

"Is it men?"

Just as softly came the answers, "Yes."

"What kind of men?" No answer, so he said, "Listen. See if you can find answers in the poem." He read it again.

Then came answers, "men who work," "brave men," "men who dare," "Men who stand fast," and "Men who suffer."

Mr. Young asked, "Can you think of any one who stood fast for truth and honor's sake? In history? In your own life? What did he do? Could it mean a mother who takes good care of her children? A father who works hard to earn a living for them? What about a student who studies hard? An honest storekeeper?"

The boys had many suggestions. Mention of an honest storekeeper reminded them of Abraham Lincoln. They mentioned him several times as an example of men who made America great. They wanted to plan an improvisation about him and the incident of walking miles to return money to a customer he had shortchanged.

Mr. Young initiated improvisation planning with questions about the store: "How does it look? What merchandise is there? How does it differ from today's stores?"

Questions about Lincoln included: "Is he tired? Worried? Is the store making a profit? Is he friendly with customers? Does he joke with them? Do they like him? Respect him? Why?"

Then came questions about customers; "Do all people who come in make purchases? Do they sit and talk? Where do they sit? What do they talk about? How do they earn a living? What names do you want to give them? What personalities belong to the different names?"

Since all members of the class were boys, they wanted to play that the shortchanged customer was a man. They named him Ben. Questions about Ben were: "What does he buy? Why does he fail to notice his change? Is he in a hurry? Why?"

The boys thought their dramatization should be in two scenes with a pause between to show lapse of time. This would give Ben time to get home.

Here are the questions Mr. Young used to help boys prepare the last scene: "What is Lincoln doing when he finds his mistake? How does he feel about it? What is he going to do? Does he decide at once? Is he sure he must go?

"Do others in the store try to persuade him to forget it? What reasons do they give? Is it a long way? How much money does Lincoln owe Ben? Does that seem to justify such a long walk?

"When others see Lincoln is determined, do they offer to help? Will one of them look after the store? What do they say about him after he leaves? Is that a good place to end the scene?"

After boys performed the dramatization Mr. Young saw need to make characters more lifelike, and to build the scene to a climax. To help the next players he asked these questions: "How does Ben show he's nervous? How does he let Lincoln know that he needs all his money? How does Lincoln show in the beginning that he, too, is worried about money, and that he is tired? Does he hesitate a little before deciding to take the long walk? What are his thoughts as he makes up his mind? How do others in the store show they wonder how he will decide? Are they proud of him afterwards?"

Historical Incident

Although Mr. Young started improvisation activity with a poem, he demonstrated also how to use historical incidents. From the decision to use the Lincoln episode this historical incident motivated the improvisation.

Appropriate incidents are found in the history of social movements as well as in political and military history. Suggestions for specific incidents come with observance of civic and religious holidays, with issuing of commemorative stamps, and famous birthdays.

Incidents of history that are suitable include: Signing of the Magna Carta; Discovery of the Pacific Ocean; Boston Tea Party; Wright Brothers Tinker with a Flying Machine in Their Bicycle Shop; Discovery of Penicillin; Joseph Lee Starts Public Recreation Movement after Seeing Children Endangered when Playing in Street; Grandma Moses Sells Her First Picture; Marshall Discovers Gold on Sutter's Creek; Signing of the American Declaration of Independence and Ringing of the Liberty Bell.

The last is suggested by the Fourth of July. Other holidays call to mind other incidents appropriate for dramatization: Christmas suggests Seeking of Shelter by Mary and Joseph; Hanukkah suggests Victory of Judah Maccabee; Thanksgiving suggests Welcoming Indians to First American Thanksgiving Dinner.

Pictures

Mrs. Hamilton, cultural arts director at a community recreation center, demonstrated pictures as a device for improvisation. She conducted art and drama activities for six- to eight-year-olds.

She began improvisation activity by display of a picture by Jan Steen. It was "The Eve of St. Nicholas." Mrs. Hamilton found it in *Story of Painting for Young People* by H. W. Janson and Dorcas Jane Janson (New York: Harry Abrams Inc., 1952). The director asked her pupils to look at the picture. It portrayed a Dutch family with several children enjoying toys left by St. Nicholas. One boy was crying because he had received a birch rod instead of a toy.

Mrs. Hamilton explained that Dutch parents tell children they receive toys when they are good. When they are not, St. Nicholas leaves a birch rod for whipping them. To help her pupils notice details she asked these questions: "What members of the family do you see? Are they happy? Why? Who is unhappy? Why? Who is in the shadow at back? What is each person saying at the moment of the picture? What do the parents' faces tell about them? Are they good parents?"

As children planned the content of their dramatization they frequently referred to the picture. It gave them ideas for characters and incidents.

For a class of twelve-year-olds Mrs. Hamilton selected two other pictures. One was "When Did You Last See Your Father?" by William Yeames, in *World Famous Paintings* by Rockwell Kent (New York: Wm. H. Wise & Co. Inc., 1932). The other, "One of the Family," by Frederick Cotman, was in the same collection.

The children in this class had previous experience with pictures in improvisations. For this session she let half the class work on each picture. On the chalkboard the director wrote these questions: "Who are the people in your picture? What is their relationship to one another? Why are they there? What is happening? What caused it to happen? How does each person feel about it? How does it all end?"

Mrs. Hamilton appointed a chairman in each group and announced, "You are to plan an improvisation suggested by the picture. Your scene will show answers to the questions on the board. Look in the pictures for clues.

She visited each group to give help that might be needed. When the improvisations were ready each group gave a presentation for the other.

Here are more paintings to motivate improvisations:

"The Happy Family" by Jan Steen in *Pictures to Live With* by Brian Holme (New York: Viking Press, 1959).

"Children's Games" by Alice Chase in *Famous Paintings* by Alice Chase (New York: Platt & Munk, Inc., 1951).

"The Graham Children" by Wm. Hogarth in *The Story of Painting for Young People* by W. H. Janson and Dorcas Janes Janson (New York: Harry N. Abrams Inc., 1952).

Instrumental Music

Music, like poems and pictures, can serve improvisation by increasing effectiveness of other devices. It can also provide the sole motivation. Music can relax children's tensions, minimize self-consciousness, and put players in the mood to dramatize.

Mrs. Roberts taught music and drama at a neighborhood center. For her creative drama class of six- to eight-year-olds she asked an accompanist to play the third and fourth movements of Beethoven's Pastoral Symphony. To the children, Mrs. Roberts said, "Mrs. Prost is going to play a selection you haven't heard before. Listen carefully." At the end of the third movement she interrupted to ask these questions: "Does the music make you feel happy, or sad? Does it make you feel like playing? What kind of play? Whirl? Jump? Run? Play tag?''

After pupils discussed answers to the questions the director said, ''Miss Prost will play that music again. This time you may run and play to show how the music makes you feel.''

When the music and playing ceased Mrs. Hamilton asked more questions to stimulate more thinking: ''What kind of people are playing in this music? Are they grownups? Teenagers? Children? Do the children play a game together, or does each child play in his own way?''

Children acted results of this discussion as Miss Prost repeated the third movement. Then they listened to the fourth movement. After it Mrs. Hamilton had questions ready: ''Did the music change? How did it make you feel? What sounds did you hear in this music? Would these sounds frighten children at play? Do they stop playing? What do they do now?''

Stimulated by the music and the discussion, these pupils created a lively dramatization. They played with abandon as they cavorted about the room. With the beginning of the fourth movement they paused to show fright at thunder and big drops of rain. Then they resumed their play by running in the rain and lifting their hands and faces to feel it. In conclusion, half the pupils played mothers who came to call the children in. Children continued to play until mothers caught them and led them indoors. Pupils did the entire scene twice so each one had opportunity to play both mother and child.

Miscellany of Devices

Many other devices exist to stimulate improvisation. Among them are cartoons, photographs, sculpture, riddles, jokes, objects like a ring of keys, assorted gloves or shoes, and sounds of rain, a closing door, and Christmas caroling.

Folk dances and ballet numbers can be just as useful as instrumental music.

Some of the most commonplace sensations can generate ideas for improvisations. These include the taste of medicine, candy, lemon, or ice cubes; the smell of escaping gas, sausages, or the ocean; the feel of sand in the eyes, a pebble in the shoe, new towels, and a piece of velvet.

7

Stories and How to Act Them

The story play leader uses creative drama techniques described in Chapter 5. Many of them are the same as for improvisation. The first task is to select stories suitable for children to act. Outlined here are carefully chosen stories and examples of procedures leaders use to help children dramatize them.

The story described first was selected by Mrs. Mack, the day care center director, who led the baby bird improvisation. One reason for choosing the story was that children had been prepared for it by the improvisation. Other reasons were interesting plot, many good parts, and incidents that could be readily dramatized.

Why the Evergreen Trees Never Lose Their Leaves, by Florence Holbrook
SOURCE: *Good Stories for Great Holidays* by Frances Olcott (Boston and New York: Houghton Mifflin Company, 1914).
CHARACTERS:
  Birds that Fly South
  Bird with the Broken Wing
  Birch Tree
  Oak Tree
  Willow Tree
  Spruce Tree
  Pine Tree
  Juniper Tree
  Frost King
  North Wind

SITUATION IN THE BEGINNING:
   Birds flying south for winter leave behind the Bird with the Broken
   Wing.
WHAT HAPPENS:
      It asks help from Birch, Oak, and Willow, but all refuse.
      Spruce, Pine, and Juniper offer a home, protection, and food.
         Frost King calls North Wind to blow off all leaves.
      The three kind trees beg to keep theirs to help the bird.
MOST EXCITING MOMENT:
   Frost King orders North Wind to spare the leaves as requested.
CONCLUSION:
   Frost King proclaims the three trees shall never lose their leaves.

   Mrs. Mack told the story to the twenty-five children under her direction. She liked the story, and she showed her feeling for it as she told it.
When she finished she didn't move. Neither did the children. Then she
said quietly, "Isn't it a good story?" They thought it was. Quickly she
suggested, "Let's make a play out of it."

   Several asked if they could be the Bird with the Broken Wing. She
answered that they would decide that later. "First we have to plan the
play. Who is in this story?" They mentioned birds, trees, Frost King,
and North Wind.

   To plan the first scene Mrs. Mack used these questions: "Who begins
the story? Do birds play in the forest before they fly away? Do they play in
much the same way as the birds who found the baby bird? How do they
know when to fly south? Could it be the sound of the North Wind?"

   Mrs. Mack let the children practice making North Wind sounds. Then
she continued her questioning: "Do birds stop their play to listen? Does
one bird hear the sound first and alert the others? Do they feel cold? Do
they talk to one another about the flight to the south? How do they get
ready? Does their leader check their wings? Does he give the signal to
start?" Answers came quickly to some questions. Others required discussion.

   The director then organized her charges to dramatize the short introductory scene. They named as forest boundaries the same tree and clump
of grass that served their previous improvisation. To fly south they would
run to the sandbox, circle it, and return to Mrs. Mack. This would put
children in position to plan the next scene.

   There were parts for every child. Mrs. Mack assigned particular responsibilities to some children. There was one who acted as leader; another signaled time to begin the play by saying, "Cheep cheep." A third heard the North Wind and cautioned all to listen.

Just before the players took their places Mrs. Mack used questions for a quick review: "Where do you wait for the play to begin? Where do you go when you fly south? What's the signal to fly away? Where do you go as the scene ends?"

After children played the scene, the director promoted improvement with this question: "Was your play like the story?"

One child responded, "The two boys who left us to play tag weren't acting the story. They were supposed to fly south." This was solved by having the private game of tag in the forest before the flight started.

Mrs. Mack asked, "What can birds do to show they enjoy their play in the forest?" This brought suggestions to fly over a wide area, not to crowd at center, and to hold up heads as though they liked to look at the trees and smell the fresh air.

The director added to their suggestions. "You should take more time to listen to the wind to be sure you hear it. Stop playing, and listen. Think about what that sound means."

To stimulate planning the next scene Mrs. Mack asked questions about plot: "Who comes as soon as the birds leave? Is the little bird flying? Why not? Does the bird limp? How does the bird feel about being alone? Does it cry? Get mad? Do you like this bird? Do you want to give it a name?" Children decided to name the bird "Candy."

Again came the questions: "Which tree does the bird speak to first? Will Birch help? Why not? Similar questions reviewed refusal of Oak and Willow. Is the bird polite when it asks for help? How does Candy feel after three trees say 'No?' What does she do?"

To organize children for dramatization Mrs. Mack asked where the three trees should stand. She assigned parts. While players took places she spoke to the observers. "What kind of day is it in the forest? Is there a little breeze? Does it make a sound in the trees? What kind of sound?"

Some observers answered, "Sh-sh-sh-." Others made a soft humming. The director liked the combination and asked them to repeat it as a signal for the players to begin. They continued it until Candy began to speak.

After this scene was played Mrs. Mack asked Candy to tell the next player how she could do better. Candy warned the next player not to forget to protect her broken wing at all times.

Mrs. Mack asked the three trees for their suggestions for improvement. Birch said, "Oak and Willow talked just the way I did. I think they should be different." This comment gave opportunity for character study.

The director said, "All we know about the trees is what they say to Candy. Birch won't help because she has her own birds to look after. Are there any birds there now? So is that a good reason not to help? Have you known people who talked about what they had to do, yet they didn't do much? Do they complain? How do people talk when they complain?" Every one answered with a whine.

Then came a discussion of Oak. "It is also worried. What about? Oak is afraid of losing its acorns. Do you think Oak is stingy? Would the acorns make good food for Candy? How does Oak spend its time?" Children thought Oak would be guarding and hiding its acorns and looking around for thieves.

Similar discussion of Willow revealed that Willow thought itself better than other trees. One child said, "Willow wants everybody to admire it."

Another suggested, "It would always be trying to make itself look prettier."

Before children repeated the scene Mrs. Mack asked questions about Candy: "Does Candy get sadder and more discouraged? How does she feel after the third refusal? Be sure to show that as you play." That ended the session for the day.

Next day Mrs. Mack began by asking, "What had happened in our play when we stopped?" This brought a quick review. She continued, "Now we're coming to the best part. Candy is sad, but help is coming. Three trees offer to help. Who remembers the names of these kind trees?" They remembered Pine.

"The others are Spruce and Juniper. Have you seen a spruce tree? Does it have low branches? What can a tree with low branches offer a bird that can't fly? Yes, a cozy home within its reach.

"How is Pine different? Remember the Pine says, 'I am big and strong.' What help does Pine offer?"

Similar questions were asked about Juniper. Then came other questions: "Does Candy accept offers of all three trees? Is she surprised?

Happy? Does she say 'thank you?' What else does she say?

"What do selfish trees think about all this. Do they pay attention to it? Are they ashamed?"

Before the children acted this scene Mrs. Mack helped them decide where the three evergreen trees should stand. Then she assigned the parts.

After acting the scene they planned the climax and conclusion. Mrs. Mack began, "Candy thinks her troubles are over. Are they? Who comes to the forest? North Wind comes, but who comes before? Does he rule the forest in winter? Does he look over the trees to see if it's time to call North Wind? I'll be North Wind. All of you be Frost King, and call me." She took a few steps away. "I'm far away. Call so I can hear. Call like a king."

They didn't sound like kings. "Try again. When you say 'Ho' hold that 'O' for a long time." This got better results. "Does North Wind come at once? Does he come quietly, or with bluster? What sound does he make?" Children practiced the sound. "Does he bow to the king? Does he look to the king for his orders? What are they? Does North Wind like his job? The story says 'It called out in its frolic.' Frolic means having fun. How does he frolic while he works?

"To which trees does North Wind go first? Does he blow off their leaves? What happens when he reaches Spruce? Has any tree ever asked him to spare its leaves? Is he surprised? What does he do? What does Frost King say? Does the same thing happen when he reaches Pine and Juniper? Do Candy and the trees wonder how Frost King will decide? Are they worried?

"What does Frost King say? Yes, say it together. These three trees shall never lose their leaves."

After assigning roles Mrs. Mack asked observers to notice whether players made the scene exciting. "Can they make us wonder whether Candy keeps her home?"

After the performance of that scene observers told why it was exciting. They thought it was because Frost King looked back and forth trying to decide. North Wind was quiet. All the players looked at Frost King.

Mrs. Mack asked, "What are Frost King's thoughts while he tries to decide. Stay where you are, and play you are Frost King thinking about his answer."

Then they played the story from beginning to end.

Here is a summary of Mrs. Mack's procedures.

1. After telling the story she divided it into sections for planning and playing.

2. With her questions she reviewed what happened in one scene at a time.

3. She promoted discussion of how characters felt as well as what they did.

4. She created extra characters with particular responsibilities.

5. She broke into planning periods to let the entire group interpret a sound or character.

6. She gave responsibilities to observers.

7. She made locations definite so players knew where to go.

8. With questions and comments she helped children to improve in succeeding performances.

In the following examples leaders follow similar procedures. They are not always described with the same detail as above. Examples are selected to show unique opportunities offered by specific stories. They demonstrate a variety of approaches so the activity is never characterized by monotony.

The Little Pine Tree Who Wished for New Leaves
SOURCE: *Folk Tales Children Love* by Watty Piper (New York: Platt and Munk, 1934).
CHARACTERS:
    Little Pine Tree
    Fairy
    Robbers
    Winds
    Goats
SITUATION IN THE BEGINNING:
    Little Pine Tree wants beautiful leaves instead of needles.
WHAT HAPPENS:
    Fairy offers her any kind of leaves she wants.
    Little Pine chooses gold leaves, but robbers steal them.
    She then chooses glass leaves, which the winds shatter.
    She asks for plain green leaves, and goats eat them.
MOST EXCITING MOMENT:
    Fairy grants Little Pine's wish to have her own needles back.
CONCLUSION:
    Little Pine says, ''Needles are best for a little tree like me.''

Miss Fisher, a playground director, told this story to five- and six-year-olds. At its conclusion she said, "All of you play you are Little Pine Tree. You are crying because you don't like your sharp needles. I'll be Fairy." She listened to their crying, then said, "What's the matter? Why do you cry?" They told her, each in his own way, and all speaking at once.

"What kind of leaves do you want?" she asked.

Some children answered, "Glass." Others correctly said, "Gold."

Miss Fisher kept them to the story line by saying, "I'll bring you gold leaves." With a big movement of her arms she seemed to shower them with golden leaves. "How do you like your gold leaves, Little Pine Tree?" She included the entire group in her question.

Changing quickly from the role of Fairy to leader she asked, "What happens to the gold leaves?" In the same way, they discussed episodes of glass and green leaves.

Then children were ready for individual roles. They decided on the location of Little Pine Tree and the direction from which Fairy entered. After playing the first episode they discussed Little Pine Tree's feelings with each disappointment. Miss Fisher also asked how Fairy felt about all this. She asked the goats how they felt when they found green leaves within easy reach.

"And the robbers," she asked, "are they surprised to see gold on a tree? Do they sneak in so they won't be seen? What are the winds doing as they come in? Do they break off the leaves, or knock them off by accident?"

Since the story offered many roles all the children could participate in each performance.

Little Miss Muffet
SOURCE: *The Real Mother Goose* (Chicago: Rand McNally and Co., 1916).
CHARACTERS:
    Little Miss Muffet
    Spider
SITUATION IN THE BEGINNING:
    "Little Miss Muffet sits on a tuffet
    Eating her curds and whey."

WHAT HAPPENS:
"Along comes a spider and sits down beside her."
MOST EXCITING MOMENT:
Little Miss Muffet runs away.
CONCLUSION:
Spider sits alone on the tuffet.

A kindergarten teacher, Miss Okama, spoke the rhyme to her pupils, then asked them to speak it with her. She asked questions about spiders: "What do they look like? How do they move?"

To recorded music children moved about the room as if they were spiders. Some crawled on hands and knees. Others walked on hands and feet. A few stood upright and walked with arms outstretched. They wiggled their fingers in menacing fashion. One or two bared their teeth in a tigerlike grin.

Then they sat in a circle and talked about Miss Muffet. Miss Okama said that curds and whey were a little like cottage cheese. Then she asked, "Do you think Miss Muffet has ever seen a spider before? How close is this one when she sees it? Is she afraid? Does she get more frightened as it comes closer? How close is it when she runs away?" The discussion that followed each question was short.

Miss Okama asked the children what Miss Muffet did with her bowl and spoon when she ran away. One wanted her to carry them with her. Another thought they should just slide off her lap. One boy said, "She throws them at the spider."

Seated in their circle all the children played that they were Miss Muffet and ate their curds and whey. Miss Okama inside the circle acted the spider and moved toward first one child and then another until all of them were frightened away.

Next, half the children played spider, and the other half were Miss Muffet.

There was a little more discussion. Miss Okama asked, "Does Miss Muffet look back at the spider as she runs? How does the spider feel when he is left alone?"

Before the end of the session children played individual roles as they pantomimed the story in the poem.

The Elephant's Child, by Rudyard Kipling
SOURCE: *Just So Stories* by Rudyard Kipling (Garden City, New York: Doubleday and Co., Inc., 1956).
CHARACTERS:
Elephant's Child
Parents
Kolokolo Bird
Bi-Colored-Python-Rock-Snake
Aunts and Uncles
SITUATION IN THE BEGINNING:
Elephant's Child lived long ago when elephants had bulgy noses instead of trunks.
WHAT HAPPENS:
He asks questions until all his relatives spank him.
When they will not tell him what Crocodile eats for dinner, Kolokolo Bird urges him to find out for himself.
He journeys to the great, grey-green, greasy Limpopo River.
Aided by the Bi-Colored-Python-Rock-Snake he finds Crocodile and asks his question. Crocodile declares he'll have Elephant's Child for dinner, and he clamps his teeth over Elephant's Child's nose.
As they struggle and pull, the nose stretches.
MOST EXCITING MOMENT:
With help from Bi-Colored-Python-Rock-Snake Elephant's Child pulls the hardest, and Crocodile lets go of his nose.
CONCLUSION:
Elephant's Child finds his nose so useful that all his relatives have Crocodile stretch their noses.

Mr. Harloff, recreation director at a settlement house, told this story to six- and seven-year-old boys. When he concluded he repeated some of the appealing words of the story. They were "great, grey-green, greasey Limpopo River," "Bi-Colored-Python-Rock-Snake," "Kolokolo Bird," "whisking and frisking his long nose," and "Led go by dose." He spoke the words with all the enjoyment he felt for them. He invited the boys to repeat the words with him. They soon caught his pleasure in the sound of the words and the feel of them on the tongue and lips.

Mr. Harloff had a homemade drum. On it he beat a slow, heavy rhythm. To its accompaniment boys moved about like elephants with long trunks. He increased the tempo of the drum beat and suggested that boys "whisk and frisk" on the way home from Crocodile.

Preparations for spanking episodes came next. The director formed the boys into groups of three. In each group, number one boy played Elephant's Child. He bent over to receive a spanking. Number two boy raised his hand to give it. Number three clapped his hands as the blow fell. The boys practiced until they could coordinate the clap with the blow. It looked and sounded as if relatives were giving Elephant's Child a severe spanking. Mr. Harloff showed the spanker how to stop his hand just before it touched Elephant's Child. The director moved from group to group to help the boys. He counted and moved his hand to indicate the rhythm. Boys changed places so each had a chance to play clapper, spanker, and one who got spanked.

There followed a discussion of the opening incident. Boys reviewed the questions Elephant's Child asked, and invented additional ones. Mr. Harloff asked how Elephant's Child felt about all these spankings. When they played the opening scene the boys used the spanking procedures they had practiced.

Other scenes were planned and played. The nose-stretching incident called for preparation. Boys decided on this procedure: Elephant's Child held his nose between the palms of his hands, and extended his fingers held close together. Crocodile clamped his extended fingers over Elephant's Child's fingers. As both pulled, Elephant's Child's extended his arms to indicate his lengthening nose. Bi-Colored-Python-Rock-Snake wrapped his arms around Elephant's Child's legs to help him pull.

The boys concluded their play with a decision by the relatives to visit Crocodile and have their noses stretched.

Where Love Is God Is, by Leo Tolstoi
SOURCES: *Ivan the Fool and Other Tales* (New York: Oxford Press, 1931).
   What Men Live By: Russian Stories and Legends (New York: Pantheon Books, 1943).
CHARACTERS:
   Martin, a poor cobbler
   Street Cleaner
   Woman and Child
   Soldier
   Apple Woman
   Street Boy
   Tea Seller
SITUATION IN THE BEGINNING:
   Martin has dreamed Christ will visit him in his shop today.

WHAT HAPPENS:

As Martin looks for Christ he sees Street Cleaner shivering at his work and invites him in for a cup of tea. To the next visitors, a poor woman and child, Martin gives money and warm clothing. He sees Street Boy steal apples, pays for them, persuades Apple Woman to forgive Boy, and Boy to carry her basket. He calms a poor, angry tea seller and buys some of her tea. Disappointed that Christ has not come he reads his Bible.

MOST EXCITING MOMENT:

He hears a voice say, ''Martin! Martin! Inasmuch as you have done it unto the least of these, my brethren, you have done it unto me.''

CONCLUSION:

Martin realizes his dream has come true.

Miss Miller, a teacher of religion, told this story to ten- to twelve-year-old boys and girls. They were studying the biblical injunction, ''Love thy neighbor as thyself.''

After the story Miss Miller started discussion with, ''Did Martin show love of neighbor? Toward whom? How?'' These questions drew from pupils a review of characters and plot. To promote study of Martin she asked, ''How did he greet visitors? How did he show love by his words, tone of voice, and the way he listened?''

Discussion lasted only a few minutes . Creative drama was new to these children. Miss Miller wanted them to get to dramatizing so the thrill of it would sustain their interest.

For their first acting experience she chose the apple-stealing episode. It was short and easy to remember. It offered roles for three players. It involved snatching, chasing, and catching—all movements familiar to children. Movements were exciting enough to draw children's attention from themselves and minimize self-consiousness.

Before starting dramatization Miss Miller asked, ''How does Apple Woman feel as she stands selling apples? How does Boy feel when he sees apples? Is he hungry? Does he sneak up and run?''

Children agreed on the location of the Apple Woman, the entrance to Martin's shop, and his workbench. Three pupils immediately volunteered to play the scene. They played with absorption and vigor. The next group of three grew rowdy during the chase.

Miss Miller interrupted their playing to ask questions. She wanted them to think about and feel what they were portraying . . She asked, ''Does this boy steal just to play a prank? Or does he need food? Does

Apple Woman need money to buy food for hungry children at home? Is she good to forgive? Is he good to carry her heavy basket of apples?''

After boys and girls played this scene several times the teacher led discussion of the entire story. She asked, ''How does Martin's kindness change each visitor to his shop?'' She showed how this change in the character was the climax of his scene. She asked, ''What character changes from cold to warm? From worry to relief? Who changes from arrogance to humility? How does he show this change? Who changes from anger to calm? What causes the change in her?''

Then children talked about the biggest change of all, the climax of the story. This was Martin's change from eagerly expecting Christ and disappointment over His not coming, to joy in hearing the Voice say, ''Martin! Martin!'' This helped prepare pupils to act all the scenes of the story.

Another teacher used this story to solve a problem of beginning and advanced pupils in one class. All joined in discussion. Experienced students took turns playing Martin. In this role they could give support and guidance to new students, who played the smaller parts of visitors to the shop.

How Boots Befooled the King
SOURCE: *The Wonder Clock* by Howard Pyle (New York: Harper Brothers, 1887).
CHARACTERS:
    Farmer
    Peter ⎫
    Paul ⎬ His sons
    Boots ⎭
    Crockery Vendor
    King
    Councillor
    Cook
    Princess
    Ladies in Waiting
SITUATION IN THE BEGINNING:
    Peter and Paul, Farmer's older sons, belittle Boots and make him do menial tasks.
WHAT HAPPENS:
    Peter and Paul in turn try to fool King and so win his daughter in marriage as he has promised. They fail and receive a whipping. To their disgust Boots goes to try his luck. He pays a crockery vendor

to break her pottery when he signals by blowing in his hat. Boots fools King by making him believe the hat is magic. King refuses to keep his promise until Boots does two tasks. Boots performs one by fooling Councillor. The second is to identify Princess whom Boots has not seen.

MOST EXCITING MOMENT:

Boots springs a mechanical mouse, which causes Princess to faint and Ladies to look after her. So Boots recognizes Princess.

CONCLUSION:

Boots marries Princess and invites his relatives to the castle.

Mrs. Johnson, a sixth-grade teacher, let her class play this story. Her pupils had participated for many months in creative drama. She wanted them to have the fun of playing this story's humorous incidents and characters.

Pupils recognized the need for an introductory scene. It must show how Peter and Paul ridiculed, and even abused, Boots. To guide planning Mrs. Johnson asked these questions: "Do Peter and Paul look down on Boots because he does housework while they work in the fields? Would he like to work outdoors? Does he try to please them? Do they ever praise him?

"Could this opening scene be one in which Boots serves breakfast to his Father and Brothers? How do they learn about King's proclamation? Do you want to invent a character who stops by to tell the news? Do Peter and Paul want to go to the castle? Does their father encourage them? Does Boots want to go? What do the Brothers say to that? Do Peter and Paul start out? Is that a good place to end the first scene?"

The sixth-graders played this scene and the scenes in which each boy tried to fool King. They were disapponted because their scenes were not as funny as in the story.

Mrs. Johnson said, "That's because you don't show how each character feels about what others say and do. Events are not as funny in themselves as in the way people react to them. Reactions among characters are called interplay. To appreciate how important this is, try acting a scene without any interplay. Begin where Boots tells the king his hat is magic. Play your own parts, but pay no attention to other players. Don't look at them. Don't listen to them except to know when to speak."

Children followed her directions. The complete lack of interplay that they demonstrated made the scene ridiculous. It was no play. It seemed like three people giving monologues. Players fully appreciated need for interplay. They must learn how to use it.

To help them learn Mrs. Johnson used the same scene. "Crockery Vendor, do you hate to break those dishes even if Boots paid you to do it? Do you want to earn the five dollars? Show both feelings, one at a time, before you break the dishes. Do you hesitate when he signals for the breaking? Do you wonder if he knows what he's doing?"

Then she turned to Boots, "How do you feel when she hesitates? Does your plan depend on her breaking the dishes? Do you show you're worried when she hesitates? Do you blow again into your hat to be sure she sees the signal? What else could you do with the hat? Yes, wave it. You want to be sure she sees."

Again Mrs. Johnson spoke to Crockery Vendor. "What do you think when you see him blowing and waving? Do you realize you must break dishes to earn five dollars? Do you break all at once? Do you stop when you're half through, hoping you can save some?

"And Boots, are you pleased when she begins to break dishes? Do you almost panic when she stops in the middle of the job? How do you signal that she is to continue?

"Now King," said the teacher, "Do you believe Boots when he says he has a magic fooling hat? Are you disgusted? Do your feelings change when Crockery Vendor breaks her dishes? Are you worried that Boots might win the Princess? Do you watch him? Do you have to contrive a scheme to keep the Princess?"

Mrs. Johnson had some final questions for Boots. "What are you doing while King is thinking? When he offers you one hundred dollars do you take it immediately? No, you show how precious that hat is? How do you show that? Do you look at the King out of the corner of your eye?"

This discussion and practice of interplay resulted in the best acting these pupils had done.

The North Wind and the Sun
SOURCE: *The North Wind and the Sun* by Brian Wildsmith (New York: Franklin Watts, 1964).
CHARACTERS:
    North Wind

      Sun
      Traveler
      People
      Animals
      Plants

SITUATION IN THE BEGINNING:

North Wind and Sun try to prove which is stronger by testing which one can make Traveler remove his cape.

WHAT HAPPENS:

North Wind blows so hard that all creatures, plants, and people are affected, but he can't get the cape off Traveler.

Sun beams such warmth that every one enjoys it.

MOST EXCITING MOMENT:

When Traveler feels Sun's warmth he takes off his cape.

CONCLUSION:

Sun's gentle warmth proves stronger than North Wind's force.

A Sunday school teacher read this story to a primary class. She sat on a low stool. Pupils sat on the floor as close to her as they could comfortably get. Every time Mrs. Martin turned a page she held up the book so children could see the picture.

To help them observe carefully she asked questions like these: "What are people doing in the picture? Why? Do you see animals? What kind? Do you see plants? Can you tell what kinds? Do you see Traveler? Where is Sun? What is Traveler doing? Does he seem happy? Where is his cape? What is North Wind doing?"

The questions resulted in valuable discussion as well as close observation of pictures. Discussion took place when Mrs. Martin paused for children to look at pictures.

When she finished the story she asked, "How does North Wind blow?" Most children puffed out their cheeks and puckered up their lips and blew. Some just puffed. Others made a loud "Oo-oo-oo" sound.

Mrs. Martin said, "Now, stay just where you are and play you are North Wind. I'll be Traveler. See if you can blow hard enough to get my cape off."

The children stayed in their compact group and blew. Mrs. Martin walked back and forth in front of them. She clutched an imaginary cape about her shoulders. Then she gestured for silence. "It's time for North Wind to give up. What does he do? Show me how you feel. Are you tired?

Are you disappointed? Are you mad?''

The teacher then pointed to a large circle marked on the floor. ''This is the path of the sun. You play Sun. Walk around the circle, and warm me with your beams. See if you can get my cape off.''

She stayed inside the circle. Children showed many ways of portraying Sun. They raised their arms and waved, moved them in great circles, and brought them down in sweeping movements. Slowly the children walked and smiled on Traveler.

She smiled in return and showed she liked the sun's gentle beams. Then she grew so warm she unfastened her cape. It hung on her arms. Finally, she exclaimed, ''I am too warm. I must take off this cape.'' She went through motions of doing so and of folding it over her arm.

With the next performance a child played Traveler. After that all the parts were played by children. Those who watched created North Wind sound effects.

The Snake
SOURCE: *Fifteen Fables of Krylov* by Guy Danuels (New York: Macmillan Company, 1964).
CHARACTERS:
  Snake
  Zeus
  Birds
  Animals
SITUATION IN THE BEGINNING:
  Snake is unhappy because the only sound he makes is a hiss, and it frightens everyone away.
WHAT HAPPENS:
  He goes to Zeus, ruler of the gods, and asks that his hiss be changed into a song. Zeus grants the wish. Snake crawls into a tree and sings his new song. Birds and animals enchanted by its beauty come to listen.
MOST EXCITING MOMENT:
  They see in Snake's open mouth the fangs which they know can kill them so they run away.
CONCLUSION:
  Snake realizes that his fangs, not his hiss, are the cause of other creatures' fears.

Miss Padillo led a group of eight-year-olds who had previous experience with both improvisation and story play. As soon as she told this story she introduced a discussion of snakes. Pupils understood that a snake's hiss was a warning. His fangs were the great danger.

These pupils were attending camp for the entire summer. They had seen snakes and had learned which were dangerous. They improvised an introductory scene that showed Snake stealthily pursuing birds and animals. When they saw him they fled in terror. Snake thought his hiss was the cause of their flight. After a few experiences of being left alone he decided to go to Zeus. Miss Padillo explained that ancient people believed Zeus gave each animal its unique powers.

To help campers plan the next scene Miss Padillo asked these questions: "What is Zeus doing when Snake arrives? Is he busy with other animals? How does he feel about Snake's visit? Does he wonder what he would do if all creatures asked for changes? Is Snake timid about approaching Zeus? Is he polite? Does he try to make Zeus feel sorry for him? Does Zeus ask questions before granting Snake's request? What movement does he use when he bestows the gift of song? What kind of song is it?"

The children wanted a high, lilting song. As they interpreted it the song sounded like a robin. "Cherrup! Cheer! Cheer!" Together all children played Snake trying out his new song.

Then they planned the episode of birds and animals coming to listen. For this, Miss Padillo helped campers devise specific responsibilities for different creatures. One creature was to hear the song first and summon others. A second was to listen and determine which tree the sound came from. A third resolved to climb the tree for a look at the singer. He rallied others to follow. A good role was that of the creature who first noticed that Snake was the singer. A fifth character of importance was a bird who saw the fangs and spread the alarm.

All other creatures practiced listening to the various items of news and reacting to them. This practice helped players coordinate their acting with one another. They gained a skill in interplay and ensemble work.

Working together players increased the climactic effect of exciting moments. Miss Padillo helped them build to the main climax by making each successive reaction a little bigger than the one before. As the scene neared the story's climax children moved faster, used bigger gestures, spoke with greater volume, and made sudden pauses.

In playing the final scene the first bird to hear the song summoned other creatures. They came slowly and quietly, listenintg as they came. As they neared the singer they moved faster. When they discovered Snake was the singer they chatted about him. When the fangs were seen, there was a gasp of fright. This was followed by shrieking and shouting and frantic movement as all but Snake fled. The scene ended with Snake's realization that his song was as terrifying as his hiss.

The Blind Men and the Elephant
SOURCE: *The Blind Men and the Elephant* by Lillian Quigley (New York: Charles Scribner's and Sons, 1959).
CHARACTERS:
   Six Blind Men
   The Rajah
SITUATION AT THE BEGINNING:
   Six blind men set out to see the Rajah.
WHAT HAPPENS:
   They walk one behind the other with the smallest in front.
   The leader bumps against an elephant in the palace courtyard.
   Having never seen an elephant each feels it to determine what it's like. The leader feels its side and says, "It's like a wall."
   The second feels its trunk and says, "It's like a snake."
   The third feels a tusk and says, "No, it's like a spear."
   The fourth feels a leg and says, "No, it's like a tree."
   The fifth feels an ear and says, "No, it's like a fan."
   The sixth feels the tail and says, "No, it's like a rope."
   They argue until they are so angry they begin to fight.
MOST EXCITING MOMENT:
   The Rajah stops the fight and explains that each has felt only one part of the elephant.
CONCLUSION:
   On their way home the six agree that to learn the truth they must put all parts together.

Mrs. Duffy told this fable to her den of eight-year-old Cub Scouts. The boys wanted to act the story. But there were eight of them and only seven parts. Mrs. Duffy asked, "Can't we have seven blind men instead of six?"

"Yes," said one boy immediately. "He can feel the elephant's stomach and think it's like a rag bag." This idea suited all the boys.

Mrs. Duffy explained that a Rajah was a high official in India.

She asked these questions about being blind: "How would you walk if you couldn't see? Would it help to have someone walk in front of you?'' She asked the boys to walk about with their eyes shut to get a feeling of blindness. Then they walked in single file with the shortest boy in front. They realized his responsibility as leader. He also faced dangers since he was the first to bump into obstacles. Those behind called out suggestions and criticisms.

Mrs. Duffy suggested that the boys improvise an opening scene to show that the men were blind. It should also explain why they decided to go to see the Rajah. The boys responded with a scene that showed the blind men at their daily occupations. This resulted from a discussion of various ways blind people could earn a living. One was a musician.

While he played a musical instrument a tourist entered. He listened with such pleasure that he gave the musician a gold piece. The musician was generous. He wanted to share his good fortune and suggested that the gold piece offered the means for all of them to go to the Rajah's palace. The scene ended as they lined up and set forth.

Before they played the second scene Mrs. Duffy asked these questions: ''How do the men feel when they start out? Are they afraid? What do they talk about on the way? Do they laugh and joke? Does their excitement increase as they near the palace? Do they talk about it? Do they hope to meet the Rajah?''

One boy thought they should talk about elephants and hope to encounter some.

The boys walked in a large circle to make their journey.

Before they performed the palace scene Mrs. Duffy asked questions to help them remember the story: ''Which part of the elephant does the leader touch? What does he think it's like? She asked the same questions about each blind man's experience with the elephant. Then all of them practiced feeling each part of the animal mentioned in the story.

When they came to planning the argument Mrs. Duffy helped by asking another series of questions: ''Are the men mad when each first declares what the elephant is like? Would each man repeat several times what he thought? Would their talk grow louder? Would it have to be very loud to attract attention from the Rajah?''

Before enacting this scene the boys discussed the layout of the courtyard. Mrs. Duffy asked, ''Which way do the blind men come from? Where is the elephant? Where is the Rajah when he hears the argument? Does he watch the men a minute before he intervenes? How does he get the men's attention? How does he show he's a person of authority? Does each man explain his opinion to the Rajah?''

After acting this scene the Cubs planned the conclusion. The den mother again asked questions: ''Do the men feel foolish when they learn their mistake? Do they thank the Rajah? How do they make up after the quarrel? How do they feel as they line up to start home? How does the play end?''

Little Briar Rose

SOURCES: *Grimm's Fairy Tales* (Chicago: Follett Publishing Co., 1968).

   Grimm's Fairy Tales by Joseph Scharl (New York: Pantheon Books, 1944).

CHARACTERS:

   King
   Queen
   Court Ladies
   Nurse
   Good Fairies
   Wicked Fairy
   Little Briar Rose
   Cook
   Kitchen Boy
   Prince

SITUATION IN THE BEGINNING:

   King and Queen welcome Good Fairies and Court Ladies to the christening of their baby, Little Briar Rose.

WHAT HAPPENS:

   Fairies, except one, present gifts of beauty and virtue.
   Wicked Fairy enters in anger because she was not invited.
   She promises Briar Rose will prick her finger on a spinning wheel when she is sixteen and shall die
   The Good Fairy who has not yet presented a gift says that Briar Rose shall not die, but sleep for one hundred years.
   On Briar Rose's sixteenth birthday Wicked Fairy causes the girl to prick her finger on a spinning wheel.
   Briar Rose sleeps. So does everyone in the castle.
   After one hundred years a prince finds her.

MOST EXCITING MOMENT:

   Briar Rose awakens.

CONCLUSION:

   Everyone in the castle awakens, and the King invites all to a feast of celebration.

Miss Burns conducted a program of creative activities for ten-year-old girls. From this story she selected ideas for improvisation a week before she told the story. First improvisations were based on feelings of drowsiness and going to sleep. Preliminary exercises included fighting drowsiness in order to stay awake, then, yielding to it. Characterization was then introduced. Girls played different kinds of people falling asleep. On these characters falling asleep girls built a short scene.

Another situation from "Briar Rose" served for improvisation. Miss Burns described a situation for the girls to act out. She said, "One of you is having a party. While you and your quests are eating ice cream, in rushes a girl you have not invited. She says, 'You didn't invite me to your party. Just for that there'll be no party.' She knocks the dish of ice cream from the hands of the hostess.

"As you plan your improvisation you are to show answers to these questions: Are you surprised to see the angry guest? What do you and your guests do as she enters? While she's there? And after she leaves? Is she madder, or calmer when she leaves than when she entered?"

Later when the girls acted the story of Briar Rose they prepared for the Wicked Fairy scene. Miss Burns said, "Remember last week's improvisation. How did you feel when the uninvited guest broke the dish that held ice cream? Do the guests at the christening feel the same way about Wicked Fairy? Would their feelings be even stronger? Of course. The other meant only spilled ice cream. This means death."

When the girls reached the scene in which everyone goes to sleep Miss Burns asked, "Do you remember the various ways in which people go to sleep? Use what you remember to make this scene convincing."

Planning the final scene brought a new situation. In the story, Prince kisses Briar Rose's hand, they fall in love, are married, and live happily ever after. The girls had not acted any stories that involved a romantic ending. Miss Burns did not want to ignore the lovely conclusion. Neither did she want it to degenerate into embarrassment or sentimentality.

Before planning the awakening scene Miss Burns prepared the girls for it—gave them ideas for interpreting it. She said, "You know we sometimes have to make changes in a story so we can act it. This story concludes as Briar Rose and Prince are married and live happily ever after. We haven't time in a play to show a wedding and living happily ever after. But we do want to show that Prince admires Briar

Rose for her beauty and gentle ways. She should show her gratitude for his courage in finding her and breaking the spell.

"Let's plan how to do this so it makes a good play. As soon as castle folk awaken, where do they go? Wouldn't King and Queen rush immediately to Briar Rose? Do others follow them? So Prince and Briar Rose hear them coming as soon as Briar Rose awakes. As they come in would they cheer for Prince? Do you want someone to say, 'Hurrah for the Prince?' And all of them love Briar Rose. What about a cheer for her too? Try it, all of you. 'Hurrah for the Prince! Hurrah for Briar Rose!' Say it as though you're glad to shout after sleeping one hundred years."

This preparation let the girls know they would not have to act a love scene. So they were not hampered by apprehension. After practicing the cheer they planned the entrance of Prince. Miss Burns asked these questions to help them think about the plan: "When Prince sees Briar Rose does he think her beautiful? Does he stand an instant to admire her? Does he think of the sadness of her sleeping for one hundred years? Is it this sadness as well as her beauty that makes him want to kneel and kiss her hand?

"Now what about Briar Rose? Is she startled to wake from her long sleep and see a stranger there? Would he reassure her? Would he say he had come to rescue her? That he had cut his way through the dense forest? Would she thank him? When others rush in, are they surprised to see Prince? Does Briar Rose tell them he is their rescuer? When do they shout? When does King invite all to the feast? Who leads the way? Who comes next? Do people cheer as they go?"

The girls played the story with great pleasure and some skill. Miss Burns suggested they repeat it for their mothers. This would not be putting on a play. It would demonstrate acting stories so mothers could see what they had been doing.

Miss Burns also suggested that they make some costume accessories. These would help the mothers identify characters. The girls made gold paper crowns for King, Queen, and Briar Rose; a white paper cap and apron for Nurse, a headband with a star for each good fairy, a black paper witch hat for Wicked Fairy. For Prince they made a belt of brown paper. At one side was attached a sheath to hold a hunting knife made of stiff silver paper. Each Lady in Waiting wore a tall, pointed, pastel-colored paper hat. From its point hung narrow crepe paper streamers. For Cook and Kitchen Boy there were chef caps made of white paper—a tall one for Cook and shorter one for Kitchen Boy.

Before the girls presented their demonstration Miss Burns explained to their mothers that this was a story play. It was not a play in which players memorized dialogue and pantomime.

The Pomegranate Seeds
SOURCE: *Tanglewood Tales* by Nathaniel Hawthorne (Chicago and New York: Rand McNally and Company, 1913).
CHARACTERS:
    Ceres, goddess of plants
    Proserpina, her daughter
    Sea Nymphs
    Pluto, god of riches under earth
    Fishermen
    Farmers
    Villagers
    Birds
    Fountains
    Phoebus, sun god
    Quicksilver, messenger of the gods.
    Jupiter, king of the gods
SITUATION IN THE BEGINNING:
    As Ceres leaves to watch over earth's plants she admires her daughter, Proserpina. Pluto waits nearby hoping to steal the child to brighten his underground kingdom.
WHAT HAPPENS:
    As Proserpina plays with Sea Nymphs, Pluto whirls her away. Trying to locate her daughter Ceres questions Sea Nymphs, Fishermen, Farmers, Villagers, Birds, and Fountains. Finally, Phoebus tells her the child is with Pluto.
    Ceres forbids any plant to grow until her daughter is returned.
    Famine brings suffering to all creatures of earth. People, animals, even the gods beg Ceres to lift her curse. When she refuses they beg help from Jupiter. He declares that if Proserpina has eaten no food in Pluto's realm she must be returned. Jupiter sends Quicksilver to bring the girl.
MOST EXCITING MOMENT:
    Prosperina returns but can stay only six months of each year because she ate six pomegranate seeds in Pluto's realm.
CONCLUSION:
    Ceres declares the earth shall be green with growing plants during the six months Proserpina is with her. The rest of the year the earth shall be barren.

Miss Metzler, a playground director, chose this story for her advanced drama group. Participants were boys and girls, eleven and twelve years old. After telling the story to them Miss Metzler said, "Two things are important to Ceres. What are they?"

Answers came quickly: "Her daughter." "Her growing plants."

"As the story opens," said Miss Metzler, "Ceres is leaving to look after the plants. How can you show she hates to leave Proserpina?"

Children suggested that as Ceres walks away she turns to look at Proserpina and wave to her. Miss Metzler said, "Let's play this farewell scene. I'll be Proserpina. All of the girls will play the role of Ceres. You are to leave me here and walk down the lawn to the trees. Spread out. There's room for all of you to play at once. Walk as if you are the goddess of all growing things. Show that you hate to leave Proserpina."

When the girls returned, one of them said, "It was such a long way. I couldn't think of things to do."

Miss Metzler commented, "What Ceres does is determined by what she is thinking. What are her thoughts?"

Among the answers were: "How good Proserpina is!" "I wonder what she'll do while I'm gone."

Miss Metzler asked, "Does she also think about her work in orchards and fields?" This gave the girls additional ideas for pantomime as they walked the seventy-five feet to the tree.

Then it was the boys' turn. Before letting them play Pluto Miss Metzler mentioned a problem. "The story says Pluto had long wanted Proserpina in his underground palace. How can we show this?" The solution was to improvise a scene before the entrance of Ceres and Proserpina. Pluto would walk in and look around. "How can he show he admires Proserpina? Can he find something that belongs to her and show he treasures it?"

Children decided that he found her scarf on a bench. He should hold it up, look at it, carefully fold it, and put it back.

"How can he show he is planning to steal the girl?"

The boys thought Pluto should bring several guards with him and hide them behind bushes. All the boys participated in this scene. They entered from the corner of the building so they had a long space to cover. After making the long entrance once, the boys found they needed ideas for pantomime. Miss Metzler helped them with a discussion of the thoughts of Pluto and his men during their walk.

In planning the rest of the scene Miss Metzler asked, "How long does Pluto hide before trying to steal Proserpina?" It was decided that he should wait until after Ceres left. He should peek out from his hiding place once or twice. He sees Ceres go and the Sea Nymphs come to play.

"How do they play?" asked Miss Metzler. "Do they just run about, or do they play a game?"

The boys approved a suggestion that the Sea Nymphs play Hide and Seek. They said, "When Proserpina is 'It' the Sea Nymphs will be out of the way, and Proserpina will have her eyes hidden. Then he can steal her."

This idea inspired another participant to think of a way to capture Proserpina. He said, "While Proserpina has her eyes closed Pluto and his guards surround her. They make a big circle. She looks up and sees them. She tries to run, but they close the circle." These suggestions worked well in performance. Then it was time to end the session.

Next day the boys tried covering another long space. They played Quicksilver, messenger of the gods. They played him, first, as he ran to answer Jupiter's summons, and again, when he carried Jupiter's message to Pluto. Quicksilver's dash across the lawn differed from Pluto's sneaking entrance and the majestic walk of Ceres. Children realized how much they could show about a character by the way he walked or ran. They also got used to the big movements needed when they played in a large space.

They participated in another long walk when they acted the suffering people who came to plead with Ceres. Before they started, Miss Metzler asked how these people felt, what they were thinking about as they approached the goddess. Then she played Ceres and watched them approach. Her firm, cold-hearted refusal helped children feel the people's disappointment. As they walked away they showed their grief and despair.

Then came ths scene of Proserpina's return. Again the full length of lawn was used. Miss Metzler prepared children for this scene charged with emotion. She did not want them to be embarrassed by the reunion of mother and daughter. She asked, "What people are waiting to see Quicksilver bring Proserpina?" The boys and girls knew the answer was Ceres and the suffering people. "Who else?" Then they remembered that animals and even the gods were there.

"Who is the first to see Proserpina coming?"

"Ceres," came the ready answer.

"What are her thoughts now?"

Answers included "She's back?" "She's safe." "I was afraid I'd never see her again."

Miss Metzler's next questions were; "What do the suffering people think when they see Proserpina? Do they tell Ceres she must break the spell? What kind of gesture does Ceres use to end the famine?"

The leader gave all the children opportunity to play Ceres breaking the spell. She said, "Spread out so you have plenty of room. I'm Jupiter. I say, 'Ceres, your daughter has been returned. Now, break the spell. 'Ready!'"

Responses varied. Some children lifted their hands as though lifting plants from earth. Others spread arms and hands in a gesture of bestowing a blessing. One girl seemed to take seed from her pocket and scatter it with a great sweep of her arm.

Then came a question about what Proserpina was thinking as she ran toward her mother. These thoughts were suggested: What a big crowd! Everyone is here! Where is my mother? Now, I see her. Does she see me? I'll wave to her. Oh, how good to be back!

These thoughts contained ideas for Proserpina's pantomime as she ran. By the time she reached her mother the two of them were lost in the general rejoicing over breaking of the spell.

At a subsequent session these boys and girls acted the story in its entirety. They used dialogue as well as pantomime. They had learned a great deal from acting first the scenes that required big movement.

The Perfect Tribute
SOURCE: *The Perfect Tribute* Mary Shipman Andrews (New York: Charles Scribner's Sons, 1916).
CHARACTERS:
    President Lincoln
    Edward Everett, a famous orator
    Secretary of State Seward
    Justices of the Supreme Court
    Audience at Gettysburg
    Warren Blair, a Southern boy
    Carter Blair, a Confederate officer
    Guards at Prison Hospital
SITUATION IN THE BEGINNING:
    President Lincoln and other officials are traveling to the Gettysburg

Cemetery dedication. He is trying to write a speech to be given there but is not satisfied with it.

WHAT HAPPENS:

Edward Everett delivers the oration of the day and receives tremendous applause. Lincoln gives his speech for which he receives no applause—only absolute silence. Disheartened over his supposed failure he takes a walk and meets Warren Blair. Warren without knowing Lincoln is president asks him to draw a will for his wounded soldier-brother.

MOST EXCITING MOMENT:

The brother without knowing who Lincoln is tells him that the president just made one of the great speeches of history. Carter Blair says, "It was so great the audience gave him the perfect tribute of absolute silence."

CONCLUSION:

Lincoln realizes that his speech reached the hearts of his audience. Carter Blair realizes his ambition of putting his hand in the hand of Abraham Lincoln.

Miss Metzler chose this story for her advanced drama group after it completed "The Pomegranate Seeds." The quick change from ancient myth to American history challenged pupils' interest. This seemed real to them. It required no big movement. Its struggle was not with physical force, but within the mind and heart.

Before Miss Metzler told the story she selected ideas from it for improvisation exercises. Her pupils were seated around large tables. She said, "You are going to do an improvisation without leaving your tables. Here is the situation. Your teacher has just told you to write a composition. You want to do well, but you don't know what to write. After you try a few sentences you are displeased with them. You make yourself finish the task, but you're disappointed in what you write."

This proved difficult for the pupils. After one performance Miss Metzler tried to stimulate their thinking with these questions: "When you're not sure how to do something do you work quickly and smoothly? Do you start and stop as you try different ways? Do you sit quietly? Do you fidget or doodle?

"Does your posture change as you grow discouraged? Do your eyes tell when you get an idea? Do they show when the idea proves disappointing? What do you do with your pencil and paper? Your hands? Feet?

Shoulders?'' Miss Metzler concluded, ''Use all of them to show how hard you try, and how discouraged you are.''

After giving pupils another try at the improvisation Miss Metzler asked, ''Would you like to hear a story about a president of the United States, who struggled to write a speech?''

The story moved them deeply. For dramatization it divided naturally into four scenes: (1) Lincoln writing the speech on the train; (2) Gettysburg dedication ceremony; (3) meeting Warren Blair; (4) drawing the will in the hospital.

When children worked on the speechwriting scene they found themselves prepared by their improvisation. Then came consideration of the men with Lincoln on the train. Questions included: ''What positions do these men hold? What do they think of themselves? Of Lincoln? Do they show these thoughts in the way they stand, sit, move, and talk? What do they talk about?''

To plan the second scene Miss Metzler asked her students to think about the people in the audience at Gettysburg. ''Why have they come? Are there people of many ages? Occupations? Walks of life?'' This discussion promoted great interest in playing members of the audience. Some children played they were wounded soldiers. There were mothers and children, farmers and merchants. All the pupils except two boys played they were in the audience. These two played Everett and Lincoln.

They discussed Everett's speech. Most of the children had heard extravagant speeches of patriotism. Edward Everett's player improvised a short speech that seemed appropriate. As to Lincoln's Gettysburg Address the children had heard it and knew at least the first sentence. The Lincoln player gave what he remembered and improvised the rest.

The speech scene resulted in exciting interplay between audience and speakers. After Everett's speech the people applauded vigorously and long. To Lincoln they paid close attention. When he concluded they stood spellbound.

The meeting with Warren Blair was easy to plan and play. To guide children's thinking Miss Metzler asked these questions: ''When you fail do you like to be alone? Is that the reason Lincoln goes for a walk? Does he feel sorry for Warren in spite of his rudeness?''

The hospital scene was more difficult. To prepare for it there were questions about Captain Carter Blair: "Do you like him? Why does he admire Lincoln? Is he grateful to Lincoln for drawing the will? What does he want very much to do?"

Then came questions about Lincoln in the hospital scene: "How does he feel when Carter first refers to his speech? Does he feel worse then than at any other time? Can he believe it when Carter says the president made one of the great speeches of history? Does he think he has heard incorrectly? Does he rejoice the way people did in Ceres and Proserpina? Has anyone else known his sadness? Does any one else know his joy? How does he show it?"

In telling the story Miss Metzler did not mention the gravity of Carter's wound. She said only that he had been wounded. She made it Lincoln's story. When he learned that his speech reached the hearts of his listeners, and when Carter laid his hand in Lincoln's, the story was over.

This example shows eleven- and twelve-year-olds dramatizing the story. It is just as appropriate for teenagers and adults.

The Queen of Hearts
SOURCE: Mother Goose.
CHARACTERS:
   King of Hearts
   Queen of Hearts
   Knave of Hearts
SITUATION IN THE BEGINNING:
   The Queen of Hearts
   She made some tarts
   All on a summer's day.
WHAT HAPPENS:
   The Knave of Hearts
   He stole those tarts
   And took them clean away.
MOST EXCITING MOMENT:
   The King of Hearts
   Called for the tarts
   And beat the knave full sore.
CONCLUSION:
   The Knave of Hearts
   Brought back the tarts
   And vowed he'd steal no more.

A drama specialist, Mrs. Baines, engaged a group of recreation directors in playing the story of this rhyme. It was to prepare them to lead the activity at the recreation centers where they worked. They could use this poem with participants of almost any age.

Mrs. Baines began the session by reading the poem. To help directors see its dramatic possibilities she made some comments: "The poem describes what three persons did. It gives no clue as to why they did it. Their motives are a mystery.

"The first mystery concerns the Queen. Why does she bake tarts? In most castles the cook bakes tarts. Why doesn't the cook do it here? What made it desirable for the Queen to bake tarts?"

Mrs. Baines was prepared to suggest solutions if the directors did not. They might not be as responsive as children. But the mystery challenged three directors. Each had a solution. One thought the cook was away. Another suggested that the Queen's hobby was baking tarts. The third director thought the Queen baked tarts to please the King. Mrs. Baines asked the group to postpone decision about the Queen until other mysteries were discussed.

She asked, "Why do you think the Knave steals the tarts?" She explained the word, knave. Although it has come to mean a mischief-maker its original meaning was just a boy, any boy. Mrs. Baines continued, "Do the names, King of Hearts, Queen of Hearts, and Knave of Hearts suggest the relationship of these three characters?"

Several directors answered in a chorus, "Father, mother, and son."

"If this Knave is the son of a King why does he have to steal tarts? Can't he have them for the asking?"

Answers to this question came quickly. They included: "The Knave is forbidden to eat tarts because he is fat." "He and his playmates see the tarts and take them for a party." "Since the cook often gives him treats the Knave thinks no one will mind if he helps himself."

Mrs. Baines asked for further consideration of the Knave. "How old is he? Are other people involved with him in the theft?" The directors decided he was about nine, and that his playmates helped him steal the tarts.

The group considered the King. Mrs. Barnes asked, "Why does the

King beat the Knave—beat him full sore? Does that seem extreme punishment for stealing tarts?'' No answer. ''Why does the King personally give the beating? Can't a servant do it?'' The directors were not ready with ideas about the King. Mrs. Baines tried again, ''What makes the crime serious enough to deserve the punishment?'' Mrs. Baines waited. She stood quietly so she, too, could think about the problem.

Then came several suggestions: (1) This was a second offense and so required severe punishment. (2) The King has asked the Queen to bake tarts because it was his birthday. (3) Servants in the kitchen doted on the Knave. He boasted to them that he could do anything he pleased, and he pleased to take the tarts.

Mrs. Baines asked directors to consider one last mystery before they began to act. ''Why doesn't the Knave eat the tarts after he steals them?''

Almost in unison her listeners answered, ''He doesn't have time.''

Pinning participants down to final decisions Mrs. Baines asked, ''Where does the opening scene take place?'' All agreed that it was the palace kitchen. ''What people are there? What are they doing? Why?'' Directors agreed that the people there were a cook, an assistant cook, and a scullery maid. They were preparing dinner to celebrate the King's birthday.

This was satisfactory. Questions followed to establish the characteristics of the three in the kitchen. ''Are the cook adnd her assistant good cooks? Do they like their work? Do they like the Knave? Do they welcome his visits to the kitchen?''

''Yes,'' came the unanimous answer to these four questions.

The same answer was given to the following questions: ''Is there a difference between the attitude of the cooks and that of the scullery maid? Does she like the royal family's visits to the kitchen? Does she pay proper attention to her work?''

In answer to Mrs. Baines, questions about the Knave's character directors agreed that he was generous, liked attention, and that he was upset when he didn't get his way.

From here on, questions came in quick succession. Answers were short, and agreement among directors almost immediate.

For decisions about the Queen the leader asked, ''Does she know much about cooking? Does she like praise? Is she devoted to her family?

Considerate of servants? Fond of parties? Does she give the Knave whatever he wants?'' Again the answers were ''Yes.''

These were the questions about the King: ''Does he like being King? Having a birthday dinner? Having the Queen bake tarts? Is he anxious to rear his son properly? Is this the reason he administers strong punishment? Is he genuinely fond of the boy? Is he impulsive?''

There followed a few questions about people in the palace—lords and ladies and playmates of the Knave.

By this time characters were so definite that they stimulated ideas for incidents. As soon as incidents were suggested Mrs. Baines organized the directors for dramatization of the opening scene. They selected a playing area and arranged it as a kitchen. It contained a work table, an oven, and a window shelf to hold the tarts. There were two entrances—one into a hall and the other outside.

Directors later based a script on their improvisation. Their play is included in the last section of this book.

Part Four

Theatre

8

Putting on Plays

When children put on plays for an audience they engage in theatre. It is also called formal drama, scripted drama, and play production.

An audience is the main difference between creative drama and theatre. To entertain an audience is the immediate goal of theatre. This gives rise to its unique characteristics:

1. *It has form.* From the word *form* comes the name *formal drama.* Form lets each player know what to say and do. He memorizes the form to present it for an audience.

The form of a play is found in its script. In the same way the form of a building is dictated by its blueprint, and the form of a symphony, by its score. A script contains a list of characters, their entrances and exits, time and place of each scene, dialogue, and suggestions of pantomime.

2. *Theatre requires exact preparation.* Each player rehearses the specific character he plays in a performance. Actors rehearse scenes many times so they can be done with exactness in performance. Technical duties are assigned, rehearsed, and executed with exactness. Rehearsals and performances are scheduled for definite times and places.

3. *Projection is essential to theatre.* To project means to stick out. The

performance of a play must stick out enough to be seen and heard by its audience. Players learn to speak and move so the audience can see and hear all that occurs onstage.

What Putting on Plays Means to Children

The principal of an elementary school once said, "I know of no activity that stimulates children to as much constructive effort as does the preparation of a play."

Another principal was urged to make play production a subject in the curriculum. His answer was, "No. Children have too much fun in it to get credit for it."

Theatre activity can help participants develop skills in speaking and moving useful for daily life. Anticipation of performance exerts a force for self-discipline that keeps children trying. Performance lets them test their ability and control. They can learn more from this self-testing than from praise, blame, or report cards. Being part of a good performance can provide thrills that are high points in a child's life.

It Is Not Professional Theatre

Plays children present have a purpose that differs from professional theatre. Both have the immediate goal of entertaining an audience. The professional theatre does this to make a profit. The long term purpose of children's performance is to delight and develop the players.

Difference in purpose results in different practices. No admission fee should be charged for performances by children. Such fees put them under tension, and take away the privilege of giving to a community that gives much to them.

Their performances should not be long enough to justify a charge. Children should present only short plays—never more than thirty minutes, usually only ten to twenty. Short plays let children avoid strain of long rehearsals. Working on only short plays permits time to be devoted to other forms of drama.

Children's plays are often presented as part of another event. This again differs from professional theatre, which people attend just to see a play. Children may give their plays at a party, a meeting, an assembly, a holiday observance., or demonstration. Such events provide an audience for the children's play. Otherwise, it is often difficult to recruit spectators for their plays.

Another difference between professional and children's activity is in assignment of roles. The theatre offers parts only to the best actors it can obtain. For children's performances roles are given to the less skilled as well as to the most proficient players.

This is like football games a school schedules for B and C teams. They are expected to play a creditable game, but competition is selected to suit their ability. In the same way performances are arranged for less skilled actors. Such arrangement gives them the thrill and incentive of performance. Yet, they are not in a situation that might embarrass them or bore an audience.

In professional theatre the same actor stars in many productions. The same child does not play the biggest role in a series of children's production. No matter how skilled he becomes he has no more than a fair share of participation opportunity.

These differences relate to players. There are also differences in facilities and supplies. The place of a professional performance needs to be large enough to insure a profit. Better suited to children's need is a small place. They have enjoyed presenting plays on improvised stages with little equipment. The activity deserves good facilities and supplies. But it does not depend on them. No director should be deterred from starting a play because he lacks resources of professional theatre. Lack of resources should constitute a challenge instead of frustration. After children achieve some degree of excellence they may earn community support for improved resources.

A Performance Worthy of an Audience

No matter what the physical resources are, children should present a play worthy of an audience. The face that it is not put on by professionals is no excuse for shoddy performance. If children present a play it should be good theatre. Here are the standards it should meet:

1. The script is worth efforts of players and attention of audience.

2. Physical appearance and voice of each player are suited to his role. For example, players cast as young children are not taller than those cast as their parents.

3. The audience can see and hear what occurs onstage.

4. Players know their lines and pantomime.

5. They act with sincerity that comes from understanding; assurance that comes from adequate rehearsal; and with enthusiasm that comes from feeling the play's story.

6. Performance starts on time and proceeds without interruption.

7. Players enter on time.

8. Technical crews discharge responsibilities properly and on time.

9. Neither they nor offstage players are seen by the audience.

10. Costumes contain no incongruities. For example, blue jeans do not show below robes of the Three Wise Men.

11. Hand properties are in place as required by the play.

12. Scenery and stage properties are anchored so they neither wobble nor fall.

13. A front curtain if used is pulled on time and in the right direction. Players do not peek from behind it. These thirteen points are a checklist to which directors refer during weeks of rehearsal. If a production does not meet these standards it is not ready for an audience.

To Serve the Good of Players

The person who directs children's plays needs another set of standards. These are to help him guide rehearsals and performances to serve the good of players. He has an obligation beyond putting on good entertainment. He wants the activity to provide fun and education for players. To work toward this purpose the director should:

1. Show enthusiasm for play and players.

2. Avoid rehearsals that are too long for children.

3. Provide activity for players who have to wait between scenes in which they rehearse.

4. Teach players how to study a part.

5. Assign, dignify, and recognize work of technical staff.

6. Protect successful players from becoming too satisfied.

7. Bolster confidence of timid players.

8. Make performance an exciting climax to a period of valuable preparatory activity.

9. Keep players aware of discipline imposed by theatre.

10. Insist that players

a. Attend rehearsals with regularity and promptness.

b. Study their roles.

c. Memorize lines and pantomime.

d. Cooperate to achieve a good performance.

e. Accept decisions of director.

Pitfalls to Be Avoided

The director of children in a play needs a third set of standards. These warn him against procedures harmful to players. To avoid such pitfalls the director

1. Should NOT humiliate players when he corrects them.

2. Should NOT subject them to his temperamental outbursts.

3. Should NOT label certain children as talented and give them extraordinary consideration.

4. Should NOT let players appear "cute" by mere imitation of adult mannerisms.

5. Should NOT make unnecessary changes in direction.

6. Should NOT urge players to project until their throats are strained or their movements foreign to children.

7. Should NOT permit hectic atmosphere or helter-skelter activity backstage during rehearsal or performance.

8. Should NOT plan plays so frequently that the same children are constantly under pressure of performance.

Organizing to Put on A Play

The preparation of a play should be so organized that it motivates valuable preparatory activity. First, children should participate in creative drama. Some of this should be based on situations from the play selected for them to present. Next, participants practice to develop their voices and bodies for play production. Only after these activities do they begin to rehearse a play.

These three activities—creative drama, practice of theatre skills, and rehearsal—should precede the performance of a play. It is easy to include all three when children participate in drama two or three times a week over many months. This schedule can be followed by some elementary schools, playgrounds, settlements, community centers, and cultural arts institutions.

For other agencies such a schedule is impossible. Scouts, Y.W.C.A., and Sunday schools may meet organized groups of children only once each week. The weekly meetings must include a variety of activities. Temptation exists for leaders with such limited time to restrict drama opportunity to rehearsing and presenting a play. This procedure has denied children some of drama's most valuable experiences and has even done harm.

Here are possible solutions to the problem of limited time. A play selected or invented for performance under these conditions should have playing time of only five or ten minutes. With Cub Scouts it may be only a playlet presented at a pack meeting.

Before rehearsals begin, a part of each meeting is devoted to creative drama. In part, ideas for improvisation should be taken from situations in the play. The story of the play may be told and acted before players know it is from a play to be presented.

Then a few minutes of each meeting are devoted to practice of theatre skills. This can be valuable if it lasts no more than five minutes at each meeting. After rehearsals start, most of the meeting time for three or four weeks is devoted to them. Perhaps an extra meeting can be scheduled for dress rehearsal.

The same solutions may apply to other situations where time is limited. These include daily vacation Bible schools, day camps, and resident camps where children stay only a week or two.

The organization of a children's drama program should not include play contests. When children come together to present plays for one another the occasion should be a festival, not a competition. Contests put unnecessary pressure on players and expose them to unnecessary disappointments. When players do a good job they should not be concerned with winning over other players.

How to Choose a Play

The director chooses the play for production before starting sessions that are to culminate in a performance. Early selection permits him to use material from the play for creative drama and practice of skills.

The director should be able to answer "Yes" to the following questions about the play he selects:

1. Does it tell a good story?
2. Does the director like it?
3. Does it offer a sufficient number of interesting roles?
4. Do the story's incidents build logically to an exciting climax and a satisfactory conclusion?
5. Are lines of the play worth the effort to memorize?
6. Does the play suit the ability of players?
7. Can it be prepared in the available time?
8. Are available resources adequate to stage the play?

Arrangements with Play Publishers

When choosing a printed play the director contacts its publisher to obtain permission to produce. This may involve payment of a royalty fee—usually five or ten dollars on the short play that children produce. Permission may require only purchase of a certain number of scripts.

Fees vary according to the circumstances under which plays are presented. Complete information should be given the publisher when permission is requested.

No arrangement with a publisher is needed when children develop a story dramatization into a play. To do this they record dialogue in a script. Then they rehearse it as they would a printed play. The play *In the Kitchen Again* is an example.

On occasion an interested playwright creates a play for children in whom he is interested. This situation involves no publisher.

And Now, The Director

Children should refer to the one who directs their plays by his proper title. He is the director. He assigns responsibilities, gives instruction in how to perform them, checks to see that they are properly performed, and coordinates the efforts of all participants into a performance worthy of an audience. He also recruits an audience and arranges for its comfort and pleasure.

9

Lead-up Activities

Lead-up activities help children develop theatre skills, and prepare them to rehearse a play. These activities are a means to develop players' voices and bodies for theatre and for daily life. With these activities children can learn terminology that enables them to take direction. The activities should be introduced gradually before rehearsals begin. They should be varied and occupy only a small part of class time.

Bridging the Gap Between Playmaking and Putting on Plays

Directors have used various methods to introduce play production to a creative drama group. One director did it just after a successful story play. She said, ''Some time would you like to work on a story play until it was so good you could invite your friends to see it?'' Then she asked, ''What would we have to do before they could enjoy our play?'' At length she drew from children these suggestions, which she wrote on the chalkboard: Players have to

1. Know exactly what to say and do. (They can't make it up in front of an audience.)
2. Act so the audience can see what they do.
3. Speak so the audience can understand what they say.
4. Make the play's story live for the audience.

The director explained, "We'll have to practice to be able to do all this. When you can, we'll rehearse a play for an audience."

Players Learn to Move about the Stage

Stage Locations. To teach stage locations this director said, "We said we must know what to do. That means, first, knowing where we should be, and how to get there. We have to learn the names of different places on the stage."

She had previously drawn chalk lines on the stage floor to mark it into nine equal squares. "Each of these squares has a name," she said as she stood in the center square. "Can you guess the name of this one?"

Children first said, "middle" and then, "center."

She quickly announced, "Center is its name." One child wrote a big C in the square. Continuing to stand in the center square the director extended her right arm to the side. "Is this my right arm, or my left?" When children answered correctly she announced, "So this square at the right of center square is called *right center.* Some one wrote RC in the square. It was easy for children to guess *left center* for the next square. The director explained that squares got their names from their location to the right or left of the actor. She added, "It doesn't matter whether it's right or left of the audience. The audience doesn't use the stage."

Next, the director walked away from children to the square behind center. She explained that stages long ago were higher at the back so the audience could see better. "So," she said, this square is not called *back center* but *up center.* Using the same method the director named the other locations.

To help them remember, the director let them play games with the locations. She asked one boy to move as he chose to various stage locations. The rest of the class divided into two teams called the name of each location as he stopped. The team calling it first and correctly scored a point. Five points for one team won the game.

With the next exercise three children stood close together on the stage. Other pupils took turns calling locations. The three repeated the location called. Then walking fast and close together they went to the new location. This was played until all had opportunity to follow directions.

Cues. A director should begin teaching about cues by explaining the word. It means a signal to do or say something as previously planned. When a player memorizes lines and movement he also memorizes cues. They let him know when to speak and move.

More often than not a cue is the last three words of another player's speech. It may also be another player's movement, gesture, change of facial expression, a sound effect, a wave, or handshake.

Whatever the cue is, every player must be on the alert for it. Responding to it is called *responding on cue.* Here are some exercises that let several children practice cues at the same time:

1. Director: "You will stand"
Response: Children rise.
2. Director: "Your king lives."
Response: "Long live the king.
3. Director: "Hurry! Get started."
Response: Children cross down right.
4. Director: "Wait. Come back."
Response: Children cross up left

Then children practice response to cues in couples. They do each exercise twice so each child has opportunity to give the cue and to respond to it.

1. Cue: Father raises hand
Response: Son says, "Don't spank me."
2. Cue: Red Riding Hood says, "What makes your eyes so big?"
Response: Wolf says, "The better to see you, my child."
3. Cue: Baby Bear says "Some one's been sleeping in my bed, and she's still here."
Response: Goldilocks jumps up and runs away.

Making an Entrance. A player entering the stage to play his role is said to be making an entrance. Observance of certain procedures helps him to use his entrance to make the play's story live. Here are procedures that should effect a good entrance:

1. The player enters on cue.
2. He keeps his eyes at eye level.
3. He moves with assurance (if in keeping with character).
4. He enters in character.

5. He shows how he feels about coming.

To practice these procedures children work in couples. One gives the cue, and the other makes an entrance. Then they change places and repeat the exercise. Here are situations that let children practice making an entrance:

1. Cue: Prince says, "Let the music begin."

Cinderella enters ballroom for the first time.

2. Cue: Scrooge says, "Bob Cratchit, come here!"

Bob enters to answer the command of miserly Scrooge.

An entering player usually crosses the stage in front of a player already there. This requires the onstage player to make a counter cross or balance movement so the entering player does not hide him from the audience. His move should not look like a game or marching maneuver. So the onstage player finds some reason in the play's story that seems to cause him to move. Here is a situation in which dramatic reasons may be seen to balance the movement of an entering player:

Cinderella enters the ballroom and crosses in front of the Prince. He stands as though spellbound until after she passes him. Then he moves in the opposite direction to balance her movement. He moves slightly down stage as well as to the side. This puts him on a level with her so she does not have to turn her back to the audience to speak to him. The story offers him three reasons for this move. They are: (1) He thinks her so beautiful he wants to get a better view. (2) He is trying to discover who she is. (3) He wants to look at her from the other side to see if she's real.

The Prince can choose whichever reasons he wants and act accordingly. Showing a reason for the balance is called motivating it. Before practicing the following exercises children should discuss dramatic reasons that motivate the balance.

1. Tom Sawyer stands and admires the fence he has just painted. Aunt Polly crosses in front of him to inspect his work. What motive does the situation give Tom for a counter cross?

2. A toymaker sits at his workbench. A customer enters and crosses in front of him to look at toys. What reason does the situation give him for rising and balancing her cross?

Players Work to Improve Their Speaking

The director with good speech habits of his own sets an example that helps players improve their speech. They tend to imitate both his voice quality and his enunciation.

Posture. Players begin to work for better speech by working for better posture. The director explains and demonstrates so players know what constitutes good posture. He also explains its importance for speaking.

One director, Miss Espey, started posture work with an exercise she called "Puppet on a String." She said, "I'm a puppet master. In this hand I hold strings fastened to the tops of your heads. When I lift my hand I lift you to your tallest position." She raised her hand. "Do you feel the pull on top of your heads? Does it lift your head above your chest? Does it lift your ribs? Are you longer than you were from your ribs to your hip bones? When I lift you to your tallest position do your arms hang easily and straight?"

She lowered her hand. "Does this make you slump? That won't do." She lifted her hand. "Take the tall puppet position." Holding her hand high she moved among the children to correct individual faults. One girl held her chin too high. Miss Espey moved it to the right position and said, "You feel the pull of strings too near the front of your head. They're attached almost back to the crown."

A boy's shoulders were tense and high. Miss Espey gave him this exercise. "Hold your shoulders up to your ears. Push them as high as you can. Now, let them drop with a flop. Relax."

Children need these exercises to develop awareness of posture and to improve it. For all exercises they stand in the tall puppet position.

SHOULDER LIFT. Raise shoulders high while counting to five. Hold five counts and drop shoulders suddenly and completely. Rib cage should remain as high as when shoulders were high, but shoulders should be relaxed.

Breathing. Speaking requires breath, and breathing needs a good supply of air. A director should demonstrate how the right posture makes room for more air. Children can demonstrate for themselves how lifting the rib cage lets them take in a greater supply of air. Here is an exercise that lets them feel it.

FINGER CRUNCH. Hold fingers together outstretched. Put as many as possible between bottom of rib cage and hip bone. Let rib cage slump. Fingers are either squeezed or forced out. This position doesn't leave room for them. Neither does it leave room for sufficient supply of air.

FILL THE BALLOON. Place palms of hands on ribs at sides. Little fingers are down. Inhale on five counts. Hold five counts. Exhale on five counts. Push hands against body to force out last bit of air and collapse rib cage.

Directors should caution children against too much rise and fall of the chest during these exercises. They should explain that air is not stored in the chest, but lower where the rib expansion occurs. Players should frequently repeat "Fill the Balloon." It can strengthen breathing muscles. So can the following.

BLOW OUT THE CANDLES. Place palms of hands on ribs so finger tips meet in front over diaphragm. Inhale slowly. Feel expansion of ribs. Exhale in series of short, sharp puffs as if blowing out candles. Blow out as many as possible before supply of air is exhausted. Try to increase number of candles on succeeding attempts.

HUMMING. Hands on ribs with fingertips meeting in front. Inhale. Hum softly and without effort until breath is gone. Keep lips together but relaxed as breath is exhaled through nose for humming sound. Put finger lightly on lips to feel vibration there. Then place finger and thumb of one hand on either side of the bridge of nose to feel vibration there. Place fingers lightly on forehead to feel vibration. Try to increase it in each place. Increased vibration means a more resonant tone.

INDIAN CALL. Intone the syllables OO NEE VAH on one breath. It should sound like an Indian call from a hilltop. Divide class into two groups with one group at each end of the room. The first group intones the call. The other group answers. Vary this by having first group intone only first syllable. Second group echoes it. They do the same with other two syllables.

In all of these exercises children try only for easy, relaxed tone. They make no effort to increase volume. If the director sees evidence of tension in the neck muscles he speaks to the player. "Easy here. This is not the place to work hard. Make your ribs and abdomen do the work. Tighten abdominal muscles. They make the air last.''

Practice of these exercises should be for short periods only. Five minutes at a time are enough, but the exercises should be done frequently.

Poems. Speaking lyric poems often improves voice quality. One reason is that such poems usually contain the singing consonants: L, M, N, NG. Another reason is the joyous spirit of a lyric poem. The way a speaker feels affects the quality of his voice. Speaking these poems should give a lift to his spirits. The following poems contain sounds and spirit that should improve children's voice quality. Participants should also enjoy the poems for their content.

> Old Burgundian Carol
> (Adapted)
> Bring along a fife
> And bring along a drum.
> Leave your cares behind
> And come, come, come.
> Play on the fife
> And play on the drum.
> Tootle-tootle-toot
> And pum-pum-pum.

> All Mine
> Oh, the wind's whining down in the canyon,
> The rain's coming down in a stream,
> And the pine's bending down with a sigh and a moan.
> Oh, I love it! I'll live it and make it all mine—
> The wind and the rain and the moaning young pine.

Enunciation. Poems can also be used to help players speak distinctly. Here are jingles that have brought such results. Children should practice them to develop flexibility of tongue and to give their speech clarity.

> Trot, My Pony, Trot
> (Mother Goose Rhyme)
> Trot, my pony, trot
> Over grass and over gravel,
> O, what fun it is to travel.
> Gallop, never stop.
> Trot, my pony, trot.

Two Hundred Horses
    Clot, clot, clot, clot
    Sounds the heavy beat
    As two hundred horses walk down the street.
    Clot-clot, clot-clot, clot-clot
    A canter swift and neat
    As two hundred horses clat-clatter down the street.

The McNed Boys
    Donald and Wilfred and Edward McNed
    Dawdled and shouted and jumped on the bed.
    Their mother was almost distracted and said,
    "Stop it! O, stop it, and get into bed."

Projection. A child who participates in theatre learns to project. Resonance of tone helps a player project his speech. The first two poems above should improve resonance. Humming and intoning vowel sounds are also effective.

Projection is aided by care in sounding each word's final consonant. There is a tendency to slight D and T when either is the last letter of a word. Practice with the last poems should help to correct this fault.

To project, players need practice in modulation. This helps them develop judgment about the volume a situation needs. Here is an appropriate exercise:

Two players sit on opposite sides of a small table and engage in this conversation. They are Alice and Grace.

> ALICE: Where are you going?
> GRACE: I'm going to market.
> ALICE: You're going to market?
> GRACE: I want to buy meat.
> ALICE: Please buy some for me.

The two then move to opposite sides of the room and repeat the conversation. The next move is outdoors where the two players stand about one hundred feet apart to speak the same lines. Before the last exercise the director cautions them, "Don't yell, but make your words intelligible."

Another aid to projection is pausing. Punctuation offers players hints that they should pause when they see commas, periods, question marks, and exclamation points. A slight pause before a prepositional phrase also helps a player get his meaning across. Pauses are necessary to let the audience think about what a player says.

Players Talk with Eyes, Face, and Body

Speech is only one of the means by which an actor conveys ideas and feeling. He communicates also by his posture, facial expression, gestures, and movement across the room. These methods of communication are called pantomime.

Eyes. By moving only his eyes a player tells something of his thoughts. To demonstrate this, children should try using their eyes, only their eyes, to convey ideas. For practice suggest that they use only eyes to communicate the thoughts in the following quotations: They do not speak. They just look.

1. "I'm interested in what you say."
2. "I hear a strange sound."
3. "I have a good idea."
4. "What are you saying?"
5. "I see something moving along the horizon."

In communicating, a person tells things with his eyes before he uses any other part of his body and before he speaks. So if actors are true to life they use their eyes before they move or speak. Here are exercises that permit players to practice this sequence of, first, eyes, then body, and last speech. Eyes move before head or hand moves. Only after movement of both eyes and body does player speak in the following:

1. Look at the door and say, "Is that door closed?"
2. Look out the window and say, "Is it raining?"
3. Look at the floor and say, "There's dirt on the floor."
4. Listen and say, "I hear someone on the roof."

A player can tell so much with his eyes that he should seek opportunities in the play's story that let him look toward the audience. He does not look *at* the audience. He looks at the space above the heads in the back row. This may be called looking front. If a player looks front without a reason in the play he may ruin its story. The following situations give a player dramatic reason to look front. He should practice them.

1. Papa Bear tastes his soup. He looks toward the audience as he thinks about the soup's temperature. Then he says, "It's too hot."

2. Cinderella watches Sisters leave for the ball. Almost as in prayer she looks front to say, "I wish I could go too."

3. Frost King looks toward the audience as he tries to make up his mind. Then he says, "These trees shall never lose their leaves."

Posture in Pantomime. Posture is a tool for pantomime. Players give information about their characters by the way they carry themselves. A player while just standing still can help to tell the play's story. In these exercises players can convey ideas by posture although they do not move.

1. Stand still like a soldier ready to do his duty.
2. Stand still like an old woman who has worked hard all day.
3. Stand still like a child afraid of thunder.
4. Stand still like a mother looking at a sleeping baby.
5. Stand still like a child looking in a candy store.

Hands. Movements of the hands in pantomime are called gestures. Players sometimes ask, "What shall I do with my hands?"

The answer is, "Don't do anything unless moving them helps tell something about character or situation." It is better to make too few gestures than too many. Here are some guidelines:

1. If you make a gesture, mean it. Don't make a start, then hesitate or draw back (unless the situation demands it).

2. Use your eyes first to show you have an urge to use your hands.

3. Look in the direction the hands are about to move. If you take something from a high shelf, look first at the shelf. If you point to the right, look right before you point.

3. Finish the gesture. Bring your hand back near the starting point of the gesture, then let it drop easily to your side. This avoids letting the hand dangle meaninglessly in mid-air. Finishing the gesture gives further proof that you mean it.

4. Move your hand before you speak. Remember the sequence: First, eyes move, then, other parts of the body, and last, speech. Let players see how ridiculous they are when they don't follow this sequence. The best way to demonstrate is to perform the sequence in reverse. Say, "Look at the rainbow!" then, point to the sky, and last, look up. This is so unnatural it is comedy.

Children practice gesture in the following situations:
1. Suffering people plead with Ceres to break the spell.
2. Toymaker says, "You may have everything in my shop."
3. "Go out that door." (Remember eye, body, then speech.")

Use of Objects. Pantomime is often concerned with objects. Players should touch them in a way that shows feeling or character. Here are exercises that permit practice with objects:
1. Tom Sawyer picks up a paint brush, dips it in the paint, and paints the fence. He wants to make the other boys wish they had a fence to paint.
2. Sleeping Beauty touches Wicked Fairy's spinning wheel. She is afraid, yet she wants to know what it is like.
3. Little Jack Horner sticks his thumb in the Christmas pie. He is proud of his accomplishment, and he likes plums.
4. Knave of Hearts steals the tarts. Although he wants them he knows he should not steal.

Exercises from the Play Selected for Production

The director does not limit exercises to those suggested here. He selects practice material from the play chosen for presentation later. He chooses situations from the play for practice in responding to cues, making an entrance, cross and balance, and pantomime. Excerpts from the play are practiced to improve voice quality and ability to project.

When children later encounter these words and situations they feel a sense of security. They have learned solutions to these problems in their lead-up activities. In this way lead-up activities not only develop players' skill. They give direct preparation for rehearsal and so may reduce the number of rehearsals necessary to prepare the play.

Getting to Know the Play through Creative Dramatization

Rehearsal time may be further reduced when lead-up activities include creative dramatization based on the play. The director uses the play's situations for improvisation. If the play is to be *A Princess at Heart* participants develop improvisations about trying on shoes. Incidents and characters grow out of shoes that are tight, loose, desirable, or unsuitable. This is advance preparation for the play's final scene.

The last of the lead-up activities is acting out the play's story. The director tells the story without mentioning its connection with the play to be rehearsed later. Participants may devote the main part of two sessions to acting this story. This acting enables children to play different characters in the different scenes of the story play. They can better understand relationships among characters. They become familiar with lines and situations. Players acquire a feeling for character that encourages sincere portrayals in performance. Their inflection when speaking lines of the script later should ring true because they understand meaning. This informal acting of the story is invaluable as an aid to memorization of lines.

Story Play Instead of a Tryout

Acting the story serves the purpose of a tryout. It lets the director judge suitability of children's physical characteristics for roles. He can assess their feelings for roles and their ability to portray characters. He judges them when their minds are on the story and are not distracted by fear of failure. Finally, children are more apt to enjoy a story play than a tryout.

A Double Cast Serves Both Players and Play

One of the disadvantages of theatre activity is that all children do not have equal opportunity all the time. This is due to the nature of a play. Some characters have bigger share than others in telling the play's story. Sometimes a good play does not contain quite enough parts for all the children in a group.

The director tries to increase opportunities. One method is to assign two children to play each role so the play has two casts. Since children should give more than one performance of a play, each cast has a chance to perform. Frequently, some of the same children are in both casts. With one cast their parts are small, and with the other, large. Each cast can help the other by performing staging tasks for it.

The two casts need not be designated as first and second. This implies that one cast is superior. Each cast can select its name from a situation in the play. For *The Wishing Shop* one cast is the Seashell Cast and the other, the Feather Bonnet Cast.

Double casts provide for emergencies. On the day of a rehearsal one child may be sick or called away by family responsibilities. It is easy to bring in the child who plays the same part with the other cast. When emergencies occur on performance day the double cast means "the play goes on."

A director sometimes has two players eager and qualified for the same role. Here is another problem that a double cast can solve. But, what if more than two children desire and qualify for the role? Then the director takes into consideration which have had greatest opportunity in other productions. The one who has had least previous opportunity gets the best part in the current play.

When opportunities also have been almost equal a director sometimes leaves the choice to luck. He must be fair. Children should be able to see objective reasons for casting. They should never have reason to think that their director caters to favorites. So there are times when he writes the name of the desired character on a slip of paper and puts it with blank papers in a bowl. Each child qualified for the role draws a paper. The player who draws the paper with the character's name gets the part.

Players should understand from the beginning that to keep their roles they must be faithful to rehearsal. The director is the judge of whether to excuse an absence. He explains when he assigns roles that players who do not accept the discipline imposed by theatre do not participate.

10

The Director Studies the Script

The director's study of the script begins before he starts lead-up activities. At that time he selects from it material for exercises to develop skill, and ideas for improvisation. His next study prepares him to conduct rehearsal.

What Are the Play's Big Moments?

To begin this study the director looks for the play's big moments. These are the speeches or pantomime essential to the play's story. In the introduction they tell who the characters are, where they are, and why they are here. Later, the big moments let the audience know what is happening. They are the times of which one might say, "The plot thickens." Each of these moments is the climax of a little scene. Out of it grows another little scene with its own moment of climax. Finally comes the biggest moment of all, the climax of the play. The director underlines in his script what is said or done at each big moment.

In *Sleeping Beauty* he would mark the following big moments:

1. KING: Fairies and Members of our Court, welcome to this christening feast.
2. WICKED FAIRY (entering): Why didn't you invite me to your feast?
3. WICKED FAIRY: And she shall die.
4. SIXTH FAIRY: She shall sleep one hundred years.
5. Beauty pricks her finger and falls asleep.

6. The Prince arrives.

7. Beauty awakes. (This is the climax of the entire play.)

With these big moments pinpointed the director is better able to (1) arrange the stage to fit the play; (2) block movement of players; and (3) invent business for players.

Fitting the Stage to the Play

It should be remembered that the word *stage* does not necessarily mean an elevated area behind a proscenium arch. It is any area that actors occupy when they give a play. It may be no more than the front of a classroom. Wherever a stage is located, its boundaries must be defined. Even if these are only imagined, players must know where they are.

After locating the stage the director locates its entrances. To do so he refers to those big moments he marked in his script. He notes that Wicked Fairy enters on a big moment when she says, "Why didn't you invite me to your feast?" At this moment the play becomes exciting. The place from which Wicked Fairy enters will heighten or diminish the excitement. Another big moment occurs at this entrance when Wicked Fairy leaves saying, "She shall die."

The director places this entrance up right. This permits Wicked Fairy to walk toward the audience as she enters. She has time and space to attract attention.

The play needs a second entrance. Through it enter King, Queen, and members of their court. The director places this entrance down right. The thrones he puts down left. This arrangement permits royalty to move in procession across the entire width of the stage. Thrones are placed on the diagonal so King looks at players and audience when he makes his proclamations. The bench on which Beauty sleeps is placed up center on a little platform so all can see her. In placing properties the director arranges them so as to encourage players to face the audience.

Another director plotted the arrangement of properties for *The Three Bears*. For the porridge scene he placed the table so its longest side was parallel to the footlights. On its upstage side was a chair facing the table. The player who sat there would face both table and audience. Next, the director put a chair at each end of the table. Players sitting there faced each other. The audience would see their profiles. These players would have to find reasons in the play to turn full face to the audience on occasion.

Players Move about the Stage

The movement of players about the stage should help to make the play's story clear, logical, and exciting. Most movement is planned, or blocked, before rehearsals begin, but changes are often made during rehearsal.

Movement Traditions. Traditions give some guidance for blocking movement. They are not rules, only guidelines. Directors observe them or ignore them depending on characters and plot. Here are some traditions.

In crossing the stage a player usually crosses in front of stage properties and other players.

Generally a player moves during his own speech rather than on the speeches of others.

The strongest position onstage is center or up center. A strong movement is from up center to down center.

Players should use the entire stage and avoid huddling in the middle.

Elevations of players should vary. Some stand while others sit. Some sit on high stools. Others kneel on chair seats or sit on low stools. A young character often perches on the arm of a chair or sprawls on the floor. Low platforms or sets of two or three steps give opportunity to place players on other elevations. The player on the highest elevation has the strongest position. Strong positions and movements should be given players when they carry big moments.

Three or more players onstage are effective if their locations mark the three points of a triangle. Two or three players may form a little group on one point. The person carrying the story forward at the moment should be at the apex of the triangle. Since most important person status shifts from one character to another the size and shape of the triangle is constantly changing. A long conversation during which no one moves is apt to be dull.

Players do not stand in a straight line like soldiers. Neither do they stand with even spaces between them. They do not huddle like a football team. Instead, they stand in little groups the way persons naturally do at a reception or on the street corner.

People are inclined to stand near those they like. Those with the same background, occupation, sympathies, or station in life gravitate together. There is a tendency for those with opposing interests to stand apart. Cinderella's stepmother and sisters stand together. Cinderella takes a position apart from them.

Movement Described in the Script. Some scripts contain explicit directions for movement. These are helpful, but a director often needs to adapt them to his own situation.

Movement Required by Plot. Some positions and movements of characters are necessary to the plot. In *Little Women* Beth toasts bread near the fireplace. So she must be there. In the same play Jo delivers a telegram to her mother. She must move close enough to her mother to hand it to her.

Movement for Clarity and Climax. Ideas for movement are found in the big moments. The movement to get the important person of the moment into strong position should not be obvious. It should not look like a succession of speakers going center to make speeches. The movement should add to the dramatic effect.

The Three Bears provides an example. How can their movement direct attention from one to another at his important moment? Papa sits center facing the audience in the porridge scene. Papa is in the strong position when he says, "Someone's been eating my porridge."

Mama does not need to move up center on her speech. She has another way of attracting attention. She turns her head left as though looking for the thief. In so doing she includes the audience in her gaze. The movement of her head focuses attention on her as she says, "Someone's been eating my porridge."

Then Baby has the speech that climaxes the scene. Before speaking he picks up his bowl, runs around the table to a place between Papa and Mama. They turn to him in surprise. Their backs are almost turned to the audience as they look at him. His own movement and position and the movement of the others direct attention to him. He gasps, "Someone's been eating my porridge." Holding his upstage position he then turns his bowl upside down to show it is empty. He says, "And she's eaten it all up."

Position and movement make the most of big moments in *Sleeping Beauty*. When the Sixth Fairy says, "I'll just wait," she moves away from the other fairies. She is now different. They have given their wishes. She has not. The audience must notice her to be ready for her wish that later changes the spell of death to sleep.

The movement of Wicked Fairy when she says, "Why wasn't I invited," has already been described. It's a walk from up right to center. She has another strong movement as she goes up right, turns, and says, "And she shall die." The dash upstage, the quick turn at the entrance before she speaks should make the audience shudder.

A little later comes the last fairy's turn to tell the story. She crosses center to comfort King and Queen. From this position she says, "The Princess shall not die, but only sleep." Then she turns to face the audience and all players. Other players turn to look at her. Both movements direct audience attention to her. If spectators miss her next line they might as well have stayed at home. She says, "She shall sleep for one hundred years."

A big moment may be marked by pantomime instead of speech. An example is the spinning wheel scene. Sleeping Beauty sees Wicked Fairy and her spinning wheel. Wicked Fairy urges the girl to spin. Beauty walks around the wheel, almost touches it, then draws back. This movement should create suspense as one wonders, "Will she touch it?"

At this moment the audience must not look at Wicked Fairy. So the directors places her seated on a low stool and her back half-turned to the audience. Beauty is above her and facing the audience. With attention on her, Beauty touches the wheel, pricks her finger, and sinks to the bench. Wicked Fairy remains motionless so everyone will watch Beauty. Only after Beauty falls asleep does Wicked Fairy pick up her wheel and go.

Beauty up center is in perfect position for the awakening scene later.

The entering prince must be careful to kneel so he does not hide her face. Then she rises, and the two walk down center as the castle folk rush in.

Temperament and Emotion Suggest Movement. Movement can portray characters' temperaments and emotions. Wicked Fairy again provides an example. Her big movements first in one direction, then another show how volatile and erratic she is.

Feelings of lords and ladies in *Sleeping Beauty* are portrayed by their movement. They are so shocked by Wicked Fairy's curse that at first they stand as though paralyzed. Then they want to do something. Not knowing what to do they move in all directions. This helter-skelter movement shows their confused state of mind.

Business Helps Bring the Play to Life

Business in a play includes various occupations and auxiliary activities in which characters engage. In life people are usually occupied with some activity. So to make a play true to life a director invents things for players to do that are appropriate to character and situation.

The occupation by which a character earns his living suggests activity. The Cobbler in the play *The Pudding Pan* cuts or sews leather or repairs shoes.

Daily routines of living suggest business. Among them are eating, putting on wraps, taking them off, combing hair, applying makeup, and picking up litter.

Recreational interests contain other hints for business. Gardening, writing letters, reading, and sewing are suitable for many characters. Business may be no more than a form of doodling—doodling with a pencil, gloves, purse, or pocket knife.

Business can be a response to weather in the play. If the day is supposed to be warm, characters fan themselves, wipe perspiration from their foreheads, and roll up their sleeves.

A condition within a character suggests business. One who suffers pain shifts and twists to find comfort. A woman in a hurry crams objects in her purse as she prepares to leave. Cinderella's vain sisters look in the mirror, arrange their hair, and admire their dresses.

Business often involves use of hand properties. These suggest activities. A king carries a scepter, puts it down, or holds it aloft. Fairies toy with their wands. Prince carries a sword that he sheathes at the sight of Sleeping Beauty.

Hand properties help players think of additional bits of business. Handling the properties gives players ideas for pantomime.

Directors can select business to indicate a character's age, interests, habits, and station in life. A character who loves books reads them, feels their bindings, and arranges them on the shelf. Misers need business with a strong box or wallet.

When a hand property is essential to plot the director devises business to make the audience notice it. Cinderella newly dressed in her ball gown needs business to call attention to her slippers. She may take one off and admire its sparkle. When she puts it on again the audience can see how easily it slips on her foot.

Players need to practice business so it does not distract from more important things happening on the stage.

11

Call to Rehearsal

Rehearsal is a time of excitement—the excitement of working toward performance. It is a time to learn and to use what has been learned. Rehearsals are not haphazard. The fun of them is concentrated work to create a performance worthy of an audience.

Rehearsal Schedule

Rehearsals take place on schedule. Class time becomes rehearsal time. If class is held only once a week, another weekly session should be added. Two rehearsals a week make a good schedule for children working on a short play. A fifteen- or twenty-minute play needs no more than nine or ten rehearsals.

Each lasts from one to two hours. The same child does not rehearse for more than one hour at a time. The director allows two hours to work with two casts, talk to players, and check on staging responsibilities. He draws up a rehearsal schedule and familiarizes all players with it.

Talking to Players' Parents

The director informs players' parents of rehearsal and performance dates. He learns immediately of any schedule conflicts. This contact is a courtesy to parents. It may be a visit or a telephone call. It lets parents know of the director's interest in their children. He has opportunity to enlist their cooperation.

He tells them about double casts and that casting is subject to change. No player owns a role. Putting on a play is a team activity. As long as players are faithful they have a place on the team. However, their places may change. Such explanations forestall disappointments when circumstances require changes in casting. The wrath of a woman scorned does not compare with that of a parent who thinks his child has been wrongfully deprived of a role.

Volunteer Leaders assist with the Production

The director needs adult or teenage volunteer assistants. He recruits them before the first rehearsal. Sources are players' mothers and teenagers interested in theatre. They should share in the excitement, receive recognition, and have opportunity to learn new skills. They are scheduled for specific times and responsibilities and given instruction in how to perform them.

Among their responsibilities are directing activity of players waiting to rehearse, assisting in procurement and preparation of properties and costumes, assuming technical staff responsibilities or supervising technical staff, and helping with costumes, make-up, and dressing room supervision at performance time.

Technical staff includes participants who work with scenery, properties, costumes, and sound effects, and do prompting. Although adults do some of this work they more often supervise children who perform the tasks.

These jobs should be offered first to children who have no roles in the play. Such responsibilities often stir children's initial interest in drama activities. Players with small parts can add some technical responsibilities to give them more activity. Often players of each cast constitute the technical staff when the other cast rehearses or performs.

First Rehearsal—Players Read the Script

Players who meet to read the script are familiar with the play's story from their story play. At this rehearsal they read lines so they can make the meaning clear and speak words correctly and distinctly.

To the rehearsal the director brings three short lists of words from the play. In the first list are unfamiliar words and phrases. The second contains proper names and other words that may prove difficult to pronounce. The third list has words and phrases to be practiced for enunciation.

Players and director sit in a compact group. After a five-minute warmup on listed words the director reads to the players the description that introduces the play. The player closest to him reads the opening speech. The next player reads the next speech. So they continue around the group. Speeches of one character are not all read by the same child. One person in his turn may get a long speech. The next may get a speech of only one word. Players make no effort to act. They read only to understand meaning.

When reading shows that a player does not understand, the director interrupts. He explains and asks questions until meaning is clear.

A mispronounced word causes another break. Director pronounces it correctly. Players repeat it. There is no embarrassment for the player who made the mistake. The director says, "Here is a word to work on. That's what this rehearsal is for."

Pauses. The play is read a second time for work on pauses. One director, Miss O'Meara, asked her players. "Why do people pause during their speaking?"

Answers were: "Thinking what to say next." "Trying to remember something." "Waiting to get a new idea."

Miss O'Meara commented, "All these answers mean that people think during a pause. You need to know what characters in your play think when you pause. Then your pantomime will make the pause mean something to the audience. Considering these thoughts will help you make the meaning of the speech clear."

The play was *Little Women*. Players were reading the scene that follows receipt of the telegram saying Father is ill. Mother says, "Be calm girls. Amy, will you send a telegram?"

Miss O'Meara said, "After she says 'girls' she thinks, 'What should I do now? Oh Yes.' Then she speaks to Amy."

The first rehearsal should include discussion of characters' thoughts in all places where meaning is not immediately clear.

As this rehearsal ends directors usually remind children of the rehearsal schedule. This is also a good time to assign roles. The reading rehearsal in addition to the story play should provide adequate basis for casting. Scripts are distributed. Players are told that circumstances sometimes make it necessary to change roles after rehearsals have begun.

To stimulate enthusiasm for the next rehearsal the director makes an announcement. "Next time we'll rehearse on the stage." He refers to the acting area as the stage even if it is only one end of a classroom. His manner lets players know that moving about the stage is a big adventure.

Second Rehearsal—Blocking Movement

The purpose of this rehearsal is to show players where to move onstage during the play. Before rehearsal time the director recruits members of a stage crew to help arrange the stage. He shows them a diagram of its arrangement. They put properties in place as indicated. The director tells the crew of its responbility to have the stage set before each rehearsal.

For warmup activity players practice making an entrance. One of the values of this warmup is that players can begin work as soon as they arrive.

After four or five minutes the director asks players in the first scene to take places onstage. Others sit nearby. The director is onstage. Referring to the script he previously marked he gives explicit directions for movement about the stage. Sometimes he demonstrates by going through the movements himself. After giving a direction he instructs players to walk through it. Then he allows time for them to record the instructions in their scripts. After marking the movement players repeat it. This puts them in position for the next move.

In conclusion the director announces, "We'll begin the next rehearsal with a review of movement. Start to memorize your lines. Learn movement and lines together. Each will help you remember the other. It's like learning the words and music of a song."

Third Rehearsal—Bringing Characters to Life

Third rehearsal is to stimulate players to think about their characters and to move and speak like them.

As he does before each rehearsal, the director checks the arrangement of the stage and confers with the stage crew.

Warmup period is devoted to exercises to develop resonant tones. Players practice humming and sustained vowel sounds.

To promote study of script and characters the director asks questions similar to those used in acting stories. He says, "Look for the answers to these questions in your script. Prove your answer by something you find in the script." Here are the questions: "How does your character look? Feel? Walk? Speak? Is he healthy and vigorous? How does he feel about other characters in the play? What does he want in life? How does he try to get it?"

Director and players sit in a compact group for this discussion. As players search scripts for answers the director says, "Look for answers in what the character does, how he does it, and what he says. Read also what other characters say about him."

Mrs. Volt, who directed ten to twelve-year-old girls in the play, *Gypsy Brew*, got the following answers to her questions.

"Dame Brand looks strong. I know because Fidalia says it." "She's about middle age because she was grown when Fidalia saw her several years ago." "She's bossy. I can tell by the way she orders everybody about." "She wants money more than anything else. The reason she wants to make nail soup is to save money."

Ordinarily players spend less than half an hour on this discussion. Then each cast rehearses the play. They review movement and make their first attempt to portray character. The director interrupts them frequently. Here are comments Mrs. Volt used during a similar rehearsal.

"You said Dame Brand was strong and bossy and unfriendly. Show it by the way you walk and stand. Try standing with your feet farther apart. Do you feel like leaning back on your heels? Does that give you a feeling of being sure of yourself?

"Repeat that line to show she thinks she is smarter than the others. Make each word emphatic. Speak quickly, but be sure to sound T and D on the end of the words. Don't hold M and N sounds. That makes Dame Brand sound too pleasant."

Mrs. Volt interrupted the girl who played Dame Kunson. "You said she wanted to win Dame Brand's favor. Do you want to sound pleasant? You are the one who sustains sounds of M and N. Try it on the line, 'Good morning, Dame Brand.' " After a player did a good bit of acting Mrs. Volt said, "Do it again. It's good. Do it that way every time."

At the close of third rehearsal every director makes an important announcement. "Memorize your lines and movement before next time. You won't carry scripts again. Your hands must be free to work with properties."

Fourth Rehearsal—What Business Does for Characterization

The purpose here is to show players how to use business.

Before this rehearsal the director appoints property man and prompter. The property man distributes properties at the beginning of each rehearsal and performance. After they are used he collects and stores them. From this time on the prompter prompts at all rehearsals and performances. The director does not act as prompter. He has more important things to do.

For warmup, players practice exercises with objects from chapter 9.

When the director says, "Players, put your scripts away," they may resist. He responds, "The prompter will give you lines if you need them." He makes no exceptions. Trying to remember lines helps players memorize them. Having to be prompted is incentive to learn them.

In conducting the fourth rehearsal of *Gypsy Brew* Mrs. Volt made sure some vegetables were there. Players needed to practice cutting and peeling. She helped them coordiante the business with their lines. She didn't want business to slow down the play. Players suggested additional business. Mrs. Volt decided when it was effective and how long it should continue.

While one cast rehearsed, the other cast listened to the suggestions and made notes. This shortened the time necessary for their rehearsal.

At the end of fourth rehearsal a director can increase interest in the fifth with this announcement. "Next time there will be a costume accessory for each player to wear.'' For the play, *Gypsy Brew,* accessories would include earrings and kerchiefs for the girls, shawls for women, and aprons and caps for children.

Fifth Rehearsal—How Pantomime Shows Character

The purpose here is to show players how to use pantomime for character portrayal.

Prior to the rehearsal the director appoints a wardrobe mistress. She immediately takes charge of accessories, and later, of all costumes. She distributes costumes to players, checks them in, and puts them away. She pins on each accessory the name of the character who wears it.

As warmup for this rehearsal players practice pantomime exercises from chapter 9.

To help players concentrate on pantomime as they enter, a director uses questions similar to some used in acting stories. The following should help with entrance pantomime: ''Why are you here? How do you feel about coming? Have you been here before? Do you know the other characters here? How do you feel toward them?''

Mrs. Volt in her fifth rehearsal of *Gypsy Brew* asked similar questions about entrances in the play's second scene. Before Dame Brand entered, Mrs. Volt asked her, ''Why has Dame Brand come here?''

The player answered, ''To find a bargain at market?''

''What does she look at as she enters?

''At the food that's for sale.''

Mrs. Volt talked to Tala and Bendell about their entrance.

''Have you ever been here before?''

''No.''

''The market place is strange to you. What do you do?''

''Look around and see what's here,'' came the answer.

To Fidalia Mrs. Volt said, ''You've been here before. What interests you the most?''

Fidalia said, ''Dame Brand.''

''Yes,'' said the director. ''You look at her. Look her up and down. Let the audience know you recognize her. Signal to Tala and Bendell behind you. Let the audience see this signal.''

To all players Mrs. Volt said, "You should use pantomime to show why you act and speak as you do. Remember you motivate actions and speeches with pantomime that shows reasons." To illustrate Mrs. Volt said, "In the first scene Tala says, 'I've found it.'' What has she found?''

The girls knew that Tala had located the town at the foot of the hill.

"What must Tala do before she says, 'I've found it'?''

"Look at the town," they answered.

"Yes, she must show she sees it before she says she sees it. When Dame Brand asks, 'Are thosse onions good and solid?' what does she do before asking?''

"Looks at the onions."

"Yes, and when Bendell asks, 'May we use this kettle?' where does she look before asking?''

"At the kettle."

Mrs. Volt continued. "All of you look at objects, but you have different ways of looking. You are different people. You have different reasons. Plan your pantomime to fit character."

From this rehearsal on, the director's position is in front of the stage. He is close enough to move there quickly to demonstrate as needed.

At conclusion of this rehearsal the director announces that all sound effects will be heard next time.

Activities for Players Waiting to Rehearse

All players work together most of the time until fifth rehearsal. They are involved in analyzing and studying. Beginning with the fifth, each cast goes through the play on its own. While offstage players wait they perform these tasks:

1. Make covers for scripts.
2. Make posters to publicize the play.
3. Record in their scripts all suggestions for acting.
4. Decorate scenery and stage and hand properties.
5. Make costumes accessories, and decorate costumes.
6. Make and decorate programs if they are to be used.
7. Prepare equipment for sound effects.
8. Make placards that announce change of scene.
9. Assist director and volunteers as needed.

Sixth Rehearsal—Teamwork

Teamwork means playing as a unit. This rehearsal is to develop interplay, or ensemble playing.

Before the rehearsal the director appoints one of the stage crew as sound effects man and another to work lights. Equipment they need is placed backstage, and working areas set aside for them. The director gives them cue sheets that list all sound or lighting effects, and the cue for each.

Warmup for this rehearsal includes posture and breathing exercises and exercises for modulation.

The director leads a discussion of teamwork in putting on a play. Players sit in a group close to the director. He begins by comparing the importance of teamwork in a play to a football game. He says, "All players on the football field play every second they are in the game. In the same way all actors must act every second they are onstage. First one player, and then another carries the ball in a football game. All other players support the ball carrier and help him move the ball forward. In the same way, first, one actor speaks, and then, another. The speaker is usually the one carrying the story forward. All other actors support him. How do they do this?"

Discussion of this problem should reveal that silent players support the speaker in these ways:

1. They look at the speaker.
2. They act as if they hear what the speaker says.
3. They show their reaction to what the speaker says. In discussing this a director may say, "Remember you wrote the thoughts of players during their own speeches. Now, write the thoughts players have while they listen to others. These thoughts will give you ideas for pantomime."

An example of such pantomime is found in the play *In the Kitchen Again*. Cook and Knave are talking.

COOK: Don't touch that cake.
KNAVE: I can if I want to. I'm the Prince. I can do anything I want to.

Three characters listen to the Knave's speech. They are Cook, Assistant, and Scullery Maid. To promote interplay the director may ask each player what he thinks about Knave's speech. Here are possible answers.

Cook thinks: Even if you're Prince you'll not spoil that cake.

Assistant thinks: What'll we do if he spoils the cake?

Scullery Maid thinks: Isn't he brave to talk like that to the head cook?

Each thought suggests pantomime for the listening player.

4. Listeners show how they FEEL about another's speech. The same conversation between Cook and Knave provides an example. The kitchen servants have feelings as well as thoughts about the Knave's speech. Scullery Maid is filled with admiration. Assistant is worried. Cook is angry.

Her anger draws a reaction from Knave. He defies her with pantomime that has a touch of arrogance. His father enters just then and completely deflates Knave. This quick change reflected in Knave's pantomime should be good comedy. It is funny only if Cook shows anger, and Knave shows defiance. This interplay is the teamwork that makes a play come alive. The listener reacts to the speaker. Then the speaker responds to that very reaction.

5. The listener's pantomime should give the speaker reason for some of his remarks. Players have already practiced pantomime to motivate their own speeches. Here they plan pantomime to motivate the speech of others. In the case of Cook and Knave, Knave should do something that causes Cook to say, "Don't touch that cake." He should either touch it or reach for it before Cook's speech. She might even grab his hand in mid-air as he reaches. This interplay makes a climax of her speech.

Another example of need for interplay is in a scene from the same play. In this scene Knave and his playmates start to eat the tarts that Knave has stolen. They hear Cook coming. All the children are afraid, but each shows fear according to his own character. To show this, Knave can try to hide the tarts. Henry could cram his in his mouth. Catherine cries, and Eleanor and Anne clutch each other. Cook, entering then reacts to the fears of the children.

At the conclusion of this sixth rehearsal the director wants to give players new interest in the seventh. He says, "We've been working on different parts of putting on a play. Next time we begin to put all the parts together."

Seventh Rehearsal—Now Fast, Now Slow, and Making Big Moments Big

The purpose to be accomplished here is to vary the play's tempo and strengthen its climactic moments.

A performance is apt to be dull if it moves always at the same speed. Tempo refers to the speed with which players speak, move, and respond to cues. The quicker the response, the faster the tempo. For slow tempo directors usually choose moments in which characters are thoughtful, relaxed, or content. An approaching climax often indicates increased tempo. This conveys tension and conflict.

The impact of the climax can also be intensified by the manner in which players speak. As they near the climax they increase its affect by greater volume, higher pitch, and sudden changes of pitch. Sudden pause can have the same affect.

At the moment of climax listening players react with increased intensity. They may sustain their positions for longer periods. How to teach variety of tempo and building toward a climax was demonstrated by Miss Lopez in her players' seventh rehearsal of *The Pudding Pan*.

In this play Cobbler and his Dame quarrel over who should return a pudding pan to a neighbor. They agree that whichever one of them speaks first must do it. Various characters enter and try to get them to speak. The play opens as their quarrel begins.

COBBLER: That was a good pudding, Dame.
DAME: Yes, but it's great trouble to take back the pan.

Miss Lopez instructed players to speak slowly and in relaxed manner on these two speeches. On the next line she asked Dame to pick up her cue quickly. The Cobbler still spoke slowly.

COBBLER: I don't call that much trouble.
DAME: (quickly): Then, why don't you do it?
COBBLER (still slowly): I'm busy.

Miss Lopez requested a break in the conversation while the Cobbler moved from table to workbench. He continued to speak slowly. Again Dame responded quickly.

COBBLER: I must finish this shoe.
DAME (fast): And I must finish my spinning.

After the Dame said ''I'' she put the pan on the table with a bang. She finished the line as she walked at a brisk pace to her spinning wheel. The Director asked Dame to repeat her last line so Cobbler could practice fast response. Both increased speed slightly with the next two lines.

COBBLER: If you were a good wife, you would take the pan back without any more talk.
DAME: If you were a good husband, you'd take it back without another word.

From this moment they gradually increased tempo. Miss Lopez indicated the tempo by using her head and hand like an orchestra conductor. Later she tapped the changes in speed with her pencil against a chair.

Miss Lopez stayed near the front of the stage. She said, ''Keep on. Listen to my directions, but don't stop the play.'' She called directions like, ''Faster.'' ''Slower.'' ''Bigger pantomime.'' ''Hold your positions.'' ''Get madder.''

When they approached the climax of the play the director gave them a countdown. This was to synchronize the directions they had discussed and practiced. The scene began with a speech by Neighbor.

NEIGHBOR: This sounds like magic.

As soon as the word *magic* was uttered Miss Lopez began to count. She had already instructed each player what he should do or say on each count.

''Ten.'' On this count Cobbler and Dame looked up to show they wondered what Neighbor meant. Doctor, Bailiff, and Landlord looked at one another as if to say, ''Now we know the answer.''

''Nine,'' intoned the director. The three moved into a loose huddle and exclaimed over the situation. Dame and Cobbler with increased fright exchanged glances that seemed to say, ''What are they going to do to us?''

"Eight." Neighbor nodded to the three in the huddle to show he knew what to do and said, "Leave it to me." The three encouragingly returned his nod.

"Seven." Neighbor turned toward Dame and fixed his gaze on her. Cobbler and Dame looked with equal intensity at Neighbor.

"Six."

NEIGHBOR: I have long suspected the Dame was a witch.

Until "six" the counting was slow to indicate a slow tempo.

Miss Lopez wanted the playing to this point to suggest the calm before a storm. With the word *witch* the storm broke, and tempo changed to breakneck speed.

"Five." Dame shuddered. Cobbler moved to the edge of his chair. The three in the huddle moved closer together as if to confer about a terrible situation.

"Four."

NEIGHBOR (picking up broom): But if a witch has laid a spell she can take it off again. (shaking broom) And witches must be made to obey.

The Dame cowered. Cobbler looked about in frenzy. The huddled three turned to watch Neighbor.

"Three." Neighbor started to lower the broom to hit Dame. Cobbler leapt toward him and caught the end of the broom. Dame dodged to escape. The other three put their arms around one another for protection. All held these positions

"Two."

COBBLER: Hold your hand! What? Beat my wife? How dare you? You villain!

"One." Dame laughed, and everybody relaxed as she explained "the cause of all the fuss."

Miss Lopez provided an example of one method of teaching tempo and climax.

At the end of the seventh rehearsal a director announces that next time players will go through the play without interruption.

Eighth and Ninth Rehearsals—Run-throughs
for Smoothness and Intelligibility

Some children's plays are so short that one run-through rehearsal is enough. This is possible because players can get through the play more than once in a rehearsal.

In this rehearsal players work for smoothness, continuity, and intelligibility. Players must not only be heard. The meaning of their words must be understood by the audience.

During the run-through the director sits in the back row of seats for spectators. Before going there he checks with all who have backstage responsibilities. Do they have cue sheets? Needed equipment? All supplies used in the play? He instructs all backstage workers that they are to

1. Be in assigned places during run-through just as during performance.

2. Be attentive to prompter and respond to his signals.

3. Cause no disturbance during run-through or performance.

The director then shows players where they will put on costumes for dress rehearsal and performance. He instructs them:

1. During run-through and dress rehearsal they will practice going from dressing room to stage at the appointed time.

2. Never will they try to get a peek at the audience.

3. Never will they be seen in costume or heard by the audience except when onstage.

It is after discharging all these duties that the director takes his place in the audience area. Two minutes after he leaves the stage prompter gives the signal to begin. Beside the director is a child who serves as messenger.

When the director cannot understand what a player says he writes instructions telling him how to improve. This is better than merely to write, "Louder." Urging children to project by saying "Louder" often results in their yelling. Typical of messages the director sends backstage are these: "I can't understand you. Put final letters on your words." "Talk to the back row of the audience." "Open your mouth wider when you speak." "Take one step to the left so you won't hide John." The messenger delivers the instruction to the player.

Directors find it difficult not to interrupt during the run-through. They see many aspects of performance that need improvement. They should remember that at this time a play's greatest need is for smoothness. It will do players good just to know they can get through without a break. The director can take them through short scenes for correction afterwards.

At the conclusion of this rehearsal the director announces the dress rehearsal.

Dress Rehearsal

Dress rehearsal is to give players an experience as nearly like performance as possible. The director invites two or three guests to give players the feeling of playing to an audience.

Just before this rehearsal begins, the director gives final instructions to the adult volunteers in charge of dressing rooms. Two minutes before rehearsal begins the director joins his guests in the audience. Again he has a messenger at his side.

In conclusion the director speaks to all participants where they are assembled onstage. He gives them a little advice and a great deal of encouragement. He lets them know he has confidence in them and looks forward with great pleasure to the performance.

12

Staging the Play

Staging includes making ready the stage, scenery, properties, costumes, makeup, and sound and lighting effects. Helping to prepare them offers children both pleasure and education. These physical resources for putting on a play add to its illusion for an audience, and its excitement for players.

Two warnings are sounded about staging: First, getting *things* ready for performance is not as important as getting actors ready. Equipment alone cannot make a play. Actors can. Directors should not become so involved with the technical side of theatre that they neglect acting. The second warning is for those who hesitate to give a play because they lack equipment or supplies. This chapter shows how to approach staging when resources are limited.

Great performances have been given in humble facilities with few supplies. Shakespeare presented most of his plays on a bare platform. If the scene was a forest, an entering player said, "Here we are in the forest." This let the audience know the locale. Classic plays of ancient Greece involved almost no scenery, properties, or attempt at authentic costuming. A successful twentieth-century play, *Our Town*, by Thornton Wilder, was written to be staged without scenery and practically without properties.

A play has only four essentials. They are a story, players, a stage, and an audience. Story, players, and audience depend on human resources. The only physical requirement is a stage.

A Stage Can Be Almost Any Place

A stage can be anyplace where actors present a play. It may be indoors or out. It does not depend on a platform or proscenium arch. It may be no more than a circle of floor or ground ringed by spectators.

Players have used for a stage such varied places as a park, a garden, a truck, a hayloft, a store window, the deck of a ship, a clubroom, classroom, gymnasium, and living room. The last, a living room, was used by the famous Abbey Players for their first productions. In the musical, *Man of La Mancha,* a play is presented in the common room of a dungeon prison.

Requirements. These are the requirements of a space that serves as a stage. It must be large enough for actors to depict the play's story. All parts of it must be within view of the audience. It needs to be quiet enough for the audience to hear what players say. This means it is protected from noise of wind, traffic, and sounds of adjacent activities.

How to Improvise a Stage

A space may need some adaptation to improve its visibility. A traditional way is to elevate players. When a stationary platform is not part of the facility it is possible to create an elevated playing area. One way is to build four- by eight-foot portable platforms and clamp them together. They may be ten to eighteen inches high and topped with heavy plywood. They serve many activities in addition to theatre. When not in use they can be stored on end.

Another way to improve stage visibility is to seat the audience on staggered elevations. Spectators may sit on the slope of a hill to watch a play on the level area below. This arrangement is improved when the hill is terraced and benches placed on the terraces. But this is not essential.

Indoors or out, seating arrangement may achieve staggered elevation for spectators. In the front row small children sit on the floor or ground. Behind them and also on the floor are taller children. Pillows or flat pads add to the comfort of these seats.

Third row spectators sit on small stools, kindergarten chairs, or low benches. Behind them is a row of folding chairs, which give their occupants the highest elevation.

A Wide Stage. Children should play on a wide stage—from twenty-five to thirty-five feet wide. It encourages free and expressive movement. It discourages them from huddling in little groups at center. The wide stage enables more spectators to be close to the stage. It is good for children to play to an audience that is close. To get more front seats and bring players closer to audience the stage is often thrust forward at center. The front line is curving instead of straight.

To Separate Stage from Audience. A stage on level with the audience needs a marker to indicate its front boundary. Both players and spectators should know the exact line that divides them. Strips of portable footlights can mark the line. So can sections of lattice or picket fence that stand only about six inches high. These are particularly appropriate when the scene is a garden.

On an outdoor stage objects anchored in the ground indicate a boundary. Twelve-inch sections of slender wooden doweling can be set in the ground ten to twenty inches apart. Each stick is decorated to suggest the locale of the play. If it is a garden a big artificial flower blooms on the top of each stick. In a play about knights silver cardboard shields lean against the pegs.

Scenery—Background for Action

Scenery creates background for the play and conceals backstage activity. It hides players until they make their stage entrances. Folding screens make suitable scenery when traditional set pieces are not available or practical. One or more screens at the back of the stage can be decorated to suggest the play's setting. Screens placed at each side can create wings for players' movement to and from the stage.

This wing arrangement is good for child players. It permits several to enter almost at once, which is often necessary in their plays. They don't have to open and close doors.

Other pieces as useful as folding screens are panels of plywood or fibreboard and lattice screens. Each piece measures no more than four by eight feet. It is held erect by inserting one end in the deep groove of a wooden base. This foundation must be wide enough to support the panel. Like folding screens the panels need to be braced and anchored so they do not wobble or fall.

An outdoor performance can take advantage of existing walls or hedges for background. New hedges have been planted to provide background and wings for an outdoor stage. When a play demands special scenery screens appropriately decorated are placed in front of the shrubs.

Decorating Scenery. Although children do not usually build scenery or attach bracing they can help with decoration. Youngsters enjoy working with paint and brush when set pieces are to be enhanced. For some productions no more is needed than to paint the pieces a new color. These provide a neutral background for the stage properties.

At other times screens and panels are decorated to suggest the locale of the play. Decorations may be a painted design, a collage, or real objects suggested by the play. An illustration of the last is a kitchen scene in which pots and pans and cooking implements are hung on a screen. Equally appropriate are pictures of pots and pans painted on the screen. With collage technique outlines of pots and pans are cut from various materials and pasted on.

A single tree painted on a panel can suggest a forest. Banners hung from the screens or painted on them create atmosphere for circus or fair. A coat of arms on the screen design gives the impression of a king's castle.

Fire Prevention. Before using any scenery or stage properties information should be secured concerning fire prevention ordinances. These may require all set pieces and properties to be flameproofed. It is a good safety measure whether required by law or not.

The Scene Shifts. The changing of scenery should be kept to a minimum in a play given by children. Their plays are too short to permit long intermissions for changing scenery. If a change is required it is wise to use the plywood panels. Designs for the first scene are painted on one side of the panels. On the back are designs for the second scene. To shift scenes it is only necessary to turn the panels around.

One way to minimize scene changes is to paint screens a neutral color and achieve different settings with a change of stage properties. This can be done by children in costume accompanied by suitable music. When the second scene is a garden scene shifters dress like gardeners or Mistress Mary. Heralds or pages carry in the throne for a castle scene. Merry Men of Sherwood put in place whatever is needed for a forest scene. Serving men and women set up table and benches for a peasant cottage.

If complete costumes are not to be had, scene shifters wear headgear that suggests the characters. The rest of their garb is their everyday clothes. A white mobcap with a deep ruffle does for serving a woman. A pointed green cap with a feather or green sprig is worn by a forester. Heralds and pages wear court hats. Gardeners wear straw hats, a fairy needs a gold headband with a star in front. Mistress Mary has a flowered hat with a bow tied under her chin.

When scene shifters have no authentic costumes a mistress of cere-monies walks down center and speaks to the audience. She says, ''We have no curtain to close while our scene changes. But each of us has brought his own curtains—our two eyes. We'll close our curtains for a minute while the scene is changed.'' With her fingers she pulls down her eyelids and waits until the crew leaves the stage. ''Now, lift your curtains. You see here the market place of Halborg.'' And she leaves the stage as players enter.

Another way to change scene is to present a group song or dance at the front of stage. During the number, changes are quietly made behind the entertainers.

When the change is a quick one a magician enters in costume and speaks to the audience:

''Abra cadabra, zim-zam-zen.
The play will start again
If you will count to ten.

With movement of his hand and his own counting he sets the rhythm for the audience count. They start slowly and softly. They increase both speed and volume until the count of ''ten'' comes in a shout. Such a count enables onstage players to be in place for a scene's opening.

Children have presented effective performances without any set pieces. To accomplish this a prologue or mistress of ceremonies has announced to the audience the name of the play and the time and place of each scene. Another method has been to place an easel on the stage at down right or down left. A large placard on the easel told where the scene took place. When the scene changed a child in costume removed the placard and put another in its place. Typical of words on the placard were: ''The Side of the Road,'' ''The King's Palace,'' ''Aunt Polly's Back-yard.''

One group of players used a wallpaper sample book instead of placards. Then the costumed attendant had only to turn a page to announce the change of scene. Methods like these are particularly effective for outdoor performances where grass and trees provide a neutral and attractive background.

Stage Properties Add to the Atmosphere

Stage properties are objects placed on the stage to suggest the scene of a play. A home scene needs furniture. A marketplace needs stalls. Properties are sometimes required by the play's story. In *The Glorious Whitewasher* Tom Sawyer needs a fence.

How to Get Properties. Before starting rehearsals a director lists stage properties needed by the play. The first step toward acquiring them is to try to borrow. Some players may have the desired property at home. A volunteer assistant may be the means of acquiring it. An item in the local newspaper or on the supermarket bulletin board may locate the needed property.

What cannot be borrowed can often be made. Useful materials for stage property construction are furniture and appliance crates, poles on which rugs are rolled, corrugated paper cartons from markets, and similar salvage material.

Furniture to be used for stage properties can sometimes be purchased from charity organization thrift shops. Adaptation and decoration are usually necessary. Frame armchairs can be gilded for thrones. Rustic picnic tables and benches can be decorated for peasant furniture. Decorating and adapting stage properties offer craft activities that most children enjoy. Both players and nonplayers participate.

Players Need Hand Properties

These objects that actors handle during the play add atmosphere and help each player feel at ease in his role. They should be obtainecd early so each player gets full benefit from practice with them. The child who plays a cripple is more convincing to himself and others when he has a crutch.

Beg, Borrow, or Make Them. Players, stage crew, adult assistants and director help to obtain hand properties. They borrow what is available, adapt what they have, and make what they can. What they can get in no other way they buy.

Making hand properties is another craft activity motivated and made more exciting by the play.

Managing Hand Properties. Once properties are obtained they are the responsibility of the property man. Before and after each rehearsal and performance he checks his stock. If any are missing or damaged he sees that they are replaced, repaired, or reported to the director.

The property man puts in place onstage the hand properties to be discovered there during the play. Backstage he puts on a table or in the property box all properties to be carried onstage. He sees that each player returns properties after using them. The director impresses the property man with the gravity of his responsibility. An otherwise good production can be ruined by lack of a hand property at the proper moment of performance.

What Will Players Wear?

Probably no aspect of a play means more to a child player than his costume. To try it on gives him a foretaste of the thrill of performance.

Like hand properties costumes help him feel his character. Wearing a costume increases his self-confidence, gives him new ideas for pantomime, and whets his zest for performance.

Costumes usually require an expenditure of money for fabric and labor even if volunteers assist. Money is well spent if it secures basic costumes that can be laundered and used repeatedly.

Basic Costumes

Costumes obtained for each production should become part of a permanent stock to be adapted for future use. They should be so designed that changes in decoration and accessories make them suitable for many characters.

An example is a dark nylon taffeta dress. It has a fitted bodice, long sleeves, moderately full skirt, and high round neck. The taffeta is durable enough to last for many washings and wearings.

The basic garment costumes a wide array of characters. With addition of a white neck ruff, mobcap, and tall pointed hat the dress suits a fairy godmother. For a witch, one needs only remove ruff and mobcap, and add a flowing cape. To costume a Puritan lady the hat and cape are taken off. White collar and cuffs are put on. These may be made of paper and attached with paper clips. With the dress a Puritan lady wears her traditional white cap.

For a court lady the above accessories are removed. The dress is decorated with a velveteen yoke that extends to a point at the front of the waistline. Decorated with braids, beads, and bows the yoke hooks over the dress at back of neck. A queen wears this and adds a long train attached to shoulders.

Without yoke and train the dress is worn by Mother in *Little Women*. She puts a band or two of cotton braid around the skirt and neck, and dons a shoulder cape when she goes out. A colonial lady removes the braid. Then tying a fichu at her throat and adding paniers to the skirt she is well dressed for a lady of her time. A dozen dresses of this type in different colors and sizes fill many costume needs.

Tights are basic garments for male characters. They provide suitable pants for kings, knights, noblemen, heralds, hunters, elves, Christmas carolers, and Peter Pan. Tights should be purchased by the dozen from wholesale houses. Smocks or tabbards worn above the tights are of such simple construction that they are quickly made.

Folk costumes of many countries are contrived with a basic stock of full skirts, and peasant blouses. Accessories and decorations are selected to fit the national costume desired. For Italy a bolero is worn over the blouse, and a sash is tied around the waist. The Spanish girl wears the same blouse and skirt. Instead of a bolero and sash she wears a dark, fitted bodice which she laces tightly over the lower front of the blouse. On her head the Italian girl probably wears a kerchief and the Spanish girl, a lace mantilla. Scandinavian girls also wear fitted bodices over blouses and skirts. They add aprons and caps.

Accessories are not limited to use with folk costumes. The Italian's kerchief is worn at other times on the head of a gypsy or the neck of a cowboy. Spanish bodice and Scandinavian apron are appropriate for a peasant woman in a fairy tale.

For fairies and other characters of fantasy or allegory there is another type of basic garment. It is a straight sleeveless sheath made of soft fabric like nylon chiffon. It can be girdled or draped or neck-trimmed in so many ways that it serves a variety of characters.

Getting costumes is one of the big worries of producing a play. The task is simplified when a store of basic garments is available.

Decorations. Although children do not usually help construct costumes they help with decorations and accessories. For craft activity this work is as appealing as making hand properties. Work is done in craft classes or by players when they have waits during rehearsal. Much value is lost if the work must be rushed through at the last minute. The valuable and pleasant activity should extend over a period of time.

Heads and Feet Are Not to Be Forgotten

Planning costumes includes consideration of heads and feet. Inappropriate caps or shoes can ruin total effect. Shoes styled in contemporary fad are conspicuous in period or fantasy costumes. For the feet of royalty of a bygone era dark socks can be turned down in neat rolls at the ankle. A cardboard sole cut to fit the wearer and placed inside the sock increases comfort. A dark oxford adorned with silver buckle suits a Pilgrim and many folk costumes.

Several players dressed alike should have identical footgear. In a production of Sleeping Beauty five fairies wore long white hose. The sixth wore hose of a deep beige shade. No spectator looking at the fairies in performance thought, "Isn't it fine that five of those fairies have matching hose?" Instead viewers continually looked at the feet and legs of the sixth fairy. All they thought of during the scene was, "Why doesn't that one fairy have hose like the others?"

Headgear is often the most distinguishing feature of a costume. A king is not a king without a crown. A chef can hardly be recognized without a starched cap. A Madonna is readily identified by a blue head drape. And an angel needs a halo.

So important is headgear that children have achieved effective performances when it represented the only attempt at authentic costuming. This is not recommended. But it can be considered if it is the only way to achieve costuming. Everyday clothes that accompany the headgear should be of inconspicuous color and design.

"Players, Take Care of Your Costumes."

This warning is important, and so is the timing of it. Given during the excitement that permeates dress rehearsal the warning may be neither heard nor heeded. Players should be instructed in care of costumes before trying them on the first time. They should understand that wearing costumes is a privilege that carries with it responsibilities.

Some directors distribute written instructions. These should also be read to the entire cast. They should include the following:

1. Before putting on costumes players wash their hands, faces, necks, and ears. They wipe off excess makeup to avoid staining costumes.

2. While wearing costumes children do not eat, run, or engage in active play. They do not appear where the audience might see them except onstage during performance. Just before going onstage they let the

wardrobe mistress give their costumes a final check. She makes sure that that every hook is hooked; every snap, snapped; every zipper closed; and every bow, tied. One unfastened hook can hold the attention of an audience as long as it is onstage.

3. Immediately after dress rehearsal and performance every player takes off his costume and puts on his own clothes. He puts the costume on a hanger or folds it and returns it to the costume mistress.

Makeup—Use a Light Hand

Makeup should be used sparingly on child players. Otherwise, it attracts attention to itself instead of the character. Audiences are close to the players. Outdoor performances in daylight make it unnecessary to use makeup except on character parts.

For a performance under stage lights makeup is needed. Even here, too little makeup is better than too much.

Character parts need some makeup to render players' appearance convincing. For example, a ten-year-old plays an old wisewoman. She needs lines on her fact to suggest wrinkles, and lines on her hands to suggest prominent bones. Her hair should be streaked with grey. If it is cut in youthful fashion it should be partly concealed beneath a cap. She may also need foundation makeup to darken her youthful complexion.

Makeup helps some characters achieve special features required by the play. Typical are a scar on the chin of a pirate, a wart on the nose of a witch, and weatherbeaten color on the face of an old seaman. These make the character more believable and help transport the audience into the world of the play.

Whenever foundation makeup changes the color of a player's skin it should be applied to all exposed skin. This includes neck, hands, wrists, and occasionally, feet and legs.

Makeup is often important on those who play creatures of fantasy. A goblin is more fantastic if his face differs from that of ordinary mortals. A green triangle on each cheek and a blue circle on his chin give him an out-of-this-world appearance.

Any three dimensional makeup like a wart, beard, or moustache should be applied securely, or not at all. A loose moustache has sent players and spectators into hysterics during performance. Even a great actor finds it difficult to save a play under these circumstances.

Making the Most of Sound Effects

The director of a children's play should make full use of sound effects. Children like to experiment with sounds. Doing so can increase their awareness of pitch and quality. Executing sound effects during performance gives them experience in timing, responding to cues, and being on the alert.

Sound effects do a great deal for a performance. They add to the atmosphere of the scene, focus attention of the audience on the play, and help the play to seem real.

Here are sounds that create atmosphere. Offstage birdcalls add to the illusion of a woodland. The wail of a coyote brings the feeling of space and loneliness to a prairie scene. The howl of the wind makes vivid the weather outside. Inner city is depicted almost as aptly by sounds of sirens and horns as by views of ambulances and cars.

Distinctive sounds are frequently used to heighten the impact of certain characters on the audience. A chain clanks on the entrance of a ghost. A high cackling laugh is heard offstage as witch enters. Tinkling music accompanies the arrival of fairies. Royalty enters to the strains of a dignified processional. These sounds are heard again when the character engages in pantomime unaccompanied by words.

A sound effect is a good way to open a children's play. Effective are sounds like these: striking of a gong, drum or cymbals, playing an arpeggio on a xylophone (even a toy), ringing of bells, ruffle of drums, and fanfare played on a trumpet or piano. The same sound is used to open each scene and at the play's conclusion.

Immediately after the play begins, a sound suggested by the plot should be heard. This brings the play to life at once. It helps quiet the rustle in the audience that often accompanies the start of a play. *The Glorious Whitewasher* is well opened by an offstage call from Aunt Polly. She calls, "To-o-om! Tom Sawyer! Come here!" The call should be loud. It is not in the script, but its addition makes a good opening.

Gypsy Brew can open with offstage birdcalls. A fanfare preceding entrance of the royal procession in *Sleeping Beauty* makes a dramatic beginning for the first scene. In *A Princess at Heart* a door should slam offstage just before Stepmother enters. The slam may indicate she has left another room, and it gets audience attention.

Various equipment can be tried out by the sound effects man. He may need assistance for this creative task. Although recordings of many sounds are available they do not provide as much fun as sounds children work out. A piano can be used for some sounds. It should be used frequently for mood music on entrances and during moments of silent pantomime.

The instruments children play in rhythm bands serve to produce sound effects. Their drums, bells, sticks, wood blocks, and triangles are the means of producing varied effects.

Children responsible for sound effects can make a host of them with their own voices, hands, and feet. They practice birdcalls and animal grunts, growls, and whinneys until the sounds are realistic. Snapping fingers, clapping hands, and stamping feet produce sounds of another kind.

The child in charge of sound effects confers with the director for help in getting equipment and for advice. He takes care of equipment. He may keep it in a box like the one for properties. He rehearses to coordinate sound effects with players' acting so his timing is precise in performance.

Enough Light

It has been stated that the audience must be able to see what happens onstage. This means there must be sufficient light to let spectators see players' faces with their changing expressions. The task of lighting is simplified because the audience is not large, and it is close to the stage.

Children often present their plays in daylight. If outdoors, the stage should be located to take advantage of the sun. It should shine on faces of players rather than on spectators. When the audience faces the sun it weakens their vision. Players who present a play indoors in daylight have to consider light from windows. Again, they should face the light.

Children once presented a short play on an evening campfire program.

The audience of young campers watched the play presented in front of the fire. The performance failed completely. With the only light that of the fire at their backs players were little more than silhouettes. To the campers, players' faces were expressionless blobs of darkness.

Children get a thrill from footlights. When used they should be accompanied by lights overhead or at the side to prevent shadows onstage.

Special lighting equipment makes demands on electric power. Before it is plugged in, available power should be checked. This prevents a stage plunged into darkness by a blown fuse.

Precaution should also be taken to prevent children's bumping into or tripping over lighting equipment. Cables strung across the floor are a hazard. Large pieces of lighting equipment should be surrounded by a barrier that protects children from running into equipment. Children should not participate in setting up lighting equipment. This is a task for adults.

13

The Excitement of Showtime

Showtime arrives. Looking forward to it keeps players at work through hours of rehearsal. They earn the thrill of playing to a full house.

The Audience and How to Get It

Players help to draw an audience. They invite their parents and other relatives, neighbors, family friends, and playmates. When relatives and friends are in the audience players need to be prepared for seeing them there. The director warns, "Your friends come because they want to see you. Your job is to make the play so interesting that they forget you. If you see them in the audience, don't wave or nod or even smile. Just act your part."

The director arranges publicity to promote an audience. Items about the play are sent to community newspapers. They should be sent two weeks before intended publication. A series of articles does much to sustain interest. Some list names of players and technical staff. Editors usually welcome material that contains names of local residents.

Here also is opportunity to recognize adults who have contributed leadership or supplies. Newsworthy articles feature unique facts about these people. Mention can be made of events in their lives that roused their interest in children and plays. Editors prefer a news story to a promotion story.

Short talks about the performance offer another type of publicity. Announcements should be made at neighborhood elementary schools. If the principal grants permission a three minute talk in every classroom can produce results. Announcements should be made in private and parochial as well as in public schools.

The director also seeks permission to announce the performance to clubs and classes meeting at the community recreation center.

Posters reach another segment of the community. Among places to exhibit them are stores, community recreation centers, schools, churches, supermarket bulletin boards, and the public library. Posters along with announcements and newspaper items increase the importance of a performance. They give players and potential spectators increased sense of the dignity of their activity.

A performance in a park or community recreation center building offers a last-minute opportunity to recruit spectators. Children dressed as town criers go about the grounds. From their shoulders hang sandwich boards proclaiming the name of the play and the time of performance. They ring bells to attract attention.

The criers stop to tell picnickers about the play. They give a personal invitation to children in the swings. They remind the leader of a day camp that it is almost showtime. She was previously invited by the director to make attendance at the play the day's finale for her campers.

To attract additional groups the performance is scheduled to start just as other activities are concluding. Children leaving the pool at the end of a swim session are invited to remain to attend the play. The crier rings his bell near the pool as swimmers leave it.

Glamour at the Entrance

As spectators arrive they should have reason to feel this performance is no routine event. It may be held in the school multi-purpose room, the community center clubroom, or under the playground pergola. But at showtime its entrance is decorated to give it glamour.

The place has a distinctive name for the day. Cut-out letters spell it out. It may be Woodland Playhouse, Hollyhock Drama Center, or Follystick Theatre.

Entrance decorations are in keeping with the name. To enter Woodland Playhouse spectators walk beneath a lattice arch twined with ivy. Ushers dress like wood nymphs. Soft music is heard from a concealed record-player. With the name Hollyhock Drama Center, tall stalks of hollyhock decorate the entrance. They spring from deep pots on either side. Ushers wear flower-sprigged dresses and sunbonnets. An accompanist at the piano plays Percy Grainger's "Country Gardens." At the entrance to Follystick Theatre stands a mammoth follystick. It is an enlarged replica of the plaything carried traditionally by court jesters. Boys in jester costumes act as ushers.

Child participants have shown imagination and resourcefulness in naming and decorating their playhouses. One group met at a small playground. The only space for performance was an outdoor basketball court. Children arranged an entrance near one of the goals. They twined its post and metal ring with vines and named the place Jack and the Beanstalk Playhouse.

Another group had to present its plays in a horseshoe court. Although the stakes could have been a handicap they were used to advantage. On the day of performance children attached a giant paper sunflower to bloom on top of each stake. Stakes were wound with green paper and decorated with paper leaves. The name Sunflower Performances appeared above the entrance.

Other players used a clubroom for their theatre. Above the doorway they fastened strings of bright pennants, fanned them out and taped the other ends of the strings to the floor. This was called The Circus Ring, and clowns served as ushers.

In many instances names and decorations continued for years. They carried on a tradition. Every performance day brought glamour that distinguished the place from everyday.

All this is an adaptation of a custom used in Shakespeare's time. On the day his company presented a play, a large flag flew from the staff above the playhouse. The flag gave a festive look and helped attract an audience.

Wiggling Children and How to Control Them

The audience at a children's play frequently includes little brothers and sisters. To keep them from wiggling, squealing, and lying down in the aisle can be a problem.

Planning is necessary to prevent the interruptions they can cause during performance. It is wise to seat the youngest children near an exit. The usher shows them to seats at such locations. He explains to their companions, "The children may get tired. If you sit here you can easily take them out."

Little children should not sit on folding chairs. Their wiggling can cause the chairs to collapse. The possibility of injury is obvious. The scream of a frightened child added to the crash of the chair can disrupt a performance.

Care in seating spectators can minimize other disturbances. Children have been known to attend with intent to provide their own entertainment. Nine- to twelve-year-old boys entering in a noisy group bear watching. They should not be seated in the front row. There they have the greatest opportunity to distract players. A "Reserved" sign on the first two rows of seats enables ushers to use discretion in seating guests there.

The adult volunteer in charge of ushers stands near the rear of the audience. If trouble appears he walks down a side aisle and looks at the troublemakers. Often this surveillance is enough to quiet them.

Of all ways to keep order the best is to present a good play. When it is well prepared, and the audience can see and hear it, there is apt to be little disruption. Another safeguard is to start on time. Distractions multiply and tensions build when spectators wait for a delayed opening.

Ushers Forestall or Rise to Emergencies

The mere presence of efficient ushers has a positive affect on audience conduct. Children make good ushers. Like all others with responsibilities, ushers need to be prepared for them. Meeting with their leader a few days before performance they learn of their obligations. These are to welcome spectators as they arrive, seat guests with consideration for audience conduct, answer questions about agency activities, and take names of children who want to register for classes.

What about Printed Programs

The value of printed programs is questionable. They have disadvantages. Rustle of program papers creates noise. They add to the problem of litter. Restless boys make them into gliders and catapult them during the performance. Money and effort to provide programs might better be spent on supplies for the play. Mimeographed programs cost less but have disadvantages, the same as above.

Here are the advantages: Programs offer a means to acknowledge by name all who contribute to the occasion. Contributors like to see their names in print, and they can keep programs for souvenirs. One copy can be placed in a group scrapbook. The program can announce activities organized by the agency that sponsors the play.

Giving the Audience Its Money's Worth

Those who attend a performance by children pay no admission fee. But they do pay by taking the time and making the effort to attend. For these expenditures they deserve good entertainment. They get it if players meet the performance standards listed in chapter 7.

Backstage at Showtime

Just before showtime everyone backstage is eager with anticipation. There is excitement, but there should be no hectic rush. Children who put on a play complete a host of tasks. Each is accomplished according to a schedule made when rehearsals began. None of them are left to the hour before performance.

This is not the time for doing. It is a time for the director's final checking. He checks to be sure all players are present in dressing rooms.

Costumes, fitted and finished, are ready. Make-up supplies are on the table. Volunteer leaders in charge of dressing rooms help with makeup and supervise the donning of costumes.

The director's next checkpoint is the stage. Clipboard in hand he confers with the property man, sound effects man, and other members of the technical staff. The prompter is ready, script in hand. Ten minutes before curtain time a messenger calls players from dressing rooms. Those onstage at opening take their places. Others wait at proper entrances.

Two minutes before curtain time the director leaves the stage to sit in the rear of the audience. Next to him sits a messenger ready to carry a message backstage if needed. From his location the director observes both play and audience. He notices reactions of spectators. Can they see and hear? At what points do they become restless? When they laugh do players wait for the laughter to reach its peak? Does the play drag at any moments? How should it be improved before a second performance?

After the Performance

Players take curtain calls only if these have been planned and re-hearsed. Then they know where to go and what to do during the call. Some directors have planned responses to curtain calls that added to the dramatic effect of the play.

After a performance of *Gypsy Brew* players walked briskly across the stage. Dame Brand showing off the nail led the procession to the feast. At the end two gypsy girls carried the kettle. As they walked all sang to the tune of ''A-Hunting We Will Go'' these words:

> To the nail soup feast we go
> To the nail soup feast we go
> We got a little nail
> And put it in a pail
> And to the feast we go.

Following *In the Kitchen Again* players skipped off the stage and once around the audience, then disappeared backstage. As they skipped they clapsed hands in groups of two or three. King and Queen were first. Then came Lords and Ladies. Next were Servants followed by Children of the Palace. Knave skipped alone at the end and held high his tray of tarts. A piano provided accompaniment for the skipping.

In curtain calls for both productions players were followed by members of the technical staff. Each carried a sign that announced his title.

As the performance concludes, the director goes backstage to congratulate players, technicians, and volunteer leaders. This is no time for criticism. That can come later at a special rehearsal before another performance.

"Let's Give It Again"

This plea is heard after almost every performance by children. They deserve a chance to give it again. Each cast should present the play more than once. Thinking about the thrill of performance motivated long and sustained effort. Children have earned and can benefit from additional performances. They learn from playing to different audiences. Greater self-confidence comes with repeat performances. The need to adapt to new situations offers valuable experience.

Extra performances mean the director must recruit additional audiences. The second performance is apt to be a children's matinee. Adults are welcome, but features are added to appeal to child spectators. A storyteller may tell stories after the short play. The first story is suggested by some feature of the play. After a performance of *A Princess at Heart* one storyteller told "The Princess on the Glass Hill." This story about a boy named Cinderlad was an interesting contrast to a play about Cinderella.

Community singing has often been part of a children's matinee. The first song was one that children knew. Then came a stunt song with all joining in the pantomime. A few children had learned it in advance. Their singing encouraged others to participate.

Readymade Audiences

The director also takes advantage of readymade audiences. They are made up of people who attend an event for some reason other than to see a play. They may not even know the occasion includes a dramatic performance. But the play should add to the pleasure of those who attend. A good play has been known to make an ordinary event into a memorable one. Events that provide readymade audiences are listed in chapter 2.

Each agency has its own readymade audiences. School plays can be repeated for several classes and assembly programs. Community recreation centers have many groups meeting there for whom children can give extra performances. These centers also organize community nights or family nights. The play is a good number on either of these programs.

Cub Scouts have a readymade audience in pack meetings. Many youth serving agency groups have opportunity to present their plays for one another. Three or four groups may assemble for the sole purpose of giving a festival of plays.

A similar festival of plays may be enjoyed by play casts from a group of churches, settlement houses, or playgrounds.

The resourceful director takes note of community events that provide readymade audiences. They make it easy to schedule several performances of each production. These events let children perform in different places under different circumstances. They must be quick to adapt. They may be likened to traveling players of old who went from one inn yard to another to present their plays for new audiences.

With additional performances children squeeze from putting on a play its last bit of value and excitement.

Part Five

Plays for Children to Put On

The Bird with the Broken Wing

(From ''Why the Evergreen Trees Never Lose their Leaves''

by Florence Holbrook)

Adapted by Maxine McSweeny

Characters:

BIRDS FLYING SOUTH
ROBIN, a bird with a broken wing
BIRCH TREE
OAK TREE
WILLOW TREE
SPRUCE TREE
PINE TREE
JUNIPER TREE
FROST KING
NORTH WIND

Scene: *A forest*

At Rise: *Bird songs are heard. They continue as music sounds for the entrance of the Trees. They enter right in stately procession. If desired, they may dance before taking their places in the forest. Birch, Oak, and Willow move up left where they stand quietly. Down right in another group stand Spruce, Pine, and Juniper.*

Music changes to an accompaniment for the entrance of the Birds. They enter right and flutter about in either a dance or an informal frolic. At its conclusion they fly off left to start their journey to the south.

Robin enters right. She hobbles center in an effort to reach the other Birds. She calls.

ROBIN: Oh, Birds! Wait! Wait a minute. Birds! Birds! *(She gives up.)* They've started south. *(Tries to lift her broken wing, but it drops useless at her side.)* I can't go with them. (Shivers) It's getting cold. Well, I can't sit down and cry. I have to do something. *(Looks around and notices Birch Tree.)* Beautiful Birch Tree.

BIRCH: Did you speak to me, little bird?

ROBIN: Yes, I did. I need help. My wing is broken. Will you let me crawl among your pretty leaves?

BIRCH: No, no. I couldn't do that. I don't know anything about broken wings. I wouldn't know what to do.

ROBIN: You don't have to do anything.

(Birch Tree doesn't answer. She is shaking out her leaves. Robin looks elsewhere for help and notices the Oak Tree.) Oak Tree!

OAK: Did someone call me?

ROBIN: I did, Oak Tree. You are stong. Will you shelter me until spring comes again? My wing is broken, and I can't fly south this winter.

OAK: Shelter you?

ROBIN: Yes. Will you?

OAK: Certainly not. I have all I can do to get my acorns ready. Besides, you might eat some of them. Birds like my acorns.

(Robin sighs and turns away. She sees Willow Tree.)

ROBIN: Gentle Willow, my wing is broken. It's getting cold. Will you give me some shelter?

WILLOW: *(Looks Robin over from head to foot.)* You are a stranger to me, little bird.

ROBIN: I've been here all summer.

WILLOW: I never have anything to do with strangers. We willows don't talk to birds we don't know. The same birds build their nests in my branches year after year.

ROBIN: (*Hobbles away from Willow.*) I don't know what to do. I can't go any farther.

SPRUCE: Little Bird!

       (*Robin turns to look at her.*)

       What's the matter, little bird?

       Why didn't you fly south with the other birds?

ROBIN: I can't fly. I'm cold and tired, and my wing is broken.

SPRUCE: Come right here. Creep close to my trunk. I can cover you with my low branches.

ROBIN: But I need a place where I can stay all winter.

SPRUCE: Well, you've found it. This branch has my thickest leaves. Creep in here.

       (*Happily Robin hobbles close to Spruce.*)

PINE: Spruce, is that a bird in your branches?

SPRUCE: Yes, it needed some shelter from the cold.

PINE: I thought all the birds had flown away.

SPRUCE: This little robin can't fly. It's going to make a winter home in my branches.

PINE: I'd like to help. My branches aren't very thick, but I am big and strong. I'll keep the North Wind away from you and the robin.

JUNIPER: What will that little bird eat when the snow is on the ground?

SPRUCE: That will be a problem. There isn't much food at this time of year.

JUNIPER: I can solve the problem. See the berries on my branches? Robin can eat them all winter long. They make the best breakfast a bird can have.

ROBIN: Thank you, kind trees. You've given me a home and shelter and food. I have everything a bird needs.

       (*Frost King enters right and surveys the forest. He inspects the trees to see whether it's time for them to lose their leaves. Then, he walks right and calls.*)

FROST KING: What ho! What ho-o-o! North Wind!

       (*Whirling and blowing North Wind rushes in right.*)

NORTH WIND: Woo-oo! I come at your call, Frost King!

FROST KING: It's time to work, North Wind. Blow every leaf from every tree in the forest.

NORTH WIND: Woo-oo! I blow! I blow!

(*He blows the leaves from Birch, Oak, and Willow.*)

FROST KING: Good. That's good, North Wind. Now for the trees on this side.

(*North Wind blows on Spruce.*)

SPRUCE: Wait! Oh, stop! North wind, blow gently. I have a little bird in my branches.

PINE: If you must blow, blow against me, North Wind. I am strong. I can keep your breath from the others.

NORTH WIND: What shall I do, Frost King? No tree has ever tried to stop me before.

FROST KING: I'll think about it. Go on to the next tree. You can come back later.

(*North Wind blows on Juniper.*)

JUNIPER: Not so hard! Not so hard! You might hurt my berries.

NORTH WIND: And why shouldn't I?

JUNIPER: I have to keep them. They are to feed the little bird.

NORTH WIND: Shall I blow them off, Frost King?

FROST KING: (*Suddenly makes up his mind.*) No. Stop. Don't touch them. These three trees shall keep their leaves this winter and every winter. They have been kind to a little bird. As a reward for their kindness they shall always be green. Come North Wind. You have done your work here. Let us go to another part of the forest.

(*Frost King and North Wind go off right.*)

ROBIN: Oh, thank you again, dear trees. I'm glad the Frost King was kind to you. I'm so happy I feel like singing.

(*Bright, bird-like music is heard. If there is no curtain players walk off right in a dignified recession. Robin walks close beside Spruce.*)

The Wishing Shop[1]

by Mildred Plew Merryman

Characters:

DADDY DOE, the man who keeps The Wishing Shop
THREE LITTLE GIRLS, who want three wishes
THREE LITTLE BOYS, who want three wishes, too
A GOBLIN
A POLICEMAN

Scene: *The Wishing Shop. At the right is a door through which customers enter. At the left is a counter with, perhaps, some shelves behind. It can be kitty-cornered, if necessary, so that all the wishes may be seen. Arrange the wishes, partly on the counter and partly around and in front of it. Any sort of nice wishes the children suggest will do—rag dolls and wooly animals and books, a sled or a shiny red wagon. Little tin dishes make good wishes, and so do big red apples; balloons, if in season, are fine. And of course the six special wishes of the six children must be there. There is a card near the counter that all can read. It says: "All Requests in Rhyme."*
The curtain rises on the empty shop, but immediately after, Daddy Doe, in a smock and skullcap and goatee, enters. He bows to his shop and sings to the tune of "Merrily We Roll Along!"

[1]From *Child Life* Magazine, Copyright 1927, 1955 by Rand McNally & Company.

195

Morning, little wishing shop,
Wishing shop, wishing shop,
Morning, little wishing shop!
Here's your Daddy Doe
Ho, my little wishes, ho!
Wishes, ho; wishes, ho!
Ho, my little wishes, ho!
Here's your Daddy Doe!

He takes out his feather duster and begins dusting the wishes.
Daddy Doe's shop is precious to him, and his dusting must
show this. He arranges and rearranges his stock, stepping
back often to get the effect. The door opens, and the Littlest
Girl comes shyly in.

DADDY DOE: Good morning, my dear! You're the very first customer today. And what may your wish be?

1ST GIRL: Oh, please, Daddy Doe, I'd like a little stick—a pep'mint stick—a little stick to lick, Daddy Doe.

DADDY DOE: Humph! a little stick to lick—let me see.

(Begins rummaging.)

It *must* be a licker, I suppose?

1ST GIRL: Oh, please, Daddy Doe!

DADDY DOE: Oh, yes! Here we are!

(He gives it to her.)

1ST GIRL: I haven't got a penny, but I've got a pricky pin.

DADDY DOE: Very well, Missy, I'll be glad to get a pin.

(She pays him, goes over to the right, sits down and begins
looking over a picture book. First Little Boy enters.)

1ST BOY: Oh, please Daddy Doe, just a minute—just a minute! Have you got a little shell with a sea song in it?

DADDY DOE: Maybe so! Maybe so!

(This expression, which he uses often, he drawls out slowly.
There is a twinkle in his eye as he says it. He hunts for the
shell, finds it, and listens for the song.)

Here's one! My, that *is* a song! Listen, boy!

1ST BOY: My father says he doesn't believe in sea shell songs, but I guess he'll change his mind when he hears *this* one!

DADDY DOE: Oh, he'll hear *that* one! Trouble is with grownups they

don't listen, and after while, when you don't listen, you lose
your listener.

1ST BOY: *(Getting ready to pay)*I—I haven't got a penny, but I've got a
slicky top!

DADDY DOE: That's very nice! I'd *like* a slicky top!
*(He takes it and the Little Boy goes over beside the Little Girl
and they look at pictures together. 2nd Little Boy and Girl
enter, speaking exactly together.)*

2ND BOY & GIRL: Oh, please, Daddy Doe, have you got a little mitten—a
little red mitten? We want it for our kitten, you know.

DADDY DOE: Humph! A little red mitten? Must be red, I suppose!

2ND BOY: Yes, sir! The others are red.

DADDY DOE: *(Hunting for the red mitten)*
Of course a kitten's mittens ought to match. Is it a front
mitten or a back mitten?

2ND GIRL: It's a left back mitten, Daddy Doe.

DADDY DOE: Oh yes! Here we are.

2ND GIRL: Oh, thank you, thank you, thank you, Daddy Doe.

2ND BOY: We haven't got a penny, so we brought a little fish.
(Offers a toy fish in payment.)

DADDY DOE: That's very nice. I need a little fish.
*(They trade, and the children go over with the other two. In
the short pause following Daddy Doe picks up his duster and
dusts, humming meanwhile the tune of his little song. At any
time, if there is a delay, he can go on with his dusting.)*

3RD GIRL: *(Entering.)*
Oh, please, Daddy Doe, have you got a little bonnet with a
pink feather on it—a pink little feather and a bow?

DADDY DOE: *(Repeating after her.)*
Some sort of bonnet with a pink feather on it—a loddy doddy
doddy—and a bow. How would *that* be now?
*(He takes the very thing out of a fancy hat box beside the
counter.)*

3RD GIRL: Ohhhh! *What* a sweety!
*(She teeters on her toes and tries it on; then remembers
paying.)*
I—I haven't got a penny—a single, single penny!

I've got a little thimble, though!

DADDY DOE: Oh, that's *much* better than a penny! I'd like a little thimble.

(He takes it and puts it on. She goes dancing back to the others to show off her wish, and 3rd Boy enters.)

3RD BOY: Oh, Please sir, please, if it isn't any trouble, could I have a little bubble, a little green bubble, Daddy Doe?

DADDY DOE: Maybe so! Maybe so!

(He begins prowling through the wishes; then very, very carefully brings out some sort of colorful box with a cover and lifts it up for the Little Boy to see. One of the plush boxes that jewelry comes in would serve nicely.)

3RD BOY: Oh, oh, oh, oh, oh! And it's green'n everything!

(He takes the box and tilts it a bit.)

DADDY DOE: Careful there, boy! That's a bubble, you know. You can't jiggle a bubble much. Once you've handled bubbles, you'll understand. Many's the bubble I've seen bought and ruined in the wrapping up.

(Carefully, the Little Boy hands over a marble in payment and tiptoes over to the others.)

1ST BOY: Have you maybe got a story in your pocket, Daddy Doe? Have you got a little story?

DADDY DOE: Maybe so! Maybe so!

(He pulls up a low chair or stool at right of stage and they group themselves around him on the floor.)

Now let's see—

(He feels in his pocket and pretends to pull out a title. Reads.)

Jack the Giant Killer!

ALL: That's too old!

DADDY DOE: Very well, very well!

(Solemnly, he feels for another one, brings it out and reads.)

The Fairy in the Radio! How's that?

ALL: That is too new!

DADDY DOE: Humph! Very well!

(Once more he fishes for a story.)

The Story of the Wishing Shop! How is that?

ALL: That's just right!

DADDY DOE: The Story of the Wishing Shop it is! Everybody knows that. We'll each tell a part!

ALL: Oh goody, goody, goody!

DADDY DOE: (*Beginning*)

Once upon a time there was an old man—

ALL: Whose name was Daddy Doe.

DADDY DOE: Maybe so. Maybe so. Well, anyway, this old man went trotting about the world, trippety trippety trot, and as he trotted he noticed that children everywhere were always wishing, wishing, wishing. "What a wishety world it is, to be sure," he thought, "and how few children get their wishes."

1ST GIRL: And so, he said to himself: "I know what would be more fun than trotting. I'll get me a wishing shop and in this wishing shop I'll keep every little wish that any child could ever, ever want." So he did.

1ST BOY: But so fast did the business grow, before long he found himself running out of wishes—especially red wishes. They were the most popular.

2ND GIRL: Finally, in despair, he went to the queen of the pixies and said: "Lady Queen, could you keep me supplied with wishes for my wishing shop?" Whereupon the Lady Queen replied—

2ND BOY: "Maybe so. Maybe so, Mr. Doe. But this you must promise me. If ever you fail to give a single child the wish for which he asks, that moment, the shop which was yours, shall become his. Should he ever fail, he, too, must pass it on."

3RD GIRL: Which, when you come to think of it, was really no more than fair, because with anything so special as a wishing shop you must expect *some* sort of catch, *especially* if you're dealing with pixies.

3RD BOY: However, Daddy Doe hasn't ever   failed yet, and *we* don't think he ever will.

(*Whereupon, a Boy in a green suit and a peaked hat, suggestive of a Goblin, bursts into the room. With his hands thrust into his pockets , his feet wide apart, very impudently he speaks.*)

GOBLIN: Quick! Quick! Quick! Give me a rickytick!

DADDY DOE: (*Bewildered*)

A rickytick?

ALL: (*Speaking one by one in quick succession*)

      Rickytick? Rickytick? Ricky? Tick? Tick? Tick?

GOBLIN: Yes, a rickytick!

DADDY DOE: Wh-what k-kind of a r-rickytick? B-big or little rickytick?

GOBLIN: A rickytick! Quick!

DADDY DOE: (*Sinking down on his chair, perfectly crushed*)

      I-I have—no rickyticks. I-I guess—the shop—is yours!

ALL: (*With a sort of moan*)

    Oh, oh, oh, Daddy Doe!

      (*At once the Goblin hops on the counter, whistling, and
      begins to disarrange things, pulling the books to pieces and
      poking his fingers in the eyes of the rag doll. The children
      stand together whispering at the right, while Daddy Doe, sits
      bent over, holding his head in his hands. Finally, the 3rd
      Little Boy leaves the group and crosses the stage.*)

3RD BOY: (*Boldly to the Goblin.*)

      So this is your shop, now!

GOBLIN: It is! It is!

3RD BOY: And are you ready for business?

GOBLIN: I am! I am!

ALL: Then quick! Quick. Quick. Give us a rickytick!

GOBLIN: (*Opening his mouth with surprise and stammering.*)

      I-I-I—why-why-I—I-guess I haven't g-g-got—any rick-
      yticks!

POLICEMAN:(*Bursting into the room.*)

      Excuse me! Have you got any goblins in here?

      (*They look at one another doubtfully.*)

     Only one sure way to tell. Stick out your tongues. All
      goblins have green tongues.

      (*Goes around counting.*)

      One, pink; two, pink; three, pink; four, pink; five, pink; six,
      pink; (*Spying the goblin*) Aha! You, young fellow, let's have
      a look at your tongue! Ha! Just what I thought! Green as
      grass! Come along, you green goblin! Come along with me!
      You're wanted by the pixie police! (*Drags him along, and
      they go out together.*)

DADDY DOE: (*Sighing with relief.*)

Oh, dear, dear, dear! What a fright I did get! What a fright!

2ND GIRL: Never mind, Daddy Doe, it's all right now. The Wishing Shop is yours, still, and I think it always will be.

(*They set about rearranging the shop.*)

2ND BOY: (*Setting everything straight again.*)

Have you maybe got a story in your pocket, Daddy Doe? Have you got another story?

DADDY DOE: Maybe so! Maybe so!

(*They gather around him as before; he reaches in his pocket, brings out a title and pretends to read it, but instead of announcing it, he chuckles and begins his story.*)

Once upon a time in the middle of a crick, lived a little rickytacky, ticky, tacky, tick!

ALL: (*Repeating after him exactly together, like a clock.*)

Rickytacky, tickytacky, ticky, tacky, tick.

(*As Daddy Doe finishes his sentence the curtain falls and by the time the children finish it is down, but they must speak so distinctly that their voices carry perfectly the last words.*)

Sleeping Beauty

by Maxine McSweeny

Characters:

HERALD
KING
QUEEN
NURSE
LADIES IN WAITING
  CORDELIA
  ADELAIDE
FAIRIES
  CRYSTAL
  WATERFALL
  BUTTERFLY
  CLOUD PUFF
  IVY
  DAWN
CLAP O' THUNDER, the wicked fairy. *(Her tall, pointed, black hat makes her look more like a witch than a fairy.)*
GOBLINS
  SLINK
  SPUNK
PRINCESS BEAUTY
KITCHEN BOY
COOK
PRINCE BERTRAM
DUKE EDGAR

Throne room of the castle. On the upstage wall is a hanging that pictures the king's coat of arms. Under the hanging is a platform. At left center is a dais that holds two thrones. They face diagonally right. The king's throne is closest to the audience. Entrances are up right, down right and down left.

Fanfare is heard off right. Enter down right a herald carrying a trumpet. He crosses to center and faces the audience. As he lifts the trumpet to his lips another fanfare is heard. Herald crosses down left and turns to face right. Processional music is heard.

The king and queen leading a procession enter down right. They proceed to their thrones and sit. Next comes the nurse carrying a tiny baby. She stands center near the queen's throne. Ladies Cordelia and Adelaide follow and stand together on the nurse's right.

Processional music changes to a tinkling melody that suggests fairy music. Fairies enter down right with skipping or light running steps. They cross in front of the thrones, circle behind them, and return down right. There they stand in a little group facing the thrones.

KING: (*Stands.*) Fairies and Members of our Court, welcome to this christening feast. We have come to honor our baby, the princess, Beauty.

(*Nurse steps forward and holds the baby for all to see. Fairies and Ladies move closer to get a better view. They make the crooning sounds of "Oo-oo" or "'A-aah" or "Isn't she darling!" that people always make when they admire a baby. The queen and nurse exclaim with the fairies and ladies in waiting. During this chorus of admiration the herald goes off down left.*)

CORDELIA: (*As babble of voices fades*) Oh, she's beautiful!

QUEEN: (*With modest honesty*) That's why we named her Beauty.

ADELAIDE: She's our little Princess Beauty. We'll always love her, won't we, Cordelia?

CORDELIA: Oh, yes. And we've brought her a present. Will you show it to the queen, Adelaide?

(Adelaide gives the queen a tiny, sparkling bracelet. Queen holds it up for the king to admire.)

QUEEN: Your Majesty, see how it sparkles.

KING: That's a bracelet worthy of a princess.

ADELAIDE: May I put it on the baby?

QUEEN: Yes, yes. She loves sparkling things.

(Adelaide fastens bracelet on Beauty's wrist. There follows the same chorus of "Oo-oo's" and "A-aah's" as before. King, Queen, Nurse, and Fairies join in. As chorus fades Crystal runs lightly to the thrones and curtsies. Adelaide and Cordelia move right to make room for Crystal.)

KING: Dear Fairy Crystal, what do you want?

CRYSTAL: May I give a present?

KING: Of course you may.

QUEEN: How wonderful to have a gift from a fairy.

CRYSTAL: *(Hesitating)* It's more like a wish than a gift. Each fairy here has power to give the princess one wish. I'll give mine now. *(Crystal walks between the nurse and the throne so she is slightly above the nurse. From this location Crystal can face both the baby and the audience. She holds her wand high above the baby. Crystal does not let her wand hide her face.)*

CRYSTAL: I wish Beauty the gift of kindness. She shall be kind to everyone she meets.

(Others fairies move into a circle down right and raise their wands so tips touch high in center of circle.)

FAIRIES: *(Holding wands high and speaking in a chorus.)* She shall be kind to everyone she meets.

(King and Queen smile their thanks as Crystal joins the circle. Fairies lower their wands. Butterfly runs lightly to the thrones and curtsies.)

KING: What do you ask, Butterfly?

BUTTERFLY: I ask permission to give my wish to the princess.

KING: Of course you may.

BUTTERFLY: *(Moves above nurse and holds wand over baby.)* My wish is for wisdom. The princess shall be as wise as she is kind.

FAIRIES: *(Raising wands to center of circle and speaking together as before)* The princess shall be as wise as she is kind.

(Butterfly returns to circle, and Cloud Puff approaches thrones.)

KING: Do you also bring a gift, Cloud Puff?

CLOUD PUFF: Yes, I do. *(Running to wishing position above Nurse she lifts her wand.)* I bring the gift of laughter. The princess' laugh shall be so merry that everyone who hears will laugh with her.

FAIRIES: *(Raising wands as before)* The princess' laugh shall be so merry that everyone who hears will laugh with her.

(Cloud Puff returns to circle. Waterfall curtsies before King and Queen.)

KING: Why do you come, Waterfall?

WATERFALL: I bring another gift. *(Moves to wishing location.)* My gift is beauty. The baby shall always be as beautiful as her name, Princess Beauty.

FAIRIES: *(Repeating ceremony as before.)* The baby shall always be as beautiful as her name, Princess Beauty.

(Waterfall returns to circle. Ivy takes her turn before the thrones.)

KING: Fairy Ivy, how can you think of another gift?

IVY: I have thought of one. *(She goes to the wishing location and raises her wand.)* Here is the gift of happiness. The princess shall be happy every moment of her life.

FAIRIES: *(In same wand raising ceremony).* The princess shall be happy every moment of her life.

(Ivy returns to circle. Dawn leaves it and walks down right, away from the other fairies. They look at her in surprise then look questioningly at one another. Ivy leaves the circle and touches Dawn on the shoulder.)

IVY: Dawn, it's your turn now. The rest of us have given our wishes.

DAWN: *(Worried.)* I know you have.

IVY: Why don't you give your wish?

DAWN: *(Frantic.)* I can't think of a wish. I want to give the baby a present. But what is left to give?

QUEEN: *(Calling gently.)* Fairy Dawn, come here.

(Slowly, sadly Dawn obeys.)

QUEEN: What's troubling you?

DAWN: It's my gift. I can't think of a wish that has not already been given.

KING: Don't worry. The princess has enough gifts.

DAWN: But I want to give her a wish.

QUEEN: Just wait. You'll think of something later. Then your gift will be a surprise.

DAWN: (*Brightening.*) Thank you dear queen. I'll just wait.

(*A clash of cymbals is heard off right. Every one is startled. Enter up right Clap o' Thunder. She stands for an instant just inside the entrance. There comes again the sound of cymbals. All in the room stop talking and turn to look at the wicked fairy. With long swift steps she strides toward the throne. The guests step aside to avoid her. Nurse moves nearer Queen. Adelaide and Cordelia go with Dawn to join the fairies. Their circle becomes more like a huddle as they draw together in fear. Clap o' Thunder stops and looks intently at the King.*)

CLAP O'THUNDER: Why didn't you invite me to your feast? I'm the fairy, Clap o'Thunder. I know magic. I'm as much a fairy as creatures you did invite.

KING: (*Rising and looking around for some way out of this situation.*) We—we-are sorry, Clap o' Thunder. (*Weakly*) We welcome you now. Stay for the christening feast.

CLAP O' THUNDER: Your welcome's too late and too weak. I don't want any secondhand welcome.

QUEEN: (*Trying to think of an excuse.*) You see, Clap o' Thunder, we have only six golden plates. We couldn't invite more than six fairies.

CLAP O' THUNDER: (*Shaking wand in the queen's face.*) Invited or not, I'm here.

KING: (*Anxious to protect queen.*) Yes, take your place with our guests. Do stay.

CLAP O' THUNDER: I shall NOT stay. But I have brought a gift. It's a fairy wish for the baby princess.

KING: Thank you, Clap o' Thunder.

QUEEN: How good of you!

CLAP O' THUNDER: I want no thanks. (*Moves to wishing location and raises her wand over baby.*) My gift is the wish of death.

ALL: (*In a buzz of frightened exclamations.*) Death! What does she mean?
The poor baby! Oh no!

CLAP O' THUNDER: Quiet! Listen to me.
(*There is instant silence.*)
When the princess is sixteen she shall prick her finger on a spindle, and SHE SHALL DIE!!! (*Throws back her head and laughs a cruel laugh. She raises her wand, waves it like a flag over her head and dashes up right. The queen grabs the baby from the nurse. The king takes a few steps after Clap o' Thunder, He stops as he sees her turn to face him at the entrance. From this distance she shakes her wand like a club at the king.*)

CLAP O' THUNDER: You won't forget my wish. And you won't forget to invite me to your next feast. I'll use all SIX of your golden plates.
(*Her terrifying laugh sounds again as she dashes out. There is another clash of cymbals.*)

KING: After her! After her! Don't let her get away.

CRYSTAL: (*Running to King and leading him back.*) No one can catch her. She's magic.

QUEEN: Oh my baby! What shall we do? What shall we do? (*Her last words are lost as every one wails over what has happened.*)
(*Nurse takes the baby. Adelaide and Cordelia help the queen back to her throne. The king returns to his. Fairy music sounds and Dawn approaches the thrones. Fairies and Ladies in waiting move right to give her room and watch what she is about to do.*)

KING: Fairy Dawn, you can save us. You haven't used your wish. Break this terrible spell.

QUEEN: Save the baby, Dawn. Break the wicked spell.
(*Every one turns to implore Dawn to help.*)

DAWN: I can't break the wish of another—But I can change it.

KING: Change it then.
(*There is a general clamor for Dawn to change the spell.*)

QUEEN: Don't let the princess die.
(*All eyes are on Dawn.*)

DAWN: The princess shall not die. She shall only sleep. She shall sleep for one hundred years.

> (*Another buzz of exclamations: "One hundred years?" "Sleep for one hundred years!" "How can that be?"*)

> After one hundred years a prince shall come from a far-off land. Only he can break the spell and wake the princess.

KING: Hear me! Hear me! I'll prevent both the sleep and the death. I'll banish every spindle and every spinning wheel in the kingdom. If there are no spindles the princess can't prick her finger on one.

> (*Everyone shouts with joy.*)

QUEEN: Husband, husband, you have saved her.

> (*The fairies do not seem so sure as others.*)

KING: And now to the feast.

> (*Music that accompanied the entrance procession is heard again. King and Queen lead guests off down right. Herald returns down left. He stands near the entrance. Music stops. Herald speaks to the audience.*)

HERALD: The baby grows into a lovely maiden. She has all the kindness, and wisdom, laughter, happiness, and beauty of the fairy wishes.

> Today is Beauty's sixteenth birthday. There is to be a great birthday party. The first to arrive is an unwelcome guest.
> (*Clash of cymbals off right. Up right enters Clap o' Thunder. Herald slips quietly out down left. Just as quietly and at the same instant Clap O' Thunder moves stealthily toward the thrones. She looks about to see if she is alone. In one hand she carries her wand. The other hand holds a little white apron and cap. She places the cap and apron on the king's throne. She sits on the throne of the queen and pounds the floor with her wand. Slink and Spunk enter up right and wait near the entrance.*)

SPUNK: Did you call us?

CLAP O' THUNDER: I did. Come here.

> (*As Goblins start toward center Slink conspicuously sticks out his foot to trip Spunk. Spunk stumbles with a clatter but does not fall.*)

SPUNK: You tripped me.

SLINK: I did not.

SPUNK: You did too. You did it on purpose.

CLAP O' THUNDER: Come here. Stop that quarreling. Bring the bench
          and the spinning wheel.

SLINK: Which do you want first?

CLAP O' THUNDER: Which did I say first?

SPUNK: The bench.

CLAP O' THUNDER: Then which do I want first?

SLINK: The spinning wheel.

CLAP O' THUNDER: No-o-o! I want the bench first.

SLINK: All right. All right.

SPUNK: Here we go.

> (*Goblins run at full speed off up right. Clap removes her
> witch hat and places it on the other throne. She picks up the
> white cap and puts it on her head. Goblins return carrying a
> slender bench. Holding it they stop inside the entrance.*)

SLINK: Clap O' Thunder, where do you want the bench?

CLAP O' THUNDER: There. On the platform. Under the coat of arms.

> (*Goblins place bench as directed. Slink lifts his end of the
> bench and drops it with a thud. Spunk does the same with the
> other end.*)

CLAP O' THUNDER: (*Jumping nervously at each thud.*) Keep quiet. Both
          of you. I don't want the whole castle to know I'm here. Quick
          now! Get the spinning wheel. And Spunk! Take this hat
          outside. (*He gets the witch hat and puts it on. Goblins put
          their fingers to their lips and sneak off up right with exagger-
          ated effort at quiet. Clap O' Thunder picks up the apron she
          previously put on the throne. She ties the apron around her
          waist and walks down left admiring herself. As she walks she
          adjusts the cap and smooths the apron. With satisfaction she
          speaks aloud to herself.*)

They'll never know me now.

> (*Goblins return with spinning wheel. A spindle wound with
> thread shows plainly.*)

Don't drop that wheel. Put it in front of the bench.

> (*Goblins obey. Slink gives the wheel a whirl.*)

SLINK: Look at it go.

SPUNK: Here! Let me.

SLINK: No. Me.

> *(As both goblins reach for the wheel Spunk pricks his finger on the spindle. He grabs the finger and holds it.)*

SLINK: *(Howling)* Ow-oo-oo! It's sharp.

CLAP O' THUNDER: *(Rushing to goblins.)* Of course it's sharp. That's why it's here. Now get out.

> *(She grabs each goblin by an ear and leads them to the entrance up right. She releases them and gives them a shove off right. Off down right several voices are heard singing "London Bridge is Falling Down." Clap O' Thunder rushes to the bench, sits down, and begins to spin. The singing ends with "My fair lady-O.")*

BEAUTY: *(Off down right.)* Now I'll run and hide. *(She runs in. After only two or three steps she sees Clap O' Thunder and stops short.)* Who are you? *(Fearful she backs toward the entrance.)* I've never seen you before.

> *(Clap O' Thunder doesn't answer. She gives full attention to her spinning. Beauty is fascinated by this strange wheel.)*
> What are you doing with that wheel?

CLAP O' THUNDER: *(Without looking up.)* Spinning.

BEAUTY: What is spinning?

CLAP O' THUNDER: I'm making thread from flax.

BEAUTY: *(Marvels at this.)* You are? How do you do it?

CLAP O' THUNDER: With this wheel.

BEAUTY: I've never seen anything like it.

CLAP O' THUNDER: *(In her sweetest voice.)* Come here and look. *(Clap o' Thunder continues to spin. Beauty, her eyes fixed on the wheel, walks slowly toward it.)*

BEAUTY: That wheel is like magic.

CLAP O' THUNDER: Don't you want to try it?

BEAUTY: I-I- don't know.

CLAP O' THUNDER: Of course you do. *(Clap O' Thunder rises and steps to one side.)* Sit right down. I'll show you what to do.

> *(Beauty sits on the bench. Hesitantly she touches the wheel. Clap O' Thunder kneels on the floor at one side of Beauty so*

as not to hide her from the audience. Clap O' Thunder places
Beauty's foot on the treadle and moves it up and down.)

BEAUTY: (*Delighted.*) Oh, it's moving.

CLAP O' THUNDER: Of course it moves. Keep pushing the treadle.

BEAUTY: Is it making thread?

CLAP O' THUNDER: It will. Faster. Go faster!

BEAUTY: (*Alarmed.*) Wait! That's too fast.

CLAP O' THUNDER: No, no! Keep it going.

> (*In fright Beauty reaches out to stop the wheel. She hits the*
> *spindle.*)

BEAUTY: (*Jumping up in pain.*) O-O-o-o-! My finger. I've hurt my
finger. I-I feel strange all over. (*She steps to one side so the*
wheel is no longer in front of her.) What—is—happening
—to—me?

> (*Clap O' Thunder crouches low and watches without making*
> *a move. Beauty's hands drop to her sides. She sinks to a*
> *sitting position on the bench. She leans toward the left so her*
> *shoulder touches the bench. Slowly she lifts her feet.*)

I can't keep awake.

> (*She lies full length on the bench. She is on her side so her*
> *face is toward the audience.*)

I just—have—to—sleep.

> (*She takes a deep breath and closes her eyes.*)

CLAP O' THUNDER: (*Jumps up and stands near Beauty's feet and looks*
toward the girl's face.) Now sleep! And sleep and sleep.

> (*Clap o' Thunder picks up spinning wheel and carries it up*
> *right. She turns back at the entrance for one last look of evil*
> *toward the sleeping princess.*)

And sleep forever.

> (*Cymbals are heard again as Clap O' Thunder dashes off up*
> *right. Beauty stirs in her sleep and settles into absolute quiet.*
> *Down right enter the king and queen. They stretch and yawn*
> *as they talk and take their places on the thrones.*)

KING: I don't know what makes me so sleepy.

QUEEN: I've never been so sleepy in the middle of the day.

KING: How can I stay awake for that birthday party? (*leaning*
back and closing his eyes.)

QUEEN: (*Drowsily.*) I wonder—where—Beauty—is. (*She gives in and goes to sleep with her head against the back of the throne.*)

(*Kitchen Boy runs in from down left. He carries a big wooden spoon which he licks with relish. Halfway to the throne he stops suddenly. He takes the spoon away from his mouth long enough to yawn. Off left the cook is heard shouting.*)

COOK: Boy! Bring that spoon back.

(*In the midst of his yawning and stretching the boy looks off left. He tries to run, but he is too sleepy to move. Still standing, his eyes close and his chin sinks on his chest. His hands hang at his sides. One hand clutches the spoon. Cook enters and sees him.*)

Wait'til I get my hands on you. You'll never run away with my mixing spoon again.

(*She raises her hand to slap the boy. Before she can deliver the blow drowsiness overcomes her. She does not even stretch. She just gives one big yawn. She and the boy sink slowly to the floor. They assume a sitting position and lean against the king's throne. They are sound asleep. Enter down right Adelaide and Cordelia.*)

ADELAIDE: Where can the girl be?

CORDELIA: I don't know. We've looked everywhere.

ADELAIDE: (*Sees Beauty on the bench.*) Look! There she is.

CORDELIA: Do you know that I feel sleepy?

CORDELIA: So do I. I can hardly keep my eyes open.

(*They stretch and yawn and sink to the floor. They lean against each other in a half-sitting position. They close their eyes and settle down for a sleep.*)

(*Herald enters down left. Remaining close to the entrance he speaks to the audience.*)

HERALD: Sleep casts its spell over the castle. Outside, the gardener sleeps. No one is awake to prune the thorn bushes. They grow into a hedge so tall and thick it hides the castle.

One hundred winters come and cover the place with snow. Ninety-nine springs melt the snow and trim the hedge with flowers. Everyone sleeps until spring returns for the hundredth time.

Then comes the prince. He has heard of an enchanted castle that holds a sleeping princess. He cuts his way through the thorn bushes and enters the castle.

(The Herald remains to watch the final scene. Prince Bertram enters down right. His companion, Duke Edward, follows close behind. They see first the cook and kitchen boy.)

BERTRAM: What has happened here? *(Walks in wonder toward the cook.)*

EDGAR: Is she dead?

BERTRAM: *(Bending over her.)* No. She breathes.

EDGAR: *(Looking at the kitchen boy.)* So does the boy. See the color in his cheek.

BERTRAM: *(Walking around the throne he sees the king and queen.)* Look at the king and queen asleep on their thrones.

EDGAR: *(Walks to Adelaide and Cordelia.)* And look at these ladies in waiting asleep on the floor.

BERTRAM: But where is the princess?

EDGAR: I don't know, but this must be the place.

BERTRAM: *(Sees Beauty.)* There! Look!

(For an instant the two stand still and look at Beauty. Slowly as if in a trance Bertram walks toward her. When he reaches her he stands near her feet so he can look toward her face. The audience can see both his face the face of Beauty. Slowly he kneels and reaches for her hand. He bends over it and lifts her fingers to his lips. Edgar remains motionless down right. He watches Beauty and Bertram. Beauty stirs in her sleep. She sighs, opens her eyes, and raises herself on her elbow. He drops her hand. Beauty looks at the prince, sits up, and looks at him more closely. She smiles. Bertram smiles in return.)

BEAUTY: Who are you?

BERTRAM: My name is Prince Bertram.

BEAUTY: Why are you here?

BERTRAM: I heard about you and came to find you.

BEAUTY: Will you stay for my birthday party?

BERTRAM: I'd like to stay.

BEAUTY: (*Looks around.*) How long have I been asleep?

BERTRAM: People in the village say it's been one hundred years.

BEAUTY: (*Sits upright and puts her feet on the floor.*) One hundred years! What do you mean?

(*He sits beside Beauty to explain what has happened. While they talk quietly to each other the others in the room begin to waken.*)

KING: (*He woke in time to hear Beauty say "One hundred years." He straightens up on his throne.*) What's that about one hundred years?

QUEEN: (*Fully awake in an instant.*) I've had such a good sleep. I feel quite ready for the party.

(*King nods and they talk quietly about the party.*)

COOK: (*Wakens and sees spoon in the kitchen boy's hand.*) So there you are. Asleep and hanging on to my spoon.

(*Cook grabs the spoon. Kitchen Boy wakens instantly, jumps up and runs in a circle. Cook chases him once around the circle and off down left. King and Queen turn to see the cause of the commotion.*)

KING: (*To Queen.*) What are they doing in here?

QUEEN: (*Horrified.*) They were sleeping on the floor.

(*As King and Queen continue to talk Adelaide and Cordelia waken. Edgar helps them to their feet. They straighten their hair and dresses and smile their thanks to Edgar. He bows in acknowledgment.*)

QUEEN: I wonder where Beauty is. It's time for her to get ready for the party.

KING: I heard her talking. She said something about a hundred years.

QUEEN: (*Sees Beauty.*) There she is. Beauty, are you all right? (*Without giving Beauty time to answer*) Who is that young man?

(*Bertram takes Beauty's hand and together they go to the king and queen.*)

BEAUTY: Mother! Father! This prince has rescued us.

QUEEN: (*To Bertram.*) Just who are you?

BERTRAM: (*Bows.*) I am Prince Bertram. I came to rescue the princess.

KING: Rescue her? From what?

BEAUTY: From an enchanted spell.

BERTRAM: All of you have been asleep for one hundred years.

KING: Asleep for one hundred years! Well, let's eat.

QUEEN: Yes, we'll have the birthday party right now. Won't you stay, Prince Bertram?

BERTRAM: Thank you, I will. (*Looks around for Edgar and motions to him. Edgar comes to Bertram's side.*) This is my companion, Duke Edgar. (*Edgar bows.*)

KING: Welcome, Duke Edgar. Please stay for the party.

EDGAR: I shall be glad to stay.

QUEEN: (*Looking at ladies in waiting.*) Adelaide and Cordelia, are you ready for the party?

ADELAIDE: Oh, your majesty!

CORDELIA: We are quite ready.

KING: Come, every one. To the birthday party.

(*Gay music is heard off right. King takes the queen's hand and holds it high as they lead the procession off down right. Following them are Bertram and Beauty. He holds her hand just as high as the king holds that of the queen. Then comes Edgar. On one side he holds high the hand of Adelaide and on the other, the hand of Cordelia. The three skip gaily off together. Last to leave is the herald. He moves with a quick marching step. When he reaches down right he lifts his trumpet to his lips. A fanfare sounds. He goes off down right.*)

A Princess at Heart

or

The Girl of the Golden Slipper

by Maxine McSweeny

Characters:

CINDERELLA
STEPMOTHER
ROSAMUND ⎱ Cinderella's stepsisters
HERMIONE ⎰
FAIRY GODMOTHER
CLEMENTINE ⎱ friends of the stepsisters
LAVONA ⎰
ROYAL GUARD WITH SCROLL
ROYAL GUARD WITH SLIPPER
PRINCE

Scene I

A family living room of long ago. An entrance up right leads to other rooms in the house. Down left an entrance opens on a hall that leads to the street. Up center is a fireplace with mantle above. A straight chair is near the hall entrance. An armchair is down right.

At Rise: *Cinderella, wearing housecleaning clothes that include apron and cap and sturdy shoes, hurries in right. She carries*

216

broom, dustpan, and dust cloth. She drops dustpan with a clatter.

STEPMOTHER: (*Off right.*) Cinderella! Cinderella! (*Her voice is strong, and she pronounces every word distinctly.*)

CINDERELLA: (*Picks up dustpan and drops broom.*) Ye-yes.

STEPMOTHER: What's going on in there?

CINDERELLA: I'm cleaning. (*Picks up broom.*)

STEPMOTHER: Well it's the noisest cleaning I ever heard. (*Enters up right.*) Thumpity-bang! Thumpity-bang! (*Sees Cinderella clinging to her housecleaning equipment.*) Cinderella! You're just standing there. Make that broom work.

CINDERELLA: I am. Right now. (*Sweeps.*)

STEPMOTHER: Well, I think you should. I don't want Hermione and Rosamund to get their skirts dirty.

CINDERELLA: (*Working hard.*) Oh no. Not those beautiful ball gowns. I'll have the floor clean in a minute. (*Stops working and looks at Stepmother.*) I only wish I could go to the ball with them.

STEPMOTHER: To the ball! What an idea!

CINDERELLA: (*Pleading.*) You know tomorrow's my birthday.

STEPMOTHER: That makes no difference. You can't go to the ball. (*Drops into armchair.*) I can't do more than get two girls ready.

CINDERELLA: (*Sadly.*) I guess you can't. (*Sighs and returns to her sweeping. She sings as she works.*)

Here comes a prince a-riding, a-riding, a-riding.

Here comes a prince a-riding for the ratson-tatson cinamon tea.

STEPMOTHER: What kind of song is that?

CINDERELLA: It's an old song. You can dance to it if you want to.

STEPMOTHER: I've no time for dancing. And neither have you. (*Tests floor with her finger.*) Is the floor clean?

CINDERELLA: Just as clean as sweeping can get it.

STEPMOTHER: Then I'll call the girls. Rosamund! Hermione! Come now, my dears.

ROSAMUND: (*Enters right and stands waiting to be admired.*) Mama! Don't I look just beautiful?

STEPMOTHER: Oh Rosamund! You do. Walk to the chair. Let me see if your hem is straight. (*Rosamund obeys.*) Yes. It's all right. You're a queen, Rosamund. Just a queenly, queenly queen.

HERMIONE: (*Entering in time to hear the last.*) Mama! You think Rosamund's prettier than I, don't you?

STEPMOTHER: Oh, Hermione! Of course not. You're my ducky, ducky dumpling. Walk over there so I get a good look at you.
(*Hermione fidgets as she walks. She twiches at her skirt, her hair, her sleeve.*)
Don't fidget, Hermione. Are you nervous?

HERMIONE: I-I don't know.

STEPMOTHER: You don't know? Why don't you know?

HERMIONE: I don't know whether I fidget because I'm nervous, or I'm nervous because I fidget.

STEPMOTHER: Oh, fidgety-fidgety fudge.

ROSAMUND: Cinderella, will you fix my hair? It's loose at the back.

CINDERELLA: Yes, Rosamund. I see what it needs. (*Arranges hair.*)

HERMIONE: Mama, I'm afraid I won't act right. I want the prince to like me.

STEPMOTHER: He will. Just flutter your long eyelashes. And laugh a little.

HERMIONE: Like this? (*She gives a simpering laugh and looks up at her mother through quivering lashes.*)

ROSAMUND: That's terrible.

STEPMOTHER: No quarreling now! You'll be the prettiest girls there.

CINDERELLA: (*In desperation*) Stepmother, won't you let me go too?

STEPMOTHER: Cinderella, no. For the last time, NO. You can bring the capes for your sisters.

(*Cinderella goes off right.*)

ROSAMUND: (*Calls after her*) Hurry, Cinderella. Lavona's father is taking us. We don't want to keep him waiting.
(*Cinderella returns with capes. Her stepsisters put them on as they move toward the hall. Stepmother follows to admire and adjust the capes. There is a chorus of "good-bye's" as girls go off left.*)

STEPMOTHER: Now Cinderella, do the dusting. Make the room look nice, and go to bed. I'm going right now. What a day! I don't know how I ever got through it. (*Goes off right.*)

CINDERELLA: (*Calls after her*) Good-night, Stepmother. (*Picks up dust cloth and tries to sing as she dusts. The song is the same, but*

her spirit is not. Half-way through the song she gives up.) I ·
did want to go to the ball.
*(There comes a flash of light followed by clashing cymbals
and tinkling bells.)*
What is it? That light! Those bells!
(Enter Fairy Godmother carrying unwrapped presents.)
Oh, who are you?

FAIRY GODMOTHER: Happy Birthday, Cinderella! *(Puts presents on
chair.)* It's almost your birthday, isn't it?

CINDERELLA: How do you know?

FAIRY GODMOTHER: It's the business of fairy godmothers to know about
birthdays. And I've brought you presents. *(Holds out a
beautiful ball dress.)* Here, my dear. Run and try this on.

CINDERELLA: *(In a daze.)* I-I don't understand.

GODMOTHER: You don't need to understand. Just do as I say.
*(She puts the dress over Cinderella's arm. Cinderella more
dazed than before drops her dust cloth and carries dress off
right. Fairy Godmother calls after her.)*
When you're ready I'll hook it for you. *(Looks around
room.)* I must do something to this room. Cinderella will
have no time to clean. *(Picks up dust cloth and dusts mantel.
From the presents on the chair she takes a candle and holder.
These she arranges on the mantel. Cinderella returns wearing the beautiful dress with her dustcap and work shoes. She
is sad.)*

GODMOTHER: Don't you like the dress?

CINDERELLA: I love it. But I can't have it.

GODMOTHER: *(Takes off dustcap and arranges Cinderella's hair.)* Why
not?

CINDERELLA: My stepmother wouldn't let me. And I've no place to wear
it.

GODMOTHER: You're going to wear it to the ball.

CINDERELLA: Tonight?

GODMOTHER: RIGHT NOW. Just as soon as we can get ready.

CINDERELLA: I can't believe it. I want to go more than anything in the
world.

GODMOTHER: *(Takes a dainty crown from chair.)* How do you like this?

CINDERELLA: It should be for a princess.

GODMOTHER: And it is. It's for you, Cinderella because you're a princess at heart. *(Reaches for gold slippers.)* Now, take off your shoes.

CINDERELLA: *(Slips off her old shoes and into the slippers.)* They fit. They're a perfect fit!

GODMOTHER: I thought they would be. *(Holds out old shoes and dust cap.)* Now get rid of these. And do hurry.
(Cinderella coming to life dashes off with the clothes and returns immediately.)

GODMOTHER: Cinderella, look at me. How do you feel?

CINDERELLA: Like-like a princess.

GODMOTHER: Good. Now, can you do as you're told?

CINDERELLA: Yes.

GODMOTHER: Then, be home by midnight. Leave the ball before the clock strikes twelve. Will you remember?

CINDERELLA: I will. I'll just charge my mind with it. I couldn't forget.

GODMOTHER: Be sure you don't. Your coach is at the door. I'll start you on your way. *(They go off left.)*

Scene II

The Next Morning

At Rise: *Enter Royal Guard with Scroll. He unrolls the scroll and reads.*

GUARD WITH SCROLL: The prince danced all evening with Cinderella. She had such a good time she forgot about the clock. When it struck twelve she remembered. She ran so fast she lost one of her gold slippers. Now you shall see what happened next morning.
(Guard goes off left. Cinderella enters right. She wears her housecleaning clothes and carries one gold slipper. She

looks about for a place to hide it. Again there come the clashing cymbals, flashing light, and tinkling bells. Fairy Godmother enters left.)

CINDERELLA: Oh, dear Fairy godmother, I forgot.

GODMOTHER: I know. And you lost your slipper.

CINDERELLA: I'm very sorry.

GODMOTHER: That's all right. I'll give you another chance. Can you do as I tell you today?

CINDERELLA: I can. Try me, and see.

GODMOTHER: Where's your ball dress?

CINDERELLA: I hid it.

GODMOTHER: Will you put it on when I tell you?

CINDERELLA: Now?

GODMOTHER: No. Not now. Later.

CINDERELLA: When?

GODMOTHER: When the prince comes.

CINDERELLA: The prince will not come here.

GODMOTHER: I think he will. When you hear he's coming, run and put on your ball dress and crown.

CINDERELLA: My stepmother won't like that. She'll yell at me.

GODMOTHER: Do you wish she'd speak softly?

CINDERELLA: Oh, I do.

GODMOTHER: I'll take care of that. She'll speak softly—very softly, after you come in your ball dress. Now I'm going.

STEPMOTHER: *(Off right.)* Cinderella!

CINDERELLA: Y-yes, Stepmother. *(To Fairy Godmother)* Please don't go. I need you.

GODMOTHER: Just do as I say. I'll be back. I wouldn't miss it—when your stepmother speaks softly. *(Tiptoes off left.)*

STEPMOTHER: *(Offstage but loud and clear)* Cinderella! It's almost noon. We've overslept.

(Cinderella looks at the slipper in her hand, realizes she has no time to hide it, holds it behind her back.)

STEPMOTHER: *(Enters and looks about the room.)* At least you finished the cleaning. *(Sees candle on mantle.)* Where did you get that candle?

CINDERELLA: I-don't-know. I guess it just came.

STEPMOTHER: Just came? A candle! What kind of talk is that? (*Notices Cinderella's hand behind her back.*) What are you holding, Cinderella?

CINDERELLA: (*Hand still behind her.*) My-my slipper.

STEPMOTHER: Your slipper! What IS going on? I can see your shoes are on your feet—not behind your back.

(*Hermione and Rosamund enter right. They yawn and stretch.*)

HERMIONE: Oh, Mama, I'm tired

ROSAMUND: I'm still sleepy. (*Almost at the same time.*)

STEPMOTHER: (*Forgets candle and slipper.*) You dear girls! Did you have a good time?

(*Cinderella puts the slipper under straight chair.*)

HERMIONE: Terrible.

ROSAMUND: The prince didn't even notice us. (*Almost together.*)

HERMIONE: He danced with some mystery girl.

ROSAMUND: She was beautiful. She wore gold slippers.

HERMIONE: And she lost one of them.

(*Cinderella tries to push slipper farther under chair. Stepmother notices her.*)

STEPMOTHER: Cinderella, what's under that chair? (*No answer*) I'll just see for myself.

(*As she goes toward chair a gong sounds off left.*)

Company! Who can that be. Cinderella, you're a sight. Run! Rosamund, see who's at the door.

(*Both girls obey. Excited chatter off left as Rosamund returns with Lavona and Clementine.*)

LAVONA: You'll never believe it.

CLEMENTINE: The most exciting thing.

STEPMOTHER: What is it? What's happened?

LAVONA: The prince. He's coming down our street.

CLEMENTINE: And stopping at every house.

HERMIONE: Will he come here?

LAVONA: Yes. Right now.

STEPMOTHER: What *are* you talking about?

CLEMENTINE: He has that gold slipper—the one the mystery girl lost. He

says he'll find her if he has to try the slipper on every girl in
the kingdom.

STEPMOTHER: And you think he'll come here?

LAVONA: Yes. Yes.

CLEMENTINE: Now. Now! (*Together. Stepsisters jump and scream.*)

STEPMOTHER: (*Paces back and forth and waves her arms about.*) Keep
calm. Everybody, keep calm. Does the house look all right?
Hermione, pick up what's under that chair.
(*Hermione starts toward chair, but the gong sounds.*)

STEPMOTHER: Wait! Hermione. Come back. Stand here, all of you!
I'll welcome him at the door. (*She goes off left.*)
(*Girls chatter and giggle and cling to one another. Their talk
sounds like, "How exciting!" "Do you think it's the
prince?" "I hope it fits me."*)
(*A fanfare of trumpets is heard. Enter Guard with Scroll.
Stepmother follows. He reads from scroll.*)

GUARD WITH SCROLL: Hear! Hear! A message from your prince. He
seeks the girl of the golden slipper. He wishes to try the
slipper on the girls in this house. (*Gong.*) The prince comes.
(*Guard bows.*)
(*Enter left the prince followed by Royal Guard with slipper.
He carries it on a satin pillow with tassels on its corners.
Prince wears same uniform as guards, but his uniform has
more gold braid.*)

STEPMOTHER: Oh, your Majesty, welcome to my house.

PRINCE: You know I wish to try the slipper on these girls.

STEPMOTHER: Of course, your Majesty.

PRINCE: (*Nods to Lavona.*) You first, please.
(*Each girl in turn tries desperately to get her foot in the
slipper. No one can. Prince turns to Stepmother.*)
Are there other girls in the house?

STEPMOTHER: No. No. That is—nobody but Cinderella.
(*Girls laugh with exclamations like "Not Cinderella!"
"What an idea!" "A gold slipper and dustcap!"*)

PRINCE: I want every girl to try. Please call her.

STEPMOTHER: Cinderella.

CINDERELLA: (*Off right.*) Yes, Stepmother.

STEPMOTHER: Come here. Right now.

> (*Cinderella in ball dress and crown enters right. She wears no shoes. She stops inside the door and smiles pleasantly at everyone. For an instant no one can speak. Stepmother recovers first.*)

STEPMOTHER: Cinderella! What's going on? Where did you get that dress?

> (*Girls gasp "Isn't she beautiful?" "The mystery girl!" "It can't be Cinderella."*
>
> *Stepmother starts toward Cinderella, but the prince steps ahead of her and takes Cinderella's hand.*)

PRINCE: Will you try on this slipper?

CINDERELLA: If you wish, your Majesty.

> (*Prince leads her to a chair. Guard with Slipper easily slips it on her foot.*)

ALL: It fits!

> (*Prince lifts her hand, and she stands. He looks at the foot without a slipper.*)

PRINCE: Where is your other slipper?

CINDERELLA: Under the chair by the door.

> (*All look toward chair. Guard picks up slipper and puts it on Cinderella.*)

STEPMOTHER: A gold slipper! I knew there was something under that chair. Cinderella, how did it get there? Your Majesty, there's been some mistake.

> (*Flashing light, clashing cymbals, and tinkling bells as Fairy Godmother enters left. She walks to Stepmother.*)

GODMOTHER: There's no mistake.

STEPMOTHER: And who are you?

GODMOTHER: (*Waves her arm back and forth above Stepmother.*) Softly, softly! Softly speak or do not speak at all.

STEPMOTHER: (*Her mouth moves as vigorously as before, but the words come in a whisper—a strong whisper.*) I can't talk. What have you done?

> (*Everyone strains to hear her words. She shakes her fist at*

Godmother and continues to whisper.) Whatever you've
done, you undo it. Can you hear?

CINDERELLA: Please, Fairy Godmother. Break the spell.

GODMOTHER: And so I will. (*Waves her arm as before and chants*.)
Speak again. Speak again. Speak with your loud clear call.

STEPMOTHER: (*Louder than ever before*.) Now! Now, you go. You've
done enough.

GODMOTHER: Yes, I'll go. I just wanted to help Cinderella celebrate her
birthday.

CINDERELLA: Oh, thank you. Thank you, Fairy Godmother.

GODMOTHER: Good-bye, my child.

(*Bells tinkle as Godmother runs off left*.)

PRINCE: (*To Cinderella*.) Is this your birthday?

CINDERELLA: Yes. And It's the best birthday I've ever had.

PRINCE: We'll have a birthday ball at the castle.

CINDERELLA: May I invite guests?

PRINCE: All the guests you want.

(*Cinderella looks happily at Stepmother, girls, and Royal
Guards*.)

CINDERELLA: I want all of you. Will you come to my birthday ball?

(*Girls answer in a chorus of exclamations: "Of course."
"We'd love to." "Oh, Cinderella, do you want us?" Royal
Guards bow to show they accept the invitation. Stepmother
says nothing and looks from one to another in
embarrassment*.)

Stepmother, please! Won't you come?

STEPMOTHER : Well, I guess I could.

CINDERELLA: I'm so happy I want to dance. Right now.

PRINCE: And so do I. A dance for Cinderella's birthday.

(*Cinderella begins to sing her song, "Here Comes a Prince
a-Riding." All join in her singing. To the tune of "Here
Comes a Duke a-Riding they sing the following words*.)

ALL SING: Here comes a prince a-riding, a-riding, a-riding.
Here comes a prince a-riding
For the girl that fits the slipper-ah-ee.
And he has found her here now, here now, here now.

And he has found her here now.
So we'll dance and sing, and merry we'll be.
(With hands clasped all skip forward and back on the first stanza. On the second they slide right in a big circle. They repeat the last stanza. As they begin to sing the repeat the prince breaks the circle. Still clasping Cinderella's hand the prince leads all off left. Hands clasped to form a long line, all sing and skip as they go.)

In the Kitchen Again

Developed from a Creative Dramatization by
Recreation Directors,
Los Angeles City Department of Recreation and Parks

Characters

HEAD COOK
ASSISTANT COOK
SCULLERY MAID
KNAVE OF HEARTS
KING OF HEARTS
QUEEN OF HEARTS
HENRY
CATHERINE ⎱
ANN   ⎱ Playmates of the Knave
ELEANOR ⎱

Scene: *The kitchen in the palace of the King of Hearts. A work table is down center; an oven is down left; an outside door is up left. Up center is a window. A high kitchen stool is up right in front of the cupboard. Down right is a doorway leading to other rooms of the castle.*

Today is the birthday of the King of Hearts. The kitchen staff works feverishly to prepare the birthday dinner; the Cook frosts the cake on the work table; the Assistant bastes the roast in the oven; the Scullery Maid polishes silver as she sits on the stool near the cupboard.

227

COOK: (*Continues to frost the cake.*) Are you getting that silver clean?

MAID: (*Holding up a knife.*) See how it shines.

(*Turns it around to catch the light.*)

Can you see?

COOK: (*Glancing up quickly.*) Yes, it will do.

(*To Assistant*)

What about the roast?

ASSISTANT: Almost done.

(*Knave passes window. Assistant sees him as she turns from the oven.*)

There's the Knave.

COOK: Now? Oh, dear!

(*Enter Knave, who presents a little bunch of flowers to Maid.*)

Oh, they're so pretty.

(*She arranges them on the cupboard shelf.*)

KNAVE: I know you like flowers.

(*Goes down center and indicates cake.*)

Is that for me?

COOK: No! It's for your Daddy's birthday dinner.

KNAVE: Is it chocolate?

COOK: Not this time.

KNAVE: Why isn't it chocolate?

COOK: Because your daddy doesn't like chocolate.

ASSISTANT: (*Warning.*) It's almost 3 o'clock.

COOK: (*To Assistant.*) We'll have to hurry.

(*As she looks away, Knave sticks out a finger to get some frosting but Cook turns in time to stop him.*)

Don't touch that cake!

(*King of Hearts passes window and hears the following.*)

KNAVE: I can if I want to. I'm the Prince! I can do anything I want.

KING: (*Entering.*) What's this?

COOK: Oh, your Majesty!

(*All curtsy.*)

KING: Thank you. (*To Knave.*) I want you to know you can't do anything you want!

(Takes Knave gently but firmly by the ear then turns to Cook.)
How's the roast?

COOK: Almost done.

KING: Smells as if it needed seasoning.

ASSISTANT: Yes, your Majesty.

KING: Come along son. Let's discuss what you can and what you cannot
do.

(They go off up left.)

COOK: *(To Assistant.)* Crush some rosemary leaves for that roast.

ASSISTANT: *(To Maid.)* Bring some rosemary.

MAID: *(Quickly bringing leaves from cupboard to Assistant who sprink-
les them on the roast.)*

QUEEN: *(Entering down right.)* Oh cook, see what I have.

COOK: *(As she, Assistant, and Maid curtsy.)* Your Majesty.

QUEEN: This is a recipe for tarts. I want to make some for the King.

COOK: *(Taken aback.)* Oh, no. You'll soil your hands.

QUEEN: That doesn't matter .

ASSISTANT: But no queen has ever done such a thing.

QUEEN: That doesn't matter either. I'm going to make tarts for the
birthday dinner.

MAID: *(Delighted to have Queen in the kitchen, she brings her an apron
from the cupboard.)*

You'll need an apron.

(Maid stands down right and admires Queen.)

QUEEN: *(Putting on apron.)* Oh, thank you.

(Moving the birthday cake to one side of the table.)

Spoons. Bring spoons and a bowl, flour and soda!

ASSISTANT: *(Getting flour and soda, calls to Maid.)*

Spoons and bowl!

(Maid quickly brings them.)

QUEEN: *(Looking in book.)* Now what does this mean? One dash two. Is
that one or two.?

COOK: No, it means one-half.

QUEEN: And this? T-S-P? What is T-S-P?

COOK: It means teaspoon. Here, you take a half teaspoonful.

QUEEN: *(To Assistant as Cook brings more supplies.)*

How do I cut it in half?

ASSISTANT: I don't know. She's the head cook.

COOK: Here, level it first. Now cut with this knife.

    (*Cook does it.*)

QUEEN: (*Stirring.*) Now what do I do?

COOK: Roll it. (*To Assistant.*) A rolling pin for Her Majesty.

ASSISTANT: (*To Maid.*) A rolling pin for Her Majesty.

MAID: (*Gets rolling pin and gives it to Assistant.*) Here!

ASSISTANT: (*Gives rolling pin to Cook.*) Here.

COOK: (*Gives rolling pin to Queen.*) Here. Now what kind of filling for
    the tarts?

QUEEN: Apricot.

COOK: Apricot? But the King likes cherry.

QUEEN: He'll like these.

ASSISTANT: Apricots aren't the right color.

QUEEN: We'll color the apricots.

COOK: (*To Assistant.*) Get the apricots. (*To Maid.*) Get the coloring.

    (*They fly to the cupboard to obey. Queen completes tarts.*)

ASSISTANT: Oh! The roast!

COOK: Take it out!

    (*Assistant does so.*)

QUEEN: (*Holding up pan of tarts ready for oven.*)

    Aren't they wonderful? I'll call the King. He must see them.

    (*Exit up left.*)

COOK: (*Frantic.*) Now we'll never have dinner ready on time. (*To
    Assistant.*) Out with the roast! (*To Maid.* In with the tarts!
    Clear the table!

    (*All work in great haste.*)

QUEEN: (*Entering, followed by King.*) Are they in the oven?

COOK: Yes, your Majesty. And be careful.

    (*She opens oven door.*)

QUEEN: See the tarts I'm baking for your birthday.

KING: (*Delighted.*) What tarts! Call all the lords and ladies. I want
    everyone in the castle to see these tarts. Maid, summon the
    whole castle.

MAID: (*Curtsies.*) Yes, your Majesty. (*Goes out right.*)

KING: Let's celebrate the baking of the tarts.

ASSISTANT: Oh, we must close the oven door.

COOK: And we must keep quiet. The tarts will be ruined.

KING AND QUEEN: (*Speaking softly as they do a little dance step.*)

> The Queen of Hearts
> She made some tarts

LORDS AND LADIES: (*Entering.*) The Queen? Has she made tarts?

COOK: Softly! Softly please!

> (*King and Queen, Lords and Ladies dance to the rhythm of the rhyme they speak. During the dance they frequently caution one another to be quiet.*)

ALL: (*Dancing as they speak together.*)

> The Queen of Hearts
> She made some tarts
> All on a summer's day

> (*As the dance ends Cook opens the oven door. All move toward the oven and look in. They hold this position as Knave appears outside window. He shows disappointment at not being a part of the celebration; then he brightens as he gets an idea and dashes off left. Cook takes out the tarts.*)

QUEEN: Are they done?

KING: To perfection. See how they're red and white and tipped with golden brown.

COOK: Shall I put them in the window to cool?

ALL: Yes!

> Yes!
> While we prepare for dinner.

KING: Make ready for the dinner. We'll celebrate with the Queen's own tarts. Come my Queen.

> (*He and Queen lead all off right in happy procession.*)

COOK: (*To Assistant and Maid.*)

> Come! While the tarts cool! We must prepare to serve the dinner.

MAID: And we'll have fresh aprons!

> (*They go off left. Knave enters up left and tiptoes along the window wall. With his back to the tarts he surveys the kitchen; sees it empty; and beckons off left to Henry, Catherine, Ann, and Eleanor.*)

KNAVE: Come on. Nobody's here.

HENRY: (*Entering and crossing to Knave at cupboard.*)

> Did you say there were tarts?

CATHERINE: (*Timidly at door.*) I don't know whether I should come.

ANN: (*Pushes past her and down center.*) I can smell tarts.

ELEANOR: (*Entering and taking Catherine's hand leads her down left.*)

> It's all right. Just for a minute. The Knave invited us, didn't he?
>
> (*Catherine nods.*)

KNAVE: (*As he and Henry look on upper cupboard shelf.*)

> They're not here. (*To Henry.*) Look below while (*Cross down left.*) I try the oven.
>
> (*Girls watch as he opens oven door.*)

ELEANOR: Are they there?

KNAVE: (*CLosing oven door.*) No.

HENRY: (*Crossing to girls at center.*)

> They're not in the cupboard.

KNAVE: Try the dining room

> (*He looks under the table.*)

ANN: Where?

KNAVE: In there. Hurry!

ANN: (*Runs right and looks off.*) No.

ELEANOR: (*Following her.*) No.

KNAVE: (*Wheeling in half circle turns up center.*)

> There! In plain sight.

ALL: (*Turning.*) Where?

KNAVE: (*Dashes to window and picks up tray of tarts. Henry and Catherine move up left to watch Knave.*)

> I knew they were here.
>
> (*Passing tarts to Henry and Catherine.*)
>
> For you and you—
>
> (*Then to Ann and Catherine as Henry crams his into his mouth and reaches for another.*)
>
> —and you and you.

CATHERINE: (*Hesitates but takes it.*) I don't know.

KNAVE: If they don't bake chocolate cake we'll eat tarts.

ANN: (*Taking a tart.*) Oh, I just love tarts.

ELEANOR: So do I.

KNAVE: If they don't invite us to the party we'll have one of our own.
　　　　(*A door slams off left. Children are startled. Henry and Ann cram the last of their tarts into their mouths leaving stains on their lips and crumbs on their cheeks. Catherine and Eleanor having eaten only a little hold their tarts behind them.*)

CATHERINE: (*Almost crying.*) I knew I shouldn't

KNAVE: (*Runs back and forth to find a hiding place for the tray. Henry points to the floor under the work table. Together they kneel and slide the tray under as Cook enters.*

COOK: (*Surveys scene from doorway then takes two or three steps into the kitchen and stops.*)
　　　　What are you doing—all of you?
　　　　(*Ann and Eleanor, hands behind backs, stand down right like statues. Henry remains kneeling near table. Catherine tries to flatten herself against wall at left center. Assistant and Maid appear in doorway. Knave rises and faces left.*)

ASSISTANT: The tarts! (*Runs to window*) They're gone!

COOK: (*Looks at window then at Knave. With slow, steady step and matching, slow, steady speech she walks toward him.*)
　　　　What—have you done—with those tarts?
　　　　(*Knave faces her in silence.*)

ASSISTANT: (*From her vantage near the window looks off down right.*)
　　　　Here comes the King.

MAID: (*With pitying look at Knave.*)
　　　　What will he do now?
　　　　(*Everyone looks for shelter. Henry scuttles left to Catherine. Ann and Eleanor, after a quick look off right, dash left to huddle with Henry and Catherine. The Assistant shrugs her shoulders and shakes her head in answer to the Maid's question and joins the Maid up left. The Knave and Cook, motionless, face each other at the table.*)

KING: (*Off right.*) And she made the tarts because it was my birthday.

LORDS AND LADIES: (*Off right.*)
　　　　Such devotion. I didn't know she could cook. Our charming Queen.

KING: (*Enters, with Queen followed by Lords and Ladies, King sees Knave.*)
　　　　My son! In the kitchen again?

KNAVE: (*Turns to father.*)

       Yes sir.

KING: And these children? How did they get in?

KNAVE: I brought them. For a party, sir.

KING: (*Looks apprehensively at the window, then at the Knave.*)

       Not with the tarts!!

KNAVE: Some of them.

KING: You shall be beaten for this.

       (*Knave turns left and bows in brave preparation for the beating. King raises his hand and gives the boy one stroke. The Queen intervenes.*)

QUEEN: Wait! Just a minute! He didn't steal all the tarts.

KING: Where are the rest?

KNAVE: (*Brings the tray of remaining tarts from under the table and hands them to his father.*)

QUEEN: He has brought back the tarts and he has been punished. Now is it all right to have the party?

KING: One thing more. (*To Knave.*) Are you through with stealing?

KNAVE: I vow I'll steal no more.

KING: (*Happily.*) Then let's begin the party.

       (*He motions all, including cooks and children to join the dance. As they dance they repeat the old rhyme.*)

ALL: The Queen of Hearts

       She baked some tarts

       All on a summer's day.

       The Knave of Hearts

       He stole those tarts

       And took them clean away.

       The King of Hearts

       Called for the tarts

       And beat the Knave full sore.

       The Knave of Hearts

       Brought back the tarts

       And vowed he'd steal no more.

       (*In conclusion All dance off.*)

The Pudding Pan[2]

by Katherine D. Morse

Characters:

COBBLER
DAME
CUSTOMER
BEGGAR
LANDLORD
BAILIFF
DOCTOR
NEIGHBOR

SCENE: *A room in Cobbler's cottage. On one side is a cobbler's bench; on the other side is a spinning wheel. Cobbler and Dame sit at a table center. They have just finished their meal.*

COBBLER: That was a good pudding, Dame.

DAME: Yes. But now it's eaten. All that's left is the pan which the baker's wife lent me. It's a great bother to have to take it back to her.

COBBLER: Oh, I don't call that much bother.

DAME: Then, why don't you do it?

COBBLER: I'm busy. (*He moves to his bench and picks up a shoe.*) I must finish this shoe.

DAME: (*Goes quickly to spinning wheel.*) And I must finish my spinning.

COBBLER: If you were a good wife, you would take the pan back without any more talk.

235

DAME: If you were a good husband, you'd take it back without another word.

COBBLER: You must take it back.

DAME: Take it yourself!

COBBLER: Listen, Wife. Let's make a bargain. The first one to speak after this will carry back the pudding pan.

DAME: Agreed! (*She puts her finger to her lips. He does the same. She spins. He hammers at the shoe. There is a knock at the door. Both jump up and open their mouths to call, "Come in." Then, remembering, they clap hands over mouths and sit. Another knock. Cobbler whistles. Dame hums. Door opens, and a customer enters. She is a proud lady.*)

CUSTOMER: Good day to you, Cobbler! I wish you to make a pair of shoes. They must be made small and fine and of the best red leather. Now shall the heels be high or low?

(*The Cobbler claps his hand over his mouth. The customer grows angry.*)

I ask you, shall the heels be high or low? Well, why do you stand there like a great dummy? Can't you answer a plain question? Indeed sir, if this is the way you treat your customers, you will lose all your trade. As for me, I am going to the cobbler who lives down the road. Good day!

(*With a stamp of her foot she marches out. The Dame laughs and points her finger in scorn at the Cobbler. He shakes his fist at her. There is a knock at the door. The Beggar comes in. He looks about slyly.*)

BEGGAR: Give a poor beggar a crumb! Ah! Yonder on the table is a fat loaf. I can see that you are kind folk who would not grudge a hungry man a crust. Since you do not say nay, I will help myself. (*He cuts a slice.*) Ah! That is so good it would be a pity to leave the rest behind. (*He puts the loaf in his bag.*) And here is a bit of cheese to go with the bread. (*He picks up the jug and starts to drink. The Dame jumps up and runs at him, shaking her stick.*) What! You grudge me a drink! (*The Dame hits him with her stick. He runs out of the door.*) Help! She's hitting me! Help, ho! (*The Dame slams the door and returns to her place in a rage. The Cobbler points his finger*

*at her and shakes with laughter. There are more knocks at the
door. The Landlord comes in.)*

LANDLORD: Good day, Good man Cobbler and Dame. I have come for
my rent, if you please. *(He looks from one to the other.)*
Well, have you both gone deaf? *(He crosses to the Cobbler
and shouts in his ear.)* I want my rent! *(The Cobbler jumps
and puts his hands over his ears.)* What, doesn't that fetch
you? Then I'll try the good Dame. *(He crosses to the Dame
and shouts in her ear.)* I must have my rent! *(The Cobbler
crosses to the Landlord and shows him his purse, which is
empty.)* Enough of this nonsense! Either you pay me my rent
or tell me why. What! You will not? Then we will see if the
Bailiff can make you talk. *(He crosses to the door, opens it,
and shouts.)* Bailiff! Ho, Bailiff! Come here. *(The Bailiff
comes in. He is fat and carries a staff.)*

BAILIFF: What is the matter here?

LANDLORD: This man and his dame will neither pay me my rent nor tell
me the reason why they will not. I think they both have a
mind to go to jail. *(The Bailiff stands in front of the Cobbler
and raps his staff on the floor.)*

BAILIFF: Come, now, my good man, do you want to go to jail? *(The
Cobbler shakes his head very hard.)*
Then why don't you speak? *(The Cobbler wrings his hands in
despair. The Bailiff goes over to the Dame.)* And you, my
good dame, do you want to go to jail, too? *(The Dame shakes
her head very hard.)* Then why don't you say something?
*(The Dame wrings her hands. The Bailiff turns to the
Landlord.)* Sir, this is very strange. It appears that they have
both been struck dumb. I think we had best call a doctor. *(The
Bailiff goes to the door, opens it, and calls.)* Doctor! Ho,
Doctor! Come here. *(The Doctor comes in. He wears spectacles
and carries a black bag.)*

DOCTOR: Who needs the doctor's care?

BAILIFF: These two poor folk here. It seems that they have both been
struck dumb.

DOCTOR: Dumb, are they? Tut, tut! That is very sad. We must look into
this. *(To the Cobbler)*: My good man, put out your tongue.

(*The Cobbler puts out his tongue.*) This tongue is neither too large nor too small, neither too wide nor too narrow, neither too short nor too long. Yet he has lost the use of it! I will give him a pill. Perhaps that will cure him. (*The Doctor gets a pill out of his bag. The Cobbler makes a face but at last swallows the pill. The Dame laughs at him behind her hand.*) There! And now, Dame, put out your tongue. (*The Dame has to put out her tongue.*) Strange! This tongue looks like a good tongue. It is neither swollen nor shrunk, neither slit nor tied. Perhaps a dose of medicine will loosen it. (*He takes a bottle from his bag and pours a spoonful. The Dame makes a face but at last swallows a dose. The Cobbler laughs in his sleeve.*) Now, Good Man and Dame, speak, I command you!

LANDLORD: Speak! Will you pay the rent?

BAILIFF: Speak! Will you go to jail? (*All stare at the Cobbler and his Dame, who do not say a word. The Neighbor opens the door and looks in.*)

NEIGHBOR: And pray, what is going on here? Does anything ail my good neighbors?

LANDLORD: Does anything ail them? Why, neither of them will speak a single word! And we know not if they be deaf or dumb or mad or all three together!

NEIGHBOR: Not speak, you say? Not speak? H'mm. (*He beckons the three men close to him and speaks in a loud whisper.*) This sounds like magic! (*The Cobbler and his Dame both start.*)

BAILIFF: Oho!

DOCTOR: Magic!

LANDLORD: What is to be done?

NEIGHBOR: (*Softly.*) Leave it to me. (*Aloud.*) In truth I have long suspected that the Dame was a witch! Now it is plain this dumbness is a spell. But if a witch has laid a spell, she can take it off again. And witches, sirs, must be made to obey! (*He crosses to the Dame and threatens her with his broom.*) Dame, I bid you take off this spell at once or I will give you such a beating as will make your bones ache! (*The Dame gives a shriek.*)

COBBLER: (*Jumping up.*) Hold your hand! What! Beat my wife!
How dare you, you villain!

DAME: Ha! Ha! Ha! Ha! Now you'll have to take back the pudding pan!
(*She dances about in glee.*)

LANDLORD: What does all this mean?

DAME: We had a quarrel, sirs—
Myself and my good man;
And if you ask the cause—
It was a pudding pan,
A simple pudding pan!

LANDLORD: Ha! Ha!

BAILIFF: Ho! Ho!

DOCTOR: Hee! Hee!

NEIGHBOR: The cause of all the fuss
Was just a pudding pan!

ALL: A simple pudding pan!

All members of the cast appear onstage and repeat in unison the five-line poem above which was spoken by Dame.

The Glorious Whitewasher[3]

by Walter Hackett

(From *The Adventures of Tom Sawyer*, by Mark Twain)

Characters:

TOM SAWYER
AUNT POLLY
JIM
BEN ROGERS
BILLY FISHER
JOE HARPER
JOHNNY MILLER

Time: *Many years ago.*
Setting: *The sidewalk outside Aunt Polly's house.*
At Rise: *The street is deserted. There is a pause, then the voice of Aunt Polly can be heard from offstage right.*
AUNT POLLY: No more argument from you, young man. The job has to be done, and that's all there is to it.

> (*Aunt Polly and Tom Sawyer enter from the right. He is carrying a large brush and a pail full of whitewash.*)

TOM: Couldn't it wait until tomorrow?
AUNT POLLY: Tomorrow's Sunday.
TOM: It's hot.

---

[3]Copyright 1949 by Plays, Inc. Reprinted by permission from *Plays, The Drama Magazine for Young People*.

AUNT POLLY: It wasn't too hot for you to skip off last night and go fishing.

TOM: That was different.

AUNT POLLY: You're to whitewash this fence.

TOM: (*Looking at the big expanse of fence.*) All of it?

AUNT POLLY: Every single inch.

TOM: Can I go swimming after I'm done?

AUNT POLLY: By the time you finish this job, it will be too late.

TOM: Maybe I can work fast.

AUNT POLLY: I doubt that. When you're finished, call me.

> (*Aunt Polly exits to the right. Tom surveys the fence and sighs deeply. He dips his brush and passes it along a plank. Unenthusiastically he repeats this. Then he stops. Jim enters from right, carrying a pail.*)

TOM: Hello, Jim.

JIM: (*Pausing*) Hello, Tom.

TOM: You going after water? (*Jim nods.*) Say, Jim, I'll fetch the water if you'll whitewash some?

JIM: Can't! Aunt Polly told me to go an' get this water.

TOM: That's the way she always talks. Gimme the bucket—

JIM: Oh, I don't dare, Tom.

TOM: Jim, I'll give you a white alley. A white alley, Jim.

> (*Tom reaches in his pocket and takes out the alley.*)
> Look!

JIM: My! That's a mighty gay alley. But Tom, I can't—

TOM: And besides, if you will I'll show you my sore toe.

> (*Tom sits on barrel and starts taking bandage off his toe. Jim, setting down his pail, bends over to watch. As the two are engaged, Aunt Polly enters from right. In her hand she carries a slipper. Swiftly she descends upon the boys. She gives Jim a whack across the rear.*)

JIM: (*Gives a yelp!*)
> Owww!
> (*Quickly picking up his pail, Jim flees, leaving at left. Aunt Polly looks threateningly at Tom, who after quickly adjusting his bandage, picks up his brush and starts painting madly. Aunt Polly exits right. Tom continues and then stops.*)

AUNT POLLY: (*Her voice floats in from right.*)

Tom! Tom Sawyer, are you working?

(*Tom falls to his work with great vigor. As he paints, Ben Rogers enters from left. Waving his arm like a paddle wheel, he shuffles along slowly. Meanwhile he eats an apple.*)

BEN: Ting-a-ling, ting-a-ling! Set her back on the starboard. Ch-chow-chow! (*Imitating a whistle.*) Whew-whew-whew! I'm the side-wheeler Big Missouri, and I'm a-ready to dock. Whew-whew! Come out with your spring line. Lively, now! Stand by that stage. Now let her go.

(*Tom has again started whitewashing, but out of the corner of his eye, he watches Ben's gyrations. Ben stops and watches Tom.*)

You're up a stump, aren't you?

(*Tom pays no heed. Like an artist, he stands back and surveys his work. He makes another stroke and then another.*)

You got to work, hey?

TOM: (*Turning around.*)

Why, it's you, Ben. I wasn't noticing.

BEN: I'm going in swimming, I am. Don't you wish you could? But of course you'd rather work—wouldn't you? Course you would.

TOM: What do you call work?

BEN: Why, isn't whitewashing work?

TOM: (*Resuming his whitewashing.*)

Maybe it is and maybe it ain't. All I know is, it suits Tom Sawyer.

BEN: You don't mean to let on you like it?

TOM: I don't see why I oughtn't to like it. Does a boy get a chance to whitewash a fence every day?

(*Tom continues to work, just as though he is very interested in his job.*)

BEN: Say, let me whitewash a little.

TOM: (*Shaking his head.*)

Wouldn't do, Ben. Aunt Polly's awful particular 'bout this fence. I reckon there isn't one boy in a thousand, maybe two thousand, that can do it the way it's got to be done.

BEN: Lemme try, please! Only just a little.

TOM: If you was to tackle this fence and anything was to happen to it, why—

BEN: Aw, lemme try it. Say—I'll give you the core of my apple.

TOM: N-no, Ben. I'm afeared.

BEN: I'll give you all of it.

> (*Tom reluctantly gives up the brush to Ben who hands him the apple. Ben starts working, while Tom, seated on the barrel, munches on the apple.*)

TOM: Be sure you do a good job, the same kind I'd do.

BEN: (*Working away.*)

> I promise. Say, this is fun.

TOM: It's serious work—I mean it takes just the right touch to do it.

> (*Tom continues to munch on the apple, while Ben works. He finishes it and makes a motion to throw the core away. Instead, he puts the remnant of the apple in his pocket. Then he settles back and nods in the sun. Seconds pass, and Tom wakes up, disturbed by the sound of whistling coming from the left. He looks up as Billy Fisher enters. Billy pauses to fix the tail of a kite he is carrying. Tom stares fixedly at the kite, then at Ben. He screws up his face and thinks hard. Meanwhile, Ben has whitewashed a good portion of the fence.*)

> That'll be enough, Ben.

BEN: (*Stopping work.*)

> Huh?

TOM: You've done 'nough.

BEN: Lemme finish.

TOM: No, Ben. If you do any more, you may get sloppy and that'll mean Aunt Polly 'll be mad.

BEN: But I like doing it.

TOM: That maybe. Buh you can't expect me to let you do the whole fence just 'cause you gave me an apple. Let me have the brush.

> (*Ben reluctantly surrenders the brush.*)

> Maybe some other time I'll let you do some more.

BEN: Golly! Thanks, Tom.

TOM: Of course I don't promise.

(Ben exits to left, giving Billy a "Hello." Tom surveys the fence, paying no heed to Billy. Billy crosses over and watches.)

BILLY: Bet you wish you were me. *(No answer.)* I said, I bet you wish you were me.

TOM: Don't bother me.

BILLY: What's wrong?

TOM: I'm busy figuring out things.

BILLY: Seems to me all you're doing is whitewashing that ol' fence.

TOM: *(Turning on him.)*

And just what do you know about whitewashing?

BILLY: I've whitewashed before.

TOM: Hah! You mean you slapped on whitewash without even thinkin' what you were doin'.

BILLY: Well, isn't that the way to whitewash—slap it on?

TOM: O'course not. Why, whitewashing a fence is—is an art. You have to know what you're doing every second. Now, my Aunt Polly could hire a man to do it, but she won't. You know why?

(Billy shakes his head.)

Because she knows that I'm the only person 'round that can do it the way it should be done.

BILLY: My ma says I'm pretty good at it.

(Tom looks unconvinced.)

Here, lemme show you.

TOM: Oh, no—not on my fence.

BILLY: Why not?

TOM: You go whitewash your own fence. Besides, I don't think you'd know how to use this kind of whitewash.

BILLY: *(Looking into pail.*

What kind is it?

TOM: A very special mixture.

BILLY: Looks like just any old whitewash to me.

TOM: That proves you don't know anything 'bout whitewash.

BILLY: Maybe I don't, but I can whitewash just as good as you.

TOM: Huh!

BILLY: Just to prove I'm right—you let me do some and I'll give you this
kite.

TOM: What do I want with an old kite?

BILLY: It's a humdinger of a kite. I'll even throw in the cord.

(*He reaches in his pocket and brings out a ball of twine.*)

TOM: Mmm! Don't know if I should. If I do, you've got to promise not to
tell a soul that I let you do it.

BILLY: (*Eagerly.*)

I promise. Lemme have that brush.

TOM: (*Handing him the brush, and in turn taking the kite and ball of
twine.*)

I think I'm making a mistake.

BILLY: I'll show you.

(*Tom sits on the barrel, examining the kite. Billy starts
whitewashing.*)

TOM: Mind you do a good job. Use plenty of wash.

(*Joe Harper and Johnny Miller enter from left, the latter
tossing a ball into the air. They stop when they see what is
going on.*)

JOE: Well, did you ever?

(*He and Johnny start laughing.*)

TOM: Look, you two, if you want to watch, it's all right, but keep quiet.

JOHNNY: What's Billy doin', whitewashing?

TOM: A special kind of job, Johnny. Isn't that right, Billy?

BILLY: Sure! Don't bother to explain to them. They wouldn't understand.

(*He continues whitewashing.*)

JOE: We thought you'd like to go swimming, Tom.

TOM: Thanks! But I'm not interested. I've got to stay and look after this
job.

JOE: You can have it.

TOM: Swimming is just where you and Johnny ought to go. It doesn't take
any brains to swim.

JOHNNY: (*Pointing at the fence.*)

And I suppose that does?

TOM: You're right, it does.

JOE: Why?

TOM: Look at the fence real close.

> (*The pair stare at it.*)
>
> Did you ever see wood just like it? (Quickly) Of course you never have. Know what kind of wood it is?

JOE: Pine?

TOM: (*Scoffs.*)

> Pine! That's Norweigan balsam—a very special kind of wood. And in order to whitewash it right, you've got to have just the right kind of whitewash. And your brush, it has to be just right, too. On top of that, the person usin' the brush has to stroke just right.

BILLY: Like me, huh?

TOM: At first I didn't want to let him do it, but I must say he's doin, a good job—better'n I expected.

BILLY: Thanks, Tom.

JOE: I bet I could whitewash that fence better'n Billy.

> (*Billy and Tom exchange looks and then both shake their heads in disbelief.*)

TOM: It's easy for you to say that, Joe, but you're just talkin' big.

JOE: You gimme a brush and I'll show you.

TOM: Not this fence.

JOE: You think I'm talkin' big.

TOM: I certainly do.

JOE: (*Turning to Johnny.*)

> Come on home with me.
>
> (*They start to exit toward left.*)
>
> Come on home with me for a minute. (*To Tom*) We'll be right back.

TOM: Don't come round here botherin' us when we're workin'.

BILLY: (*Working away.*)

> Joe and Johnny, they talk mighty big.

TOM: I know.

BILLY: To hear Joe talk, you'd think he could do everything.

TOM: Better stop talkin' so much, or you'll spoil the fence. Concentrate.

> (*Billy works faster. Tom looks off to the left.*)

BILLY: Tom.

TOM: Keep workin'.

BILLY: But, I—

TOM: You heard me.

BILLY: But I've got to sneeze.

TOM: (*Grudgingly.*)

All right.

(*Billy sneezes. There is a pause. Then Joe and Johnny rush in from left, each carrying a paint brush. They cross to Tom.*)

JOE: (*Shoving brush under his nose.*)

How about this brush? Is it all right?

TOM: (*Blandly.*) For what?

JOHNNY: (*Holding up his brush.*)

What about mine?

JOE: I took them from my father's work shed. They're good ones, aren't they?

TOM: (*Examining them*)

Yes, they're pretty good brushes. But why show them to me?

JOE: We want to help.

TOM: You mean with—?

(*Pointing at the fence*)

You mean—?

(*Joe and Johnny both nod.*)

No.

JOE: Please!

(*Billy stops working and turns.*)

BILLY: I wouldn't if I were you, Tom. I'm doing such a good job, they might spoil what I've done.

TOM: I think you're right.

JOHNNY: We'll be real careful.

TOM: I'd like to, but—

JOE: Be a good fellow.

TOM: I'm not sure my Aunt Polly would like it.

JOE: (*Making a motion*)

Want me to go ask her?

TOM: (*Hastily*)

No! She might get real mad.

JOHNNY: (*Taking ball out of his pocket*)

If you let me, I'll give you this.

(*He reaches again and takes out a piece of chalk. Tom accepts ball and chalk grudgingly.*)

JOE: (*Diving into his pocket and bringing forth several articles.*)

If you let me help, I'll give you this piece of blue bottle-glass. (*He holds it up.*)

See—You can look through it. And you can have these two aggies and twelve marbles and this brass doorknob.

(*He presses them upon Tom.*)

Is it a bargain?

TOM: (*Motioning to Billy*)

Move over.

(*Joe and Johnny start to paint.*)

Be sure and do the kind of a job I'd do.

JOE: Did you say this was special whitewash?

TOM: I did.

JOE: Seems just like any old whitewash.

TOM: That's because you don't know any better. That whitewash you're usin' is a secret mixture. and no one knows what's in it but Aunt Polly'n me. By the way, have you fellows got enough left?

(*They chorus ''Yes.*)

JOE: You think maybe you might gimme the secret formula?

TOM: I couldn't do that; its a real secret. Tell you what, though.

JOE: What?

TOM: When you get ready to whitewash your own fence let me know and I'll mix up a batch for you.

JOE: Golly! That'll be fine.

TOM: That's if you'll give me that set of tin soldiers of yours.

JOE: (*Dubiously*)

Well—

TOM: It doesn't make any difference to me.

BILLY: You better take him up on it, Joe.

JOHNNY: It's a good swap.

JOE: All right. I'll do it.

JOHNNY: You think you might do the same for me?

TOM: Well—

JOHNNY: My cat's goin' to have kittens. I'll give you one, if you say yes.

TOM: All right, I'll swap.

BILLY: Mebbe you'd like that brass whistle of mine?

TOM: Mebbe I might. I'll think it over.

> (*The three painters work on in silence for a few seconds.*)

AUNT POLLY: (*Calling from right*)

> Tom?

TOM: (*Jumping to his feet*)

> Everything's goin' fine, Aunt Polly.
>
> (*Now the fence is completely whitewashed. Billy drops his brush into the pail. The boys stand back, as though asking Tom's approval. He nods.*)
>
> Must say as how you did a pretty fair job—almost as good as I could.
>
> (*The boys smile.*)
>
> Yup, not bad at all.

JOE: Thanks for lettin' us do it.

TOM: That's all right.

JOHNNY: Mebbe we can do it again some time, hey?

TOM: I'll have to think it over. Don't want to make a habit of it, you know. Where you fellows goin' now?

JOE: Swimmin'.

BILLY: You comin'?

TOM: Mebbe after I inspect your work again.

> (*The three of them exit to the left. Tom goes to barrel and, tipping it up, puts his newly-acquired presents into it. He barely finishes this before Aunt Polly enters from right.*)

AUNT POLLY: How much have you done?

> (*Tom points to the fence.*)
>
> Well, I never! There's no getting around it, you can work when you've a mind to. Well, go along and play; but mind you, get back some time in a week, or I'll tan you.
>
> (*Tom starts to exit left.*)

Little Women

(From *Little Women,* by Louisa Alcott)
Adapted by Maxine McSweeny

Characters:
JO
AMY
BETH
MEG
MOTHER

(*The scene is the March family living room. Jo lies on the floor near the fireplace. On a low stool nearby sits Beth with her chin in her hands. In an armchair behind Beth is Meg knitting a sock. Amy with drawing paper and pencil is on the opposite side of the room. At the rear sits their mother at a writing desk.*)

JO: There never was such a cross family

AMY: You're the crossest person in it.

BETH: (*Tries to make peace.*) Birds in their little nests agree.

MEG: Don't peck at one another, children.

(*Jo sits up in a boyish manner and begins to whistle.*)

AMY: Don't Jo. It's so boyish.

JO: That's why I do it.

AMY: I detest rude, unmannerly girls.

JO: And I hate affected niminy-piminy chits.

MOTHER: Girls! Be quiet for a minute. I must get this letter off. You drive me distracted with your worries.

(*Picks up papers and goes, kissing her hand to the girls.*)

JO: (*Ashamed.*) If Marmee shook her fist instead of kissing her hand it would serve us right. We're ungrateful wretches.

250

MEG: You're old enough to behave better, Josephine. Now that you turn up your hair you should remember you're a lady.

JO: I am not. And if turning up my hair makes me one, I'll wear it in two pigtails until I'm twenty. I wish I were a boy so I could be a soldier with Father. But I have to stay home and knit like a poky old woman. (*Picks up sock and shakes it until needles rattle and ball bounces.*)

BETH: Poor Jo. You must be contented to play brother to us.

MEG: As for you, Amy, you are altogether too particular and prim. You'll grow up an affected little goose if you don't take care.

BETH: If Jo's a tomboy and Amy's a goose, what am I?

MEG: You're a dear and nothing else.

JO: Hurrah for Bethy.

AMY: My only comfort is that Mama doesn't take tucks in my dresses whenever I'm naughty as Maria Park's mother does. My dear, it's really dreadful. Sometimes she's so bad, her frock is up to her knees and she can't come to school.

MEG: If I had lovely dresses like hers I wouldn't care if they had tucks in them.

AMY: I don't think it's fair for some girls to have plenty of pretty things and other girls nothing at all.

BETH: We've got Father and Mother and each other.

JO: We haven't got Father and shan't have him for a long time.

MEG: That's the only way we can make a sacrifice. I think it's splendid of Father to go as a chaplain when he was not strong enough for a soldier.

JO: Don't I wish I could go as a drummer? (*She begins to march around the room, beating an imaginary drum. Mother returns and smiles as she watches them for a moment.*) Rub-a-dub-dub. Rub-a-dub-dub. I'd cheer all the men.

MOTHER: (*Picking up her shawl from the chair.*) I'm glad to find you so merry, my girls.

JO: Or I'd be a nurse so I could be near Father all the time.

BETH: When will he come home, Marmee?

MOTHER: Not for many months, dear. I'm going to post this letter to him now. He'll be wanting news of his little women.

JO: Oh, I'm going to try to be a little woman and do my duty here.

MEG: Are you going shopping while you're out, Mother?

JO: Please, wait 'till tomorrow, Marmee. We want to go with you and get the things for the play.

MOTHER: I'm going to mail this letter. Good-bye girls. Beth, you may start the toast for supper while I'm gone.

ALL: Good-bye, Marmee.

> (*Beth goes out and soon returns with bread and toasting fork which she holds over the coals.*)

JO: (*Marching up and down with her hands behind her back and nose in the air.*) There is so much to do about the play.

MEG: I don't mean to act any more after this time. I'm getting too old for such things.

JO: You won't stop, I know, as long as you can trail around in a white gown with your hair down and wear gold paper jewelry. You are the best actress we've got, and there'll be an end of everything if you quit the boards. (*Pacing the floor as before.*) We ought to rehearse now. (*Turning suddenly.*) Amy, we should do that fainting scene. You are as stiff as a poker in that.

AMY: (*Slightly offended.*) I can't help it; I never saw anyone faint and I don't choose to make myself black and blue, tumbling flat as you do. If I can go down gracefully, I'll drop. If I can't, I shall fall into a chair.

JO: Even when Hugo comes at you with the dagger?

AMY: I don't care if you do.

JO: Do it this way. Clasp your hands so, and stagger across the room like this. "Roderigo! Save me! Save me!" Let's try it now.

AMY: All right.

JO: Now, before I come, you are sitting by the window with your hands folded.

AMY: I'm ready. Now don't be too violent, Jo.

JO: (*Cares nothing for the warning. Beth has continued to toast bread but is now completely carried away by Jo's acting. Jo slinks across the room toward Amy, looking at an imaginary dagger in her hands.*) Ah! fair blade, you shall soon taste blood. Blo-oo-od! (*Amy begins to cringe as Jo approaches.*) Aha! my proud beauty, call for your Roderigo now. (*She touches Amy's hand with the imaginary dagger.*) Feel the cold steel!

(She laughs villainously.) Ha, ha, ha. *(Aside to Amy)* Scream, Amy, scream.

AMY: *(Petulantly)* Ow!

JO: Remember your speech to Roderigo.

AMY: *(A very poor and quiet imitation of Jo.)* Roderigo, save me, save me.

JO: Come on, Meg! It's time for Roderigo.

MEG: *(Jumping up and assuming a manly attitude.)* I come, Esmerelda, I come! And you, Hugo. Drink, drink until you die. *(She holds Jo's hands and pretends to force a cup to her lips.)*

JO: *(Shrieking)* Oh! What pain! *(She stumbles about the room and falls.)* I die! I die!

MEG: It's the best we've had yet. *(She helps Jo to her feet.)*

JO: It's better; but Amy, imagine you're about to die. Don't act as if I'm pricking you with a pin.

BETH: *(Entranced.)* I don't see how you can write and act such splendid things.

MEG: Beth, look at your toasting fork. That's Marmee's slipper instead of the toast. *(The girls shriek with laughter.)*
(Mother returns looking worried.)

BETH: Oh, Mother, was there a letter from Father at the post office?
(All the girls eagerly await her reply.)

MOTHER: *(Slowly.)* No, Bethy, there wasn't.

JO: Oh, Mother, we always hear from him on Tuesday.

MEG: He's as regular as the sun.

AMY: Perhaps the trains are delayed.

MOTHER: I hope we'll get word soon.
(There is a sharp ring at the doorbell.)

JO: I'll go, Marmee *(She hurries out and returns almost immediately in great excitement. She is holding a telegram.)*
(Frightened) It's a telegram, Marmee.
(Mother almost snatches it from her, tears it open, and reads as the girls crowd around her.)

JO: *(Reads over her shoulder.)* "Your husband is ill. If you can take him home all will be well. Come at once."

MEG ⎫ Oh, Marmee. *(They help her to sit down but she recovers herself
BETH: ⎬ immediately and gets to her feet. Everyone is thinking of
     ⎭ Father.)*

MOTHER: I'll go to him at once. (*Thinking*) Today's train leaves in an hour. I'll take it.

MEG: But, Marmee, your ticket! Where will you get the money for it?

MOTHER: I'll have to borrow it from Aunt March. Your pencil and paper, Amy! Quickly! (*Amy gives her pencil and paper, and Mrs. March hastily writes.*)

JO: She won't let us have it. She didn't want Father to go in the first place.

MOTHER: We'll try. Here, Jo, take this note to Aunt March and come back as soon as you can.

JO: I'll fly, Marmee. (*As she hurries out, she picks up the shawl her mother has dropped on the chair and puts it over her head.*

BETH: She couldn't refuse us now.

AMY: (*Sniffling.*) Oh, Marmee, I wonder how sick he is.

MOTHER: (*Gently*) It's no time for tears. Be calm, girls, and help me think. Amy, will you send a telegram saying I will come?

AMY: (*Glad to be doing something*) Of course, Marmee, and I've money enough in my little purse. (*She dashes out.*)

MOTHER: Meg, will you get down the little black trunk?

MEG: I know just where it is. (*She, too, goes.*)

BETH: Mother, sit quietly for just a minute. (*Pleading.*)

MOTHER: Yes, for a minute—just to get my breath.

BETH: Isn't it fine you have just come from town? You won't even have to change your dress?

MOTHER: (*Looking at her skirt*) No, I won't, Beth. That will save a little time.

MEG: (*Returning with the little trunk*) Here, Marmee. May we pack it for you?

MOTHER: I hardly know what to do 'til Jo gets back.

MEG: (*Trying to be cheerful*) Won't it be wonderful to have Father with us?

MOTHER: Of course it will, Meg. I am only wondering how sick he may be. You know he's not strong.

MEG: But they must think he's able to be moved or they wouldn't send for you.

BETH: We'll nurse him so carefully he'll be well in a week.

AMY: (*Returning and looking at her Mother with concern.*) Are you all right?

MOTHER: I am all right, dear. Did you send the telegram?

AMY: Yes. (*Looking around.*) Hasn't Jo come back?

MOTHER: No, not yet. (*She goes to the door to look out.*)

MEG: Is she coming?

MOTHER: I don't see her.

AMY: Oh, maybe Aunt March won't give her the money.

MOTHER: (*Worried.*) I'm sure she will. (*Walking up and down the room.*) What could have happened to Jo?

AMY: Oh, we don't know what freak notion she's taken into her head.

BETH: Amy, you know she wouldn't do anything harum-scarum now.

MEG: I guess she's getting a lecture from Aunt March. (*Turning to Mother.*) Shall I put your things in the little trunk, Marmee?

MOTHER: Of course, Meg. Put in my blue calico and some underthings.

MEG: I'll find all you need neatly laid in your bureau drawer. I'll get everything. (*She goes out.*)

AMY: Your cape and bonnet are here, Marmee. You can put them on as soon as Jo comes.

MOTHER: (*Growing more anxious.*) Where can she be?

BETH: (*Taking up her position near the door.*) I'll tell you as soon as I see her.

MEG: (*Returning with her arms full of clothing and a comb and hair brush in her hands.*)

AMY: I'll help, Meg. (*The two girls quietly pack the little trunk.*)

MOTHER: Did you remember hankerchiefs?

MEG: Yes, they're here in the corner. Help me shut it, Amy.
(*They close and strap the little trunk.*)

MOTHER: Oh! What could have happened to Jo?

BETH: (*With a sigh of relief.*) There she is.

MOTHER: If she has the money we'll leave at once. (*She picks up her cape.*)

JO: (*Enters and speaks triumphantly.*) There's my contribution. (*Hands her mother a roll of bills.*)

MOTHER: (*Looks at them hastily. She is both grateful and relieved.*) My dear, was Aunt March very cross?

JO: I didn't go to her.

MOTHER: (*Excitedly.*) Where did you get this money? Twenty-five dollars.

MEG: Jo, I hope you haven't done anything rash.

JO: No, it's mine honestly. I earned it, for I only sold what was my own. (*She takes off the shawl and all see that her hair has been cut short. Heretofore she has worn false hair in a snood, so it is easy to remove this while she is off stage and reveal the player's own short hair. The next four speeches are given almost at the same time.*)

MEG: Your hair! Your beautiful hair!

AMY: Oh, Jo, how could you? Your one beauty.

MOTHER: My dear girl, there was no need of this. (*Puts arm about Jo.*)

BETH: (*Takes Jo's hand.*) She doesn't look like my Jo but I love her dearly for it.

AMY: What made you do it, Jo?

JO: Well, I was wild to do something for Father, and I knew Aunt March would croak if we asked her for that much. As I went along, I kept thinking what I could do.

MOTHER: I'm afraid you'll regret it.

JO: In a barber's window I saw tails of hair with prices marked. One was forty dollars. Then I knew. I had one thing to make money out of.

BETH: (*Awe-struck.*) How did you dare?

JO: I told the barber my story and he cut it off quickly. I told him to hurry so I wouldn't change my mind.

MEG: Oh, Jo, you are so brave.

MOTHER: Come, girls, we have to hurry if I catch that train.

JO: (*Handing her Mother a lock of her hair and looking rather sad.*) I saved a lock for you to keep.

MOTHER: (*Taking Jo's hand for an instant.*) Thank you, dear.

MEG: Jo, will you help me with the little trunk?

JO: (*She has recovered her joyful spirits.*) Of course. We'll see you safely on the train, Marmee.

BETH: And when you return, Father will be with you.

AMY: Come, Marmee. (*As Amy and Beth lead their Mother out, she turns to speak to Jo and Meg who are following witht the trunk.*)

MOTHER: And how proud he'll be of his "Little Women."

(*They hurry out in great excitement.*)

Gypsy Brew

by Maxine McSweeny

Characters:

TALA
BENDELL } Gypsy girls
FIDALIA
MARGUERITE, who sells ribbons
CARLA, who sells vegetables
GERTRUDE, who sells grain
TESS }
ELNA } Gertrude's children
DAME EDRIS }
DAME KUNSON } customers
DAME BRAND }

Scene I

A hilltop overlooking the town of Halborg.

At Rise: *Tala enters left and looks about, goes right, and looks offstage.*
What she sees pleases her. She turns and calls off left.

TALA: I've found it. Bendell! Fidalia! Come. I've found it.
     (*Bendell runs in left*)

BENDELL: Where?

TALA: (*Points off right.*) Just down the hill. I saw it yesterday. I knew it
     wasn't far.

BENDELL: (*Looks off right.*) It looks like a good town. We can dance for
     our dinner there.

(*Fidalia enters slowly left. She looks about as though afraid.*)

BENDELL: Look, Fidalia. Tala found the little town.

FIDALIA: Is there a town at the foot of this hill?

TALA: Yes. You can see it.

FIDALIA: I thought so. I've been here before. (*Tries to remember.*) Something happened here.

BENDELL: What kind of something?

FIDALIA: (*Looks off right at town.*) Something that wasn't good. There were people there. They were mad. I'm going down this path.
Maybe I'll remember.

BENDELL: You must be thinking of some other place.

FIDALIA: I don't think so. (*Goes off right.*)

TALA: Bendell, it's market day down there.

BENDELL: Let's go down. Maybe we can earn a dinner with our dancing.

TALA: I'm so hungry.

BENDELL: And we can't go back to camp without our dinner. The old ones need the food that's there.

FIDALIA: (*Returning.*) I knew it. I remember everything now.

BENDELL: What do you remember?

FIDALIA: We camped here once—almost on this spot—when I was a little girl. The people from the town below came and drove us away.

BENDELL: Why?

FIDALIA: They don't like gypsies. Everybody came—women as well as men. I remember one fine, strong-looking woman. She kept saying, "We don't want any gypsies around here." She seemed to be important and everyone wanted to agree with her. They called her Dame Brand. She'd say, "Get out of here. Gypsies are nothing but beggars and thieves."

TALA: Why did she say that?

FIDALIA: My father said she was one of the pygmy-hearted people. He says every tribe, every nation has a few pygmy hearts. They think that a person must look like them and live like them or he's no good.

BENDELL: And I guess a true pygmy-heart like this Dame Brand would even look down on her own people.

FIDALIA: I suppose so. She's a big person down there. And no gypsy will
        dance in Halborg. That's the name of the town.

TALA: Oh, towns change and people change.

BENDELL: And maybe they've never seen a gypsy Tarantella. Come on,
        I'd like to see this Dame Brand of Halborg.

FIDALIA: What are you going to do?

BENDELL: Try the Tarantella. And if that doesn't work, I've another idea.
        Come, I'll tell you as we go. (*They go off right.*)

Scene II

*It is market day in Halborg. Three stalls display wares. Up center
is one holding ribbons and laces. The stall down right has vegetables for
sale. Bags of grain and meal are seen in the stall down left. Near center
stage is a tripod with a kettle over a fire. Slightly to left of the stall up
center is a stool. The townspeople enter from left, gypsies from right.
Music is heard offstage. Marguerite hurries in and arranges her display
of ribbons and laces. Carla enters and takes her place behind the
vegetable stand. Gertrude slips behind her stall. Her two children, Tess
and Elna, follow her in and move near Marguerite. Enter Dame Edris
who carries her knitting and Dame Kunson who has a market basket.
They stop in front of Gertrude's stall.*

MARGUERITE: *(Crying her wares.)* Get your pretty laces to show off your
        pretty faces! Pretty ruffly laces!

GERTRUDE: Elna, are you touching Marguerite's ribbons?

ELNA: Oh no, Mother.

MARGUERITE: Let them look.

GERTRUDE: They must not bother you.

DAME EDRIS: *(Sits on stool.)* Children are not a bother. It would be a poor
        town without children.

DAME KUNSON: They can be pretty bothersome when they want to, just
        the same.

TESS: Here comes Dame Brand.

        (*Flutter of excitement passes over the little group. Dame
        Kunson adjusts her cap and leans forward to look offstage.
        Tess catches Elna's hand, and the two children scamper off*

right. Dame Edris picks up her knitting and begins to work. The three stall keepers call their wares.)

MARGUERITE: Get your pretty laces
　　　to show off your pretty faces!
GERTRUDE: Oats, rye, and barley meal! 　　　Together
CARLA: Nice fresh onions for sale!
　　　Nice fresh onions!

(*Enter Dame Brand left.*)

DAME KUNSON: (*Very pleasantly.*) Good Morning, Dame Brand.
DAME BRAND: Good morning. *(She passes Dame Kunson and the grain stall and circles past the ribbon stall. Dame Kunson falls into step behind her.)*
DAME EDRIS: Good morning, Dame Brand.
DAME BRAND: Good morning.
DAME KUNSON: (*Speaking over Dame Brand's shoulder.*) Aren't those pretty laces, Dame Brand?
DAME BRAND: All right, if you like laces. *(She moves steadily on to Carla's stall.)* Are those onions good and solid?
CARLA: Do you want to try one?
DAME BRAND: I certainly do. No use paying hard money for soft onions. *(Testing the onions.)*
DAME KUNSON: (*Over Dame Brand's shoulder.*) Oh, you're right, Dame Brand.
DAME BRAND: (*Ignoring her.*) How much are these onions?
CARLA: Two pennies a box.
DAME BAND: Two pennies a box! What a price! Well—I suppose I'll have to pay it. Here, put them in my basket. *(Puts basket on counter and carefully counts out two pennies.)* One, two. This time of year you should get onions for one penny a box.
　　　(Tess and Elna call as they run in.)

TESS: Mother!
ELNA: Gypsies are coming!
　　　(There is an instant of shocked silence. Everyone stands spellbound. Then all talk at once.)

Gypsies!
Not here!   }
Where?   *Together.*
Are you sure?   }

GERTRUDE: How do you know? You've never seen a gypsy.

ELNA: But I have. I can remember when we drove them away.

MARGUERITE: (*Almost shrieking.*) Gypsies! And not a man in the town!

GERTRUDE: Oh, why did the men have to go hunting today?

MARGUERITE: What can we poor women do?

DAME BRAND: Poor women, indeed! What do you mean? I've driven
    gypsies away before, and I can do it again.

CARLA: Maybe they don't mean any harm.

DAME BRAND: What are you talking about? A gypsy would steal the
    shoes off your feet.

DAME KUNSON: And what they don't steal they beg. I've known 'em to
    beg the beans right out of the soup I was cooking for supper.

DAME EDRIS: As for me a gypsy dance would be worth a few beans out of
    my soup.

DAME BRAND: Well, they won't get a thing out of me. Now, hide
    everything before they get here.

DAME KUNSON: Yes, quick! Hide everything. Down behind the stalls.

(*The stall keepers work frantically to obey. There is a buzz of talk as they
    work.*)

I wouldn't want to lose this.
Here, take these!   }
They mustn't see this meal.   *Together.*
Oh, vegetables are so hard to hide. }

DAME BRAND: (*She and Dame Kunson scurry about giving orders.*)
    Hurry, hurry!

TESS AND ELNA: (*Peeking off right.*) They're coming. They're almost
    here.

CARLA: Dame Brand! Here! Your basket! (*Dame Brand grabs the basket
    which she left on Carla's stall. She gives Carla a sharp look.*)

DAME BRAND: I don't want to lose those onions—not at two pennies a
    box. (*She hurries across and hides the basket behind
    Gertrude's stall.*)

GERTRUDE: This last bag! Where shall I put it? There's no room.

DAME BRAND: (*Gypsy music.*) Sit on it. (*Gertrude obeys. The children sit beside her. Dame Brand stands at center. She is ready to fight.*) Not a bite of food for a gypsy! Now remember!
(*Dame Kunson stands at left of Dame Brand. Enter Bendell, Tala, and Fidalia.*)

BENDELL: Good morning.

DAME BRAND: It's not a good morning when gypsies come to Halborg.

TALA: We saw it was market day.

BENDELL: And we want to dance for our dinner.
(*Dame Kunson whispers in Dame Brand's ear. It is obvious that everyone wants to see the gypsies dance.*)

DAME BRAND: Well, you may dance—but as for dinner—
(*Music of Tarantella sounds. Gypsies dance. Children yell with glee. Marguerite sways in rhythm of dance. Dame Edris gives herself wholeheartedly to enjoyment of dance. Dame Kunson taps her foot. Even Dame Brand nods her head in rhythm. At end of dance, Tala speaks to Dame Brand.*)

TALA: We're very hungry.

DAME BRAND: You've come to a poor place for dinner. The men have gone hunting and there's no food in the town. You can see even the market place is bare.

BENDELL: Well, if we can't eat with you, you'll have to eat with us.

DAME BRAND: What would we eat with you?

BENDELL: We can always give you nail soup.

MARGUERITE: (*Shrieking.*) Nail soup! They'll kill us.

TALA: You are poor folk like us. Surely you have eaten nail soup.

DAME KUNSON: I never heard of it.

DAME BRAND: What kind of gypsy brew is that?

BENDELL: It's soup made with a nail instead of beans or a soup bone.

DAME BRAND: Soup made with a nail. Well, how's that done?

BENDELL: We'll show you.

TALA: May we use this kettle of hot water?

DAME BRAND: Well, I guess so. (*Everyone nods approval.*)

BENDELL: Just watch and you'll always have the making of a meal.
(*Holds up nail.*) See it's just a plain nail. (*Drops it in kettle. Takes stick from Carla's stall.*) Here, Fidalia, is a nice clean stick.

FIDALIA: (*She has stayed quietly near the entrance but now comes forward.*) I'll stir. We don't want it to stick to the bottom. (*Stirs.*)

DAME BRAND: (*Looking in kettle.*) It looks like plain water to me.

BENDELL: This may be a little thin. I've used the nail several times.

DAME BRAND: You mean you can use the nail again? Well, this beats all.

BENDELL: Remember the time we had nail soup with onions in it?

TALA: Oh, it was wonderful the way the onions drew the flavor out of that nail.

FIDALIA: But what we do not have, we do without.

DAME BRAND: You say onions make it better?

BENDELL: Yes, but it is good without them. (*Everyone looks at Dame Brand.*)

DAME BRAND: An onion might have dropped around here last market day. (*Goes to her basket behind Gertrude's stall.*) Yes! Here are onions—several of them. (*Returns with all the onions she can carry and drops them in the soup as fast as she can skin them.*)

TALA: Oh, you shouldn't. You may need the onions.

DAME BRAND: Well, my goodness, if I can make soup out of a plain nail, I can spare a few onions.

BENDELL: The soup would thicken faster if we had some barley or a little meal.

FIDALIA: But what we do not have, we do without.

DAME BRAND: A little meal you say?

        (*All look at Gertrude who points to the sack under her and shakes her head helplessly.*)

GERTRUDE: You might look back there. (*Pointing to her stall.*)

DAME BRAND: There must be meal in an old sack over there.

DAME KUNSON: I'll look. (*Goes behind Gertrude and returns with a scoop of meal.*) Look! I found a whole scoopful.

DAME BRAND: Put it in the soup. Don't just stand there!

        (*Dame Kunson pours the meal in the kettle.*)

TALA: Oh, do you think you should?

DAME BRAND: Keep stirring. I can't wait to taste soup made out of a plain nail.

CARLA: Would it be all right to add some carrots and turnips?

FIDALIA: Fine, if we had them.

CARLA: *(Dropping in vegetables.)* Here they are.

MARGUERITE: Oops! What a soup this will be.

DAME BRAND: And all from a plain nail.

DAME KUNSON: Doesn't it smell good?

BENDELL: Once the king came to our camp and ate nail soup with us.

DAME BRAND: The king you say? Eating nail soup? Just like this?

TALA: Just the same, except he put in a great piece of meat and some potatoes.

DAME BRAND: That settles it. I have meat and potatoes at home. We'll have soup as good as the king's. Come. All of you! *(To Tala and Fidelia.)* Bring the kettle. *(Including everyone.)* To my house for soup as good as the king's. *(She takes Bendell's hand and leads her left.)*

> MARGUERITE: Oh, Dame Brand!
> FIDALIA: To your house?
> TALA: Just think! Meat and potatoes in the soup.
> DAME KUNSON: What a feast!

Together

DAME BRAND: *(Turns at entrance.)* You wonderful gypsies! You'll always be welcome in the town of Halborg. You've taught us to make soup out of a nail.

(Dame Brand and Bendell leave followed by Tala and Fidalia carrying kettle.)

(All the townsfolk shout praise of the gypsies as they follow Dame Brand and gypsies off stage.)

> The gypsies!
> They're wonderful!
> We didn't know!
> What gypsies!

All together.

(They shout until out of sight. Dame Edris who has to stop and arrange her knitting is the last one to leave the stage. She gives the audience a knowing look.)

DAME EDRIS: What a nail!

(She quickly goes off left.)

Index

Accomplishment, thrill of, 22

Activities for waiting players, 158

Adelaide, in *Sleeping Beauty,* 202-15

Administration of Public Recreation (Hjelte), 26

"A-Hunting We Will Go," 185

Alcott, Louisa, 250

"All Mine," 137

Amy, in *Little Women,* 250–56

Andrews, Mary Shipman, 113

Ann, in *In the Kitchen Again,* 227–34; in teamwork example, 160

Aristotle, 21

Audience, control of, 183; director's observation on, 185; inappropriateness of, in creative drama, 58; reaction of, 185; recruitment of, 180; ushers for, 183

Aunt Polly, in *The Glorious Whitewasher,* 240–49; in sound effects, 177

Baby Bear, in stage movement illustration, 148

Babysitter, 11; as leader of improvisation, 78,79

Backstage, at showtime, for execution of offstage effects, 185; in creative drama, 65; location of, 65

Bakery play project, 41

Balance, or counter cross, 134

Beauty shop play project, 42

Beethoven, Ludwig van, 86

Bendell, as example of characteriza-

tion, 157,158; in *Gypsy Brew,* 257–64

Ben Rogers, in *The Glorious Whitewasher,* 240-49

Beth, in *Little Women,* 250-56

Bi-Colored-Python-Rock-Snake, 96,97

Billy Fisher, in *The Glorious Whitewasher,* 240–49

Birch Tree, in story play, 88–90; in *The Bird with the Broken Wing,* 191–94

Bird with the Broken Wing, The (McSweeny), 191–94

"Blind Men and the Elephant, The" (Quigley), 105–07

Blow out the Candle exercise, 136

Boots, in story play, 99–101

Boy Scouts, 13

Breathing, importance of, to speaking, 135,136; exercises to improve, 136

Browning, Robert, 23

Business, stage, as aid to characterization, 156; how invent, 149; memorization and, rehearsal of, 156; what it is, 149; with hand properties, 150.

Butterfly, in *Sleeping Beauty,* 202–15

Camp, 13, 28; director of, as leader of story play, 103

Camp Fire Girls, 13

Carla, in *Gypsy Brew,* 257–64

Carter Blair, in story play, 113–16

Cast, double, 142, 143; methods of

selecting, 142

Ceres, in gesture exercise, 141; in imitative play, 37; in story play, 110

Characterization, in creative drama, 64,68,91; in rehearsal, 155–58

Chase, Alice, 86

"Children's Games" (Chase), 86

Churches, 28

Cinderella, in imitative play, 36; in making an entrance, 134; in pantomime exercise, 140; in *A Princess at Heart,* 216–26

Circus, 20; in creative drama, 29; in imitative play, 35

Cleanup, in imitative play, 53; supplies for, 37

Clementine, in *A Princess at Heart,* 216–26

Climax, in story play, 104; rehearsal for, 161–63; study of, 144

Cloud Puff, in *Sleeping Beauty,* 202–15

Cobbler, as example of stage business, 149; as example of climax and tempo, 161–63; in *The Pudding Pan,* 235–39

"Columbus" (Miller), in creative drama, 61, 82

Community recreation center, setting for creative drama, 85

Congratulations, after performance, 186

Cooperation, 24; in creative drama, 57

Cordelia, in *Sleeping Beauty,* 202–15

Costume accessories, in creative drama, 109,110; in rehearsal, 156; with basic costumes, 173, 174

Costume fabrics, 173, 174

Costumes, accessories for, 173–75; care of, 175, 176; for perfor-

mances, 173–76; incongruities of, 126; in creative drama, 109, 110; in imitative play, 36; procurement of, 173–75; trimming for, 173–75; with basic garments, 173–75

Costuming of specific characters, 173, 174; of heads and feet, 174

Cotman, Frederick, 86

Crash, example of improvisation, 73

Cratchit, Bob, 134

Creative drama, as preparation for theatre, 128; as prerequisite to rehearsal, 141; characteristics of, 57,58; excelling in, 58; forms of, 58; leadership of, 59–68; place for, 59; plan in, 57; program material for, 59–63; teamwork in, 57

Creative theatre, for delight, 19–22; for development, 22–25; forms of, 26; guidelines and cautions for, 27; leader of, 29; opportunities for participation in, 28; potential of, for good or ill, 25; with other activities, 28

Criticism, of participants, 186

Crystal, in *Sleeping Beauty,* 202–15

Cub Scouts, in story play, 105–7; in theatre, 128

Cues, definition of, 66; exercises in response to, 132, 133; in creative drama, 66; sheet of, for technical staff, 159, 164

Cultural centers, 28; director of, as improvisation leader, 73

Curtain, stage, use of, 126; participants' duties with, 185, 186

Curtain calls, 185, 186

Daddy Doe, in *The Wishing Shop,* 195–201

Dagliesh, Alice, 52

Dame, in *The Pudding Pan,* 235–39;

in climax, 161; in tempo example, 161–63.

Dame Brand, in characterization study, 155–57; in *Gypsy Brew,* 257–64

Dame Edris, in *Gypsy Brew,* 257–64

Dame Kunson, in characterization study, 156; in *Gypsy Brew,* 257–64

Dance, relation of, to creative theatre, 29

Danuels, Guy, 103

Dawn, in *Sleeping Beauty,* 202–15

Day Care Center director as leader of improvisation, 77; as leader of story play, 88–93

Daylight in performances, 178

Delivery truck play project, 42

Departments of theatre arts of colleges, 28

"Development" (Browning), 23

Development of participants, 22

Director, duties of, in theatre, 130; location of, at performance, 185; location of at rehearsals, 154–65; responsibilities of, at rehearsals, 153–65; study of script by, 144–50; title of, 130

Doll show, creative drama for, 29

Double cast, activities for, 158; advantages of, 142; opportunities for players in, 142,143; rehearsals with, 156

Drama as development, 22; as delight, 19–22; combined with art, 28, 85, 86; with crafts, 40; with music, 28; with nature study, 29; with religious education, 29; with social studies, 28, 84, 85

Dress rehearsal, 165

Duke Edgar, in *Sleeping Beauty,* 202–15

Eleanor, in *In the Kitchen Again,* 227–34; in teamwork rehearsal, 160

Elementary schools, 13, 28, 34

"Elephant's Child, The" (Kipling), 96,97

Elna, in *Gypsy Brew,* 257, 264

Entrance, making an, exercise for, 134; procedures for, 133

Entrance (place) in creative drama, 65; location of, in theatre, 145

Enunciation, 137

Environment, in imitative play, 39

"Eve of St. Nicholas, The" (Steen), 85

Everett, Edward, in *The Perfect Tribute,* 113–15

Excerpt from conversation, in improvisation, 75, 76

Exercises for breathing, 136, 137; entrances, 133; movement, 132,134; pantomime, 139–41; speaking, 135,137,138; from play, 141

Experience, new, 21, in imitative play, 35, 36, 44, 46; in creative drama, 59, 78

Fanfare, as introduction to scene, 177

Fashion show play project, 43

Feelings, how to harness, 24

Festival of plays, 187

Fidalia, in *Gypsy Brew,* 257–64; as characterization study, 155,157

Fill the Balloon exercise, 136

Fire prevention, 169

First Thanksgiving Story, The (Dagliesh), 52

Flag day Observance, creative dramatization in, 29

Flameproofing, 169

Folk Tales Children Love (Piper), 93

Formal drama, 123

Frost King, in pantomime, 140; in

story play, 88–93; in *The Bird with the Broken Wing,* 191–94
Fyleman, Rose, 82

Games, as example of improvisation leadership, 79
Gesture, use of hands in, 140; exercises to improve, 140; sequence of, 140
Girl Scouts, 23
Glorious Whitewasher, The (Hackett), 240; sound effects in, 177
Goldilocks, exercise for cue response, 133
Good Stories for Great Holidays (Olcott), 88
Grab bags, in improvisation, 80
"Graham Children, The" (Hogarth), 86
Grimm's Fairy Tales, 52, 107
Guidelines and cautions, for creative theatre, 27; for theatre, 124–27
Gypsy Brew, 257–64

Hackett, Walter, 240
"Happy Family, The" (Steen), 86
Hawthorne, Nathaniel, 110
Henry, in *In the Kitchen Again,* 227–34; in teamwork example, 160
Hermione, in *A Princess at Heart,* 216–26
Hide and seek, in improvisation, 79, 80
Historical incident, example of improvisation, 84, 85
Hjelte, George, 9, 10, 26
Hogarth, William, 86
Holbrook, Florence, 88
Holme, Brian, 86
"How Boots Befooled the King" (Pyle), 99
Humming, exercise to improve breathing, 136

Imitative play, a form of creative theatre, 26; definition of, 33; encouragement of, 35; forms of, 34; leaders of, 35; as creative expression, 34; place of spectators in, 33; projects for, 40–43; space for, 33; supplies for, 33
Improvisation, definition of, 58; examples of leadership procedures for, 69–87; relation of, to story play, 58
Indianapolis 500, in imitative play, 62
Indian call, exercise for breathing, 136
Indian, in puppet play, 52; as illustration of drama, 21
Informal routine activities, 26
Instrumental music, in improvisation, 86, 87
Intelligibility, rehearsal for, 164
Interests in imitative play, 36; in creative drama, 60, 61
Interplay, in creative drama, 100, 101; rehearsal for, 159
In the Kitchen Again, Los Angeles Recreation Directors, 227–34; curtain call for, 185; example of rehearsal for teamwork, 159
Ivan, The Fool, And Other Tales, 97
Ivy, in *Sleeping Beauty,* 202–15

Janson, W. H., & Dorcas Jane, 85, 86
Jim, in *The Glorious Whitewasher,* 240–49
Jo, in *Little Women,* 250–56; in stage movement example, 147
Joe Harper, in *The Glorious Whitewasher,* 240–49
Juniper Tree, in *The Bird with the Broken Wing,* 191–94; in story play, 88, 90
Jupiter, in *The Pomegranate Seeds,*

110–13
Just So Stories (Kipling), 96

Kent, Rockwell, 86
King of Hearts, in *In the Kitchen Again,* 227–34; in story play, 116–19
Kipling, Rudyard, 96
Knave of Hearts, as example of teamwork, 159, 160; in use of objects, 141; in *In the Kitchen Again,* 227–34; in story play, 116–19
Kolokolo Bird, in "The Elephant's Child," 96, 97

Lavona, in *A Princess at Heart,* 216–26
Leaders, for competence of, 29, in creative drama, 59–68; in creative theatre, 29; in imitative play, 35, as volunteers, 152
Librarians, 13
Light, for performance, 178
Lighting equipment, hazards of, 179
Lincoln, Abraham, in improvisation, 83, 84; in *The Perfect Tribute,* 113
"Little Briar Rose," 107
Little Jack Horner, in use of objects, 141; in imitative play, 49, 60
"Little Miss Muffet," for imitative play, 49, 60; for story play, 94
Little Pine Tree, in "The Little Pine Tree Who Wished for New Leaves," 93
"Little Pine Tree Who Wished for New Leaves, The" (Piper), 93
Little Women (Alcott), 250
Locations onstage, 132
Los Angeles Recreation and Park Department, 14; Directors of, in story play, 117, as playwrights, 227–34

"McNed Boys, The," exercise for enunciation, 138
McSwigan, M., 37
Makeup, in imitative play, 37; for performance, 176
Mama Bear, as example of stage movement, 147
Marguerite, in *Gypsy Brew,* 257–64
Masks, for imitative play, 37
May Day, creative theatre as part of, 29
Meg, in *Little Women,* 250–56
Meigs, Cornelia, 23
Merryman, Mildred Plew, 195
Messengers, at dress rehearsal, 165; at performance, 185
Miller, Joaquin, 61, 82
Morse, Katherine D., 235
Mother, as promoter of imitative play, 35; as improvisation leader, 73,75
Mother Goose, characters for puppet play, 49; in story play, 94; Trot my Pony, Trot, 137
Motivation, for counter cross, 134; for speaking, 160
Movement of players onstage, blocking for, 146–49; rehearsal of, 154
"My Cat, Timothy" (Fyleman), 82

"Nation's Strength, A" (Emerson), 82
Neighborhood center, as place for improvisation, 86, 87
North Wind and the Sun, The (Wildsmith), 61
North Wind in *The Bird with the Broken Wing,* 191; in *The North Wind and the Sun,* 101–3; in story play, 88–92
Nursery School, leader of, 13

Oak Tree, in *The Bird with the Broken Wing,* 191; in story play,

88
Objects, use of, in gesture, 141
Olcott, Frances, 88
"Old Burgundian Carol," 137
Olympic Games play project, 43
"Oo-Nee-Vah," Indian call, 136
"Opportunity" (Sill), 82

Pantomime, definition of, 139; eyes in, 139; in characterization, 157, 158; rehearsal for, 157,158
Papa Bear, in pantomime exercise, 140; stage movement example, 147,148
Participants' experiences, example of improvisation, 78,79
"Pastoral Symphony" (Beethoven), 86
Paul, in "How Boots Befooled the King," 99, 100
Pausing, as essential to good speaking, 139; punctuation as guide to, 138; in reading script, 153,154
Perfect Tribute, The (Andrews), 113
Performance, as force for self-discipline, 124; audience for, 180, 181; entrance decoration for, 181; standards for, 125, 126; ushers for, 183, 184
Peter, in "How Boots Befooled the King," 99, 100
Phoebus, in "The Pomegranate Seeds," 110
Piano, for sound effects, 178; for mood music, 178
Pictures, in improvisation, 85,86
Pictures To Live With (Holme), 86
Pilgrims, in puppet play, 52
Pine Tree in The Bird with the Broken Wing, 191–94; in story play, 88–92
Piper, Watty, 93
Play contests, disadvantages of, 128
Play days, as opportunity for improvisation, 80–82, creative theatre in, 29
Playground, circus at, 20; drama class of, 22
Playground, director of, as leader of improvisation, 71; as leader of story plays, 93, 94, 110, 113
Playmaking, as distinguished from imitiative play, 57,58; as means to introduce theatre, 131; definition of, 57
Play production, 123; voice and body development for, 128
Plays, big moments of, 144, 145; choice of, 129; publishers of, 129
Pluto, in imitative play, 37; in story play, 110
Poems, as example of improvisation, 82–84; as means to improve speaking, 137
"Pomegranate Seeds, The" (Hawthorne), 110
Posters, making of, 158; use in publicity, 181
Posture, importance of, in speaking, 135, 136
Prince Bertram, in Sleeping Beauty, 202–15
Princess at Heart, A, as material for theatre lead up activity, 141, 142; playscript of, 216–26
"Princess on the Glass Hill, The," for story telling, 186
Program material, for creative drama, 59–63
Programs, printed, 184
Progress, from easy to difficult material, methods, 71
Projection, as essential to theatre, 123; exercises for, 138
Projects, for imitative play, 40–43
Prompter, assignment of, 156; readiness of, for performance, 185; duties of, 156

Properties, hand, in imitative play, 33, 38; in stage business, 150, management of, 172; procurement of, 172; rehearsal with, 156

Properties, stage, in creative drama, 65; in imitative play, 39; procurement of, 171, 172; in theatre, 171

Property man, duties of, 156, 172; in creative drama, 67

Proserpina, in imitative play, 37; in story play, 110

Publicity, to secure an audience, 180, 181

Public recreation agencies, 28

Publishers, arrangements with, to produce a play, 129

Pudding Pan, The (Morse) as example of stage business, 149; rehearsal of for tempo, 161–63; playscript of, 235–39

Puppet on a string, exercise for posture, 135

Puppets, in imitative play, 47; paper dolls as, 47; sticks as, 48; fingers as, 49; fists as, 50; projects with, 51–53

Pyle, Howard, 99

"Queen of Hearts, The," in creative drama, 60,61, 116–19; as example of development of story into playscript, 119

Questions, as aid to character study, 155; in creative drama, 64,68

Quicksilver, in "The Pomegranate Seeds," 110

Quigley, Lillian, 105

Reading rehearsal, 153

Recurrent scheduled activities, 26, 27

Red Riding Hood, as exercise for cue response, 133; telling of, 63

Rehearsal, and parents, 151,152; and volunteer leaders, 152; for blocking movement, 154; for business, 156; for characterization, 155–58; for climax, 161–63; for intelligibility, 164; for pantomime, 157; for smoothness, 164; for teamwork, 159; for tempo, 161–63; opportunities for, 128, 151; schedule of, 151; with costume accessories, 156, 157; with properties, 156

Responsibilities, of participants, in creative drama, 66, 67

Restaurant play project, 40

Rhythm band instruments, for sound effects, 178

Riley, James Whitcome, 78

Rosamund, in *A Princess at Heart,* 216–26

Run-through rehearsal, 164

Saxe, Edward, 82

Scenery, 168–71

Scouts, 128

Screens, 168, 169

Script, as material for improvisation, 141, 142; as story play preparatory to rehearsal, 141,142; as material for skill development, 141, 142; contents of, 123; study of, 144–50

Scripted drama, 123

Scrooge, exercise for cue response, 134

"Seein' Things at Night" (Riley), 78

Service station play, 42

Settlements, 28

Settlements, director of, as leader of story play, 96,97

Shifting of scenery, 169–171

Shoulder lift exercise, 135

Sill, Edward, 82

Situation in a sentence, example of improvisation, 76–78

Sleeping Beauty, as example of play's big moments, 148; as example of hand property use, 150; use of objects, 141, script of, 202–15; with fanfare for procession, 178

Smoothness, rehearsal for, 164

"Snake, The" (Daniels), 103

"Snow Treasure" (McSwigan), in imitative play, 37

Social studies, 13, 28, 61

Something burning, example of improvisation, 73–75

Sound effects, in creative drama, 66,67; in imitative play, 39, 40; in performance, 177; to emphasize character, 177

Sound effects technician, in creative drama, 66,67; in theatre, 177,178

Speaking, how to improve, 135

Special events, 27

Spectators, 167, 168

Spider, in "Little Miss Muffet," in imitative play, 49,50; in story play, 94, 95

Spruce Tree, in *The Bird with the Broken Wing,* 191–94; in story play, 88–90

Stage, arrangement of, for creative drama, 65,66; for theatre, 145; facilities that serve as, 167; how to improvise a, 167, 168; locations on a, 132; movement of players on, 146; requirements of, 167; width of, 168

Stage crew, cue sheets for, 164; preparation of to discharge responsibilities, 154; selection of, 154

Staging, elements of, 166; importance of, 166, essentials of, 166

Standards of theatre activity, for performance, 126; for good of players, 126, 127; to avoid pitfalls, 127

Steen, Jan, "The Happy Family," 86

Stories for story play, 88–119

Story of Painting for Young People (Janson), 85, 86

Story play, definition of, 58; relation of, to improvisation, 58

Story telling, after performance, 186; hints on, 63

Supplies, for imitative play, 36, 37 40

Sweaters and Jackets, example of improvisation, 71–73

Tala, in *Gypsy Brew,* 257, illustration of characterization, 157,158

Tall Book of Mother Goose, 51

Tall Book of Nursery Tales, 51

Teacher, elementary, as stimulus for creativity, 63; as leader of improvisation, 69–71; as leader of story play, 99–101

Teacher, kindergarten, as leader of story play, 94, 95

Teacher, of religion, as leader of story play, 97–99

Teacher, Sunday school, as leader of improvisation, 82

Teamwork, in creative drama, 57; rehearsal for, 159, 160

Technical staff, duties of, 152; instructions for, 164; selection of, 152

Tempo, rehearsal for, 161–63

Tess, in *Gypsy Brew,* 257–64

Thanksgiving, in puppet play, 52

Theatre, professional, characteristics of, 124, 125; as distinguished from plays by children, 124, 125

Theatre (activity), discipline of, 143; director in, 130; characteristics of, 123; form in, 123; good of players in, 126; incentive for skill development, 124; preparatory activities for, 128; pitfalls of, 127

Theatre (place), glamour at entrance of, 181,182; name of, 181,182

Thinking, fun of, 21

Three Bears, The, as example of stage movement, 147, 148

"Three Little Kittens," in puppet play, 51,52

Tolstoi, Leo, 22, 97

Tom Sawyer, as exercise for counter cross, 134; as exercise in use of objects, 141, as offstage call, 177; in *The Glorious Whitewasher,* 240-49

Traditions in stage movement, 146

"Trot, My Pony, Trot," 137

Tryout, story play as, 142

"Two Hundred Horses," 138

"Twopenny Town" (Meigh), 23

UNESCO, use of creative drama by, 59

Ushers, effect of, on audience, 183; obligations of, 183; preparation of, 183

Values, gaining a sense of, 25

Volunteer leaders, in rehearsals, 152; in performance, 152

Wardrobe mistress, 157

Warren Blair, in *The Perfect Tribute,* 113-116

Waterfall, in *Sleeping Beauty,* 202-15

Wee Willie Winkie, in imitative play, 49

What Men Live By: Russian Stories and Legends, 97

"When Did You Last See Your Father" (Yeames), 85

Where Love Is God Is (Tolstoi), 22, 23, 97

White House Conference, recommendations of, regarding creative drama, 58

"Why the Evergreen Trees Never Lose Their Leaves" (Holbrook), 88-93

Wildsmith, Brian, 101

Willow Tree, in "Why the Evergreen Trees Never Lose Their Leaves," 88-91, in *The Bird with the Broken Wing,* 191-94

Wind storm, example of improvisation, 69-71

Wishing Shop, The (Merryman), as example of double cast, 143; script of, 195

Wonder Clock, The (Pyle), 99

World Famous Paintings (Kent), 86

Yeames, William, 85,86

YWCA, theatre in, 128

Zeus, in "The Snake," 103-05

About the Author

Maxine McSweeny has had thirty-five years' professional experience with children's drama activities. She graduated from the Cumnock School, majoring in literature and drama, and studied drama and education at Columbia University, and recreation at the University of Southern California and New York University. In addition to writing and telling stories for radio's "American Story Book" program, she has written and adapted plays for the Los Angeles Department of Recreation and Parks, as well as having directed costume workshops for these productions. Her lectures on creative children's theatre have included radio, television, churches, women's clubs, Parent Teacher Associations, and university classes in recreation and drama.

Here, in nontechnical language, is shown what creative theatre means to children in terms of fun and development. These benefits are illustrated by anecdotes from the author's personal experience. Dividing drama into three categories, Maxine McSweeny gives step-by-step instructions for leading each form.

The first form is imitative play, in which children act what they want to act. The leader does not direct them when they play "fashion show" or "service station." But he encourages them by pointing out a porch to serve as a runway or grease rack. For imitative play with puppets, fingers, fists, sticks, and paper dolls provide almost instant puppets.

In creative drama, the second form, children make up and act plays just for themselves. The book shows how to promote this playmaking with poems, pictures, music, and everyday sights and sounds. To facilitate making plays from stories there are illustrations of how